Multilingual Computer Assisted Language Learning

AF749418

BILINGUAL EDUCATION & BILINGUALISM

Series Editors: **Nancy H. Hornberger** *(University of Pennsylvania, USA)* and **Wayne E. Wright** *(Purdue University, USA)*

Bilingual Education and Bilingualism is an international, multidisciplinary series publishing research on the philosophy, politics, policy, provision and practice of language planning, Indigenous and minority language education, multilingualism, multiculturalism, biliteracy, bilingualism and bilingual education. The series aims to mirror current debates and discussions. New proposals for single-authored, multiple-authored, or edited books in the series are warmly welcomed, in any of the following categories or others authors may propose: overview or introductory texts; course readers or general reference texts; focus books on particular multilingual education program types; school-based case studies; national case studies; collected cases with a clear programmatic or conceptual theme; and professional education manuals.

All books in this series are externally peer-reviewed.

Full details of all the books in this series and of all our other publications can be found on http://www.multilingual-matters.com, or by writing to Multilingual Matters, St Nicholas House, 31-34 High Street, Bristol BS1 2AW, UK.

BILINGUAL EDUCATION & BILINGUALISM: 114

Multilingual Computer Assisted Language Learning

Edited by

Judith Buendgens-Kosten and Daniela Elsner

MULTILINGUAL MATTERS
Bristol • Blue Ridge Summit

DOI https://doi.org/10.21832/BUENDG1480

Library of Congress Cataloging in Publication Data

A catalog record for this book is available from the Library of Congress.

Names: Buendgens-Kosten, Judith, 1980- editor. | Elsner, Daniela, editor.

Title: Multilingual Computer Assisted Language Learning/Edited by Judith Buendgens-Kosten and Daniela Elsner.

Description: Bristol, UK; Blue Ridge Summit, PA, USA: Multilingual Matters, [2018] | Series: Bilingual Education & Bilingualism: 114 |Includes bibliographical references and index.

Identifiers: LCCN 2018012622| ISBN 9781788921480 (hbk : alk. paper) | ISBN 9781788921473 (pbk : alk. paper) | ISBN 9781788921510 (kindle) | ISBN 9781788921497 (pdf) | ISBN 9781788921503 (epub)

Subjccts: LCSH: Language and languages--Computer-assisted instruction. | Multilingual education.

Classification: LCC P53.28 .M85 2018 | DDC 418.00285–dc23 LC record available at https://lccn.loc.gov/2018012622

British Library Cataloguing in Publication Data

A catalogue entry for this book is available from the British Library.

ISBN-13: 978-1-78892-148-0 (hbk)
ISBN-13: 978-1-78892-147-3 (pbk)

Multilingual Matters

UK: St Nicholas House, 31-34 High Street, Bristol BS1 2AW, UK.
USA: NBN, Blue Ridge Summit, PA, USA.

Website: www.multilingual-matters.com
Twitter: Multi_Ling_Mat
Facebook: https://www.facebook.com/multilingualmatters
Blog: www.channelviewpublications.wordpress.com

Copyright © 2018 Judith Buendgens-Kosten, Daniela Elsner and the authors of individual chapters.

All rights reserved. No part of this work may be reproduced in any form or by any means without permission in writing from the publisher.

The policy of Multilingual Matters/Channel View Publications is to use papers that are natural, renewable and recyclable products, made from wood grown in sustainable forests. In the manufacturing process of our books, and to further support our policy, preference is given to printers that have FSC and PEFC Chain of Custody certification. The FSC and/or PEFC logos will appear on those books where full certification has been granted to the printer concerned.

Typeset by Deanta Global Publishing Services Limited.
Printed and bound in the UK by Short Run Press Ltd.
Printed and bound in the US by Thomson-Shore, Inc.

Contents

Contributors

Antonie Alm (PhD, UCLA) is a senior lecturer in the Department of Languages and Cultures at the University of Otago in New Zealand where she teaches German language and culture, Computer-assisted language learning and Intercultural Communication. Her research on topics of social media in language learning, L2 motivation, learner autonomy and informal learning have appeared amongst others in *Innovation in Language Learning & Teaching, JALT CALL Journal and Zeitschrift für Interkulturellen Fremdsprachenunterricht*. Dr Alm is on a number of editorial review committees and works as an Associate Editor for the CALL Journal as well as the JALT CALL Journal. She is also the senior vice-president of the New Zealand German teacher association.

John Michael Alvarez is currently engaged in research of second language acquisition of secondary level Latino Persistently Emergent Bilingual Learners (PEBLs) at the University of Southern California, Los Angeles, California. Most recently, his article, entitled 'Using CLIL-Methodology: Developing Learner Motivation in Learners of English as a Second Language through Content Area Guided Reading' was published by Peter Lang in *Mehrsprachigkeit als Chance: Herausforderungen und Potentiale individueller und gesellschaftlicher Mehrsprachigkeit* (Witzigmann, S. & Rymarczyk, J., eds).

Sonja Brunsmeier is a headmaster. She worked as a research fellow at the University of Education Freiburg and University of Education Tyrol. In her PhD project, she investigated the development of Intercultural Communicative Competence in the primary EFL classroom. Her further research interests include teaching primary EFL and using literature and media in language education.

Judith Buendgens-Kosten is currently professor-pro-tem at Goethe University Frankfurt. She has completed her doctorate in English Linguistics at RWTH Aachen University, and her MA in Online and Distance Education at the Open University, UK. Her research focuses on computer assisted language learning and multilingualism.

Do Coyle is professor of languages education and classroom pedagogies and director of Research and Knowledge Exchange in the School of Education, University of Edinburgh. Her research involves bilingual pedagogies, especially in CLIL contexts and technology-enhanced learning including the use of shared learning spaces. Coyle is most known for her work in bilingual pedagogies for integrated learning using more than one language. She is a founder member of the European Graz Group which is developing an inclusive learning model for pluriliteracies education. She has published extensively in the field of CLIL and has worked tirelessly to enhance student learning.

Euline Cutrim Schmid is a full professor of applied linguistics and TEFL at the University of Education Schwäbisch Gmünd, Germany. She has a PhD in Linguistics and an MA in language teaching from Lancaster University, UK, and she also holds an MA in applied linguistics from the Federal University of Rio de Janeiro, Brazil. She teaches at undergraduate and postgraduate levels on a variety of topics including language teaching methodologies, computer assisted language learning (CALL), and applied linguistics. Her academic publications focus mainly on the use of interactive technologies in the EFL classroom and pluralistic approaches to foreign language education.

Henriette Dausend is associate professor of English at the Center for Teacher Education at Chemnitz University (Germany). She finished her Master of Education (English and PE) at the University of Vechta in 2009. After research and lecturing jobs and stays in Vechta, Frankfurt/Main, Edinburgh, and Istanbul, she got her PhD for a thesis on researching early language learning in German primary schools from the Goethe University of Frankfurt (Germany) in 2013. Her major interests are in cross-curricular teaching, multilingual learning, tablets and smartphones in teaching and learning languages, popular culture (street art and film) in teaching.

Daniela Elsner is professor of TEFL/TESOL education and research at Goethe University Frankfurt/Main, where she is also one of the directors of the Academy for Teacher Education and Research (ABL). Her research focuses on early foreign language learning and teaching, bi- and plurilingualism, CLIL and immersion, multilingual and technology-assisted learning and teaching processes, and the quality of higher education teaching. She is co-author of *Sally*, the number one textbook for EFL in the primary classrooms in Germany. In 2014 she was awarded with the national Ars Legendi Prize for Teaching Excellence in Higher Education and the 1822 University Teaching Award.

Wolfgang Hallet is professor of teaching English as a Foreign Language at Justus Liebig University Giessen, Germany. He is co-editor of a series of handbooks on teaching literature and culture, of the Giessen Contributions to Foreign Language Research (Tübingen: Narr) and a major German bimonthly journal on Teaching English as a Foreign Language (Der fremdsprachliche Unterricht Englisch). In foreign language teaching his research and publications, including several monographs, comprise study of culture-based theories of teaching literature and culture, cognition and literature, the task approach, literary competences, and multimodality theories and multiliteracies. His most recent monograph (2016) presents a genre approach to teaching foreign languages.

Annika Kolb is a professor at the English Department of the University of Education Freiburg/Germany. She holds a doctoral degree in EFL from Hamburg University. In her dissertation, she investigated the use of portfolios in the primary EFL classroom. She has worked as a language teacher in primary and secondary schools in Germany and Spain. Her main research interests are teaching English to young learners and literature (especially picture books) in language education. Current research projects include the use of story apps (digital picture books) in primary ELT, multilingualism in language teaching, and teacher education in a blended learning programme.

Gabriela Meier is a senior lecturer in language education at the Graduate School of Education, University of Exeter, UK. Having lived, worked, and studied in different linguistic regions in Europe, she speaks four languages, and has always had a keen interest in languages, social cohesion, and social justice. She obtained her PhD in 2009, based on a study of Europa-Schule Berlin. Since then, her research led to a range of publications in the field of bilingual and multilingual education, above all from a social cohesion and critical perspective. She works as a teacher educator at master's level and supervises many doctoral projects in this field.

Sílvia Melo-Pfeifer is currently a professor at the Department of Education of the University of Hamburg (Germany). She is also a member of CIDTFF (Research Centre 'Didactics and Technology in Education of Trainers') at the University of Aveiro (Portugal). Her research interests include plurilingual and intercultural (online) interaction, pluralistic approaches to languages and cultures, and heritage language education. She presently integrates the German team of the following Erasmus-Plus Projects: Koinos, EVAL-IC, and Spiral. She coordinated the educational department at the Portuguese Embassy in Berlin (Germany), between 2010 and 2013.

Oliver Meyer is professor of English-Didactics at the Johannes Gutenberg-University in Mainz. He is also a qualified teacher of geography and EFL with several years of CLIL teaching experience. His research interests include foreign language learning in mono- and multilingual settings as well as the use of educational technologies to design next-generation ecologies for deeper learning. Oliver has coordinated the work of the Graz Group and played a leading role in the development of the Pluriliteracies Model for Deeper Learning.

Heike Niesen had been working as an EFL teacher in Rhineland-Palatinate, Germany, for 10 years before she finished her PhD on 'The impact of socio-cultural learning tasks on EFL students' foreign grammatical language awareness' at the University of Luxemburg in 2014. She is currently working as a research assistant at the Department of English and American Studies at Goethe University in Frankfurt/Main. Her research interests cover linguistic heterogeneity in EFL settings, the development of pre- and in-service EFL teachers' professional vision, as well as impacts of individual language learning biographies on multilingual-sensitive EFL teaching.

Manuela Pohl is a trained teacher of English, Russian and German as a foreign language. She has several years of teaching experience in primary and secondary schools in Germany, Kazakhstan, and the UK. Currently she is working as lecturer at the chair of 'Teaching English as a Foreign Language' of Potsdam University (Germany). Her research areas include multi- and plurilingualism in the foreign language classroom and technology-enhanced language learning. She is working on this latter area for her PhD thesis on the benefits of digital media genres in the EFL classroom.

Kevin Schuck is an International Baccalaureate Head Teacher at Penta College Jacob van Liesveldt in Hellevoetsluis, the Netherlands, and a member of the original Graz Group Pluriliteracies project. His work in education now focuses on Deeper Learning and the implementation of the Pluriliteracies Model. Schuck has been working for the International Baccalaureate organization as a workshop leader in both Language A and Language B courses and as a member of the curriculum review process since 2005. He also works with Nuffic in the Netherlands as a CLIL specialist and teacher trainer. He is originally from the US where he taught both primary and secondary education including special needs and Montessori.

Rae Si'ilata (Ngati Raukawa, Tuhourangi, Fiji) is Associate Dean Pasifika and a lecturer in Biliteracy-Pasifika Education in the Faculty of Education and Social Work, at The University of Auckland. Her research interests centre on language and mixed identities; Māori and Pasifika Education; linguistically and culturally sustaining pedagogies for Pasifika and other culturally diverse learners; and teacher professional learning and development in bilingualism and biliteracy.

Multilingual CALL: Introduction

Judith Buendgens-Kosten and Daniela Elsner

The Reality of Language Learning Today

In his 2001 paper, Vivian Cook (2001: 405) argued that an 'anti-L1 attitude was clearly a mainstream element in twentieth-century teaching methodology'. He quotes Howatt's (1984: 289) history of English language teaching (ELT), in which Howatt called the monolingual principle 'the unique contribution of the twentieth century to classroom language teaching', the 'bedrock notion from which the others ultimately derive'. Regarding the first language (L1), the literature seems to engage in a form of polite fiction: The L1 may indeed exist, but as it has no place in the classroom, it is best benignly ignored. Just like the polite fiction of not having an active digestion, this polite fiction is only interrupted when a linguistic air escapes (which it may, quite regularly, in the actual classroom, even if not in the foreign language learning [FLL] literature).

It would not be fair to claim that monolingually inspired approaches reign unquestioned within theoretical discourses on foreign language learning and teaching (cf. for example Butzkamm, 1973; Cummins, 2008; Königs, 2015; Scott, 2010). Yet, many multilingual alternatives are not truly satisfactory either, as the other language (L1 or school language) mainly functions as a lifebuoy, coming into play anytime the message in the second language (L2) seems to be too difficult for the learner (e.g. some types of grammar instruction for beginners), too time-consuming (such as some types of vocabulary explanation) or socially awkward (disciplinary/organizational matters). Even though Cook provides a list of programs he considers to go beyond a monolingual focus, only a few of these language learning programs go beyond this life-saver function. These, however, are based on reciprocal/dual language learning models, valuing translation as a tool *and* a goal, and – this is the most notable part – those that focus on compound bilingualism (Weinreich, 1953; also cf. Council of Europe, 2011: 4f) rather than coordinate bilingualism.

The Reality of Language Use Today

Butzkamm (1973) and Cook (2001) criticize the monolingual principle within two-language settings. The focus is thus on the role 'the' L1 can play for 'the' L2. This book, on the other hand, is based on the assumption that a multilingual perspective of language education needs to go further than this.

Multilingualism as a word has a rich history, and is used here in the broadest possible sense, that is not as a word contrasting with *bilingual*, not as a word contrasting with *plurilingual*, but encompassing any co-existence or co-presence of two or more languages, within and without language learning contexts.

In many countries, language learning is a bedrock of education. In Europe, for example, where foreign language instruction starts increasingly early, the majority of pupils study more than one foreign language at school (Eurydice, 2017: 8). Even if learners start school as monolinguals who only speak the majority language, they are likely to acquire communicative competences in two or more foreign languages before leaving school. It is important to not just consider these foreign languages once they have been fully developed, but to also keep them in mind while or even before a child has learned them. Königs (2004: 97) calls this 'prospective multilingualism' [prospektive Mehrsprachigkeit].

Moreover, let's not forget that foreign languages are not just learned in school! Work on informal language learning practices (cf. e.g. Sockett, 2014) show how interest in a popular TV show, or a fashionable manga, can inspire practices that support foreign language acquisition. Globalization does not only mean that a T-shirt may have travelled around the globe before ending in one's wardrobe. It also means – especially considering the technical means available for legal and illegal sharing of files – that a Korean pop song and a Mexican soap opera may have fans in Belgium. In practice, actual language learning goes beyond what is reflected by national or regional curricula.

When addressing globalization, one cannot but discuss migration. Migration is hardly a new phenomenon – but today, many countries experience migration in forms that are new, either in quality or in quantity. Some, like Germany, have realized that the language learning policy that dominated earlier approaches to migration, such as the era of 'Gastarbeiter' migration in the 1950s to 1970s (Gogolin & Reich, 2001) has had a lasting negative impact on current society, and the original *Gastarbeiter*, their children and grandchildren. There is great motivation to 'get it right' this time.

Migration, of course, should not be equated to 'home language plus majority language', as language patterns can be complex. Individuals may have already been multilingual in their home countries, for example by speaking a minority language and the local majority language. They may have studied foreign languages. And migration does not necessarily imply moving 'from Country A to Country B'; people who arrive in Country B might have lived and acquired languages in quite a range of countries before.

Recent migration is not the only source of multilingualism. In Europe, over the last decades, a range of protections for 'indigenous' minority languages and national sign languages have been developed. Schooling in regional and minority languages is actively sought by many parents whose children may speak, or whom they may wish to learn, e.g. Sorbian, Frisian, Friulian or a national sign language. And not to forget those countries in which more than one national language is spoken and learned on a broader footing, such as Luxembourg, Belgium or Ireland!

In short, in many countries of the world, you can visit an average classroom and find speakers of many different languages, and at differing competence levels. And even the average 'monolingual' child has had frequent contact with other languages before they enter school, e.g. in kindergarten, while traveling, through media or when playing and talking with friends at the playground. And all of these learners are expected to learn even more languages in school.

A list of ways in which languages can be acquired and learned may imply that each of these languages is seen as a distinct unit of linguistic knowledge. Traditional notions of multilingual practices in the classroom, often based on concepts of code-switching (Legenhausen, 1991), are today complemented by the notion of translanguaging (García, 2009).

In today's world, viewing language learning and language use from a multilingual perspective is essential. A multilingual perspective[1] not only rejects a compartmentalized view of languages and language learning, it furthermore appraises all languages and any kind of language competence as meaningful (Council of Europe, 2011: 5f.). Multilingual education, understood this way, means much more than 'enlightened monolingualism' [Aufgeklärte Einsprachigkeit] (Butzkamm, 1973), and it goes beyond 'strategic bilingualism'. Instead, multilingual education stands for an enlightened multilingualism.

Introducing Multilingual CALL

With this backdrop, talking about any language learning – and this, of course, includes computer assisted language learning (CALL) – as a monolingual endeavor falls short of the reality. Yet, we lack a label to refer specifically to a non-monolingual perspective on CALL.

Following the time-honored tradition of creating acronyms for subfields of CALL (think *MALL* for 'mobile CALL', *BALL* for 'blog-assisted language learning', etc.), we suggest *MCALL* (multilingual CALL) as a label for practice and research related to language learning, acquisition and use that purposefully integrates more than one language (via plurilingual individuals and multilingual textual and non-textual environments and their affordances) in CALL contexts.

To a certain degree, the label *multilingual CALL* seems superfluously verbose. Of course, any CALL is, unavoidably, multilingual, at least insofar as it contains (at least) a learner with (at least) skills in one language, and material or tasks related to the target language. Is not, actually, any CALL a form of multilingual CALL?

Defining the component words does not help much in clarifying the notion. The meaning of *multilingual* has already been discussed above. A further and more comprehensive definition of this complex and sometimes even contested term is not possible – nor needed – in this introduction. CALL is the study and practice of teaching languages through digital media. Traditionally, the focus lay on computers as digital tools (henceforth the C of *CALL*), but today the focus has broadened to encompass a wide range of digital technologies such as tablets and smartphones, and the range of digital tools will most probably increase with ubiquitous computing and the internet-of-things.

Just combining these two notions gives us the following definition:

> Multilingual CALL is the study and practice of language learning with digital media in non-monolingual contexts or settings or using non-monolingual media. This may involve the use and/or activation of native language(s), previously studied language(s), heritage language(s) or dialect(s). Multilingual CALL can be multilingual due to the multilinguality of learners, due to the multilinguality of group of learners (including telecollaboration or CMC settings) or due to the multilinguality of teaching material/tasks.

As clear as this definition may seem at first sight, as unclear it is on second sight. Can *any* use of digital media in foreign/second language classrooms or, vice versa, any use of more than one language in digital environments, be considered as MCALL? Is the average European classroom (with a diverse range of speaker backgrounds and a slowly increasing amount of digital media used in instruction) an example of multilingual CALL? Are bilingual online dictionaries examples of multilingual CALL?

Multilingual CALL can be the result of a didactic *design* process, which explicitly considers dimensions of multilingualism and of technology in language learning, either in research or in practice (such as teaching or material development). At the same time, multilingual CALL may also *emerge* from existing language ecologies and digital ecologies in the classroom as well as in non-formal and informal settings. In other words, it is a consequence of features of the learner group and/or the teaching environment. If these factors are taken into account in describing and analyzing language learning/acquisition, work on such settings would certainly qualify as MCALL, just as much as a multilingually aware CALL design would.

Multilingualism and CALL: A Match Made in Heaven, or a Marriage of Convenience?

If language learning should be viewed from a multilingual perspective, so should CALL, as CALL is primarily language learning (using computers and similar tools), and what applies to language learning can seldom be ignored in CALL without peril. But, is there a special relationship between CALL and multilingualism, a relationship that justifies a volume specifically on their connection, rather than a subchapter in a text primarily on non-CA language learning?

From the perspective of *emergent* MCALL, multilingualism and CALL just tend to co-occur. Often, both multilingualism and technological assistance in language learning are present at the same time (especially in informal/non-formal, but also increasingly in formal contexts). When technology is as much a place as a tool (cf. the multilingual niches created by blogs, Buendgens-Kosten, 2016), ecological, not relationship-based, metaphors come to mind.

In discussions of *designed* MCALL, though, the metaphors of a marriage of love and a marriage of convenience come in handy. Often, in designed MCALL, the technology is seen as a way to compensate for 'deficiencies' of individuals: A teacher may not speak the languages of their students, a learner may not be literate in their mother language, so technology is used to bring information (e.g. L1 texts, audio support for texts) into the classroom. This is, indeed, computer-assisted multilingual language learning, with the technology taking the role of an assistive technology.

In informal speech, calling something a *crutch* is often done disparagingly. In learning contexts, though, assistive technologies are of value, as they can level an uneven playing field. The digital text in diverse L1s of students means that they, too, can have L1 input in class, not only those who happen to speak an L1 spoken by the teacher. The audio support means that students can use their previously learned or previously acquired languages, including L1s, regardless of the amount of formal education they had in these languages, providing more opportunities for students speaking less recognized languages or students with interrupted educational careers. Technology, in these contexts, is an *enabler* for MCALL.

Yet, for the romantically inclined researcher, the question remains: Are there scenarios where the CALL in MCALL does more than 'just' level the playing field, increase access and democratize multilingual learning?

In the context of creating multilingual identity texts (second language acquisition [SLA] setting), Cummins (2008: 71) refers to technology as an amplifier: 'Although not always an essential component, technology acts as an amplifier to enhance the process of identity investment and affirmation. It facilitates the production of these texts, makes them look more accomplished and expands the audiences and potential for affirmative feedback'.

Whether technology is seen as an enabler or as an amplifier for multilingual CALL – or, for that matter, as a place or social event – it is meaningful to discuss how technology enriches multilingual language learning, as well as how multilingual practices enrich CALL.

This volume might be a first step toward this – a needed step, as we will outline in the following section.

The Need for a Multilingual Turn in CALL

While, very slowly, the multilingual reality within the classroom is arriving in the literature for FLL and second language learning (SLL), with some people having started to refer to a 'multilingual turn' in language education (Conteh & Meier, 2014; May, 2014), multilingualism seems not yet to have arrived in CALL research to a meaningful degree. While both CALL and multilingualism in language learning receive ever-increasing attention, the interstices between the two – that is, MCALL – remain understudied.

The following example will show how dramatic this effect is. Within CALL, even the words *plurilingual* or *multilingual* rarely appear in the current literature. For Figure I.1, we assessed the frequency of the words 'multilingual*', 'plurilingual*' and 'bilingual*', (a) in all 2015 issues of *CALL* journal, (b) in all 2015 issues of *ReCALL* journal, (c) in all 2015

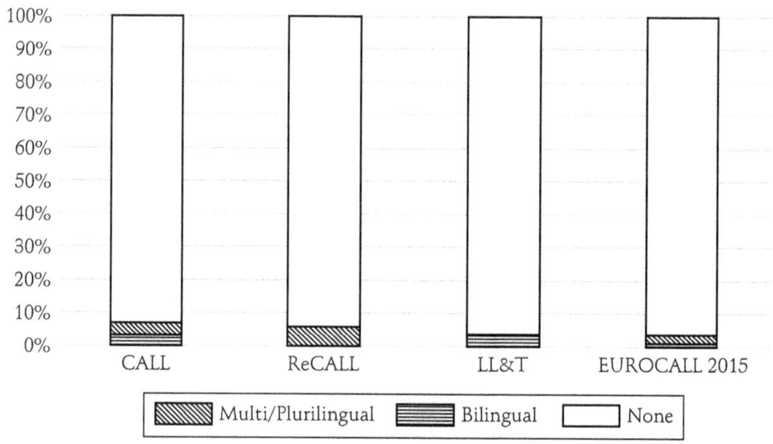

Figure I.1 Frequency of multilingualism-related words in CALL publications, 2015

issues of *Language Learning & Technology* and (d) in the abstracts of the EUROCALL 2015 conference. All parts of the papers/abstracts, with the exclusion of the reference lists, were considered.

As Figure I.1 shows, the percentages are very low. In absolute numbers: two papers in *CALL*, one paper in *ReCALL*, one paper in *LL&T* and a total of eight papers at the EUROCALL conference, within 2015, even mentioned the words *multilingual*, *plurilingual* or *bilingual*. And even these very low absolute numbers present a certain over-estimation, as the mere presence of a word was checked, not the relative importance of that word, as can be demonstrated by a quick analysis of the content of these publications.

Roughly, the studies fell into one out of four categories:

(1) using multilingual CALL-based input (e.g. captioning, bilingual concordancers, bilingual dictionaries);
(2) creating, or documenting, a space for multilingual practices (e.g. Facebook, telecollaboration tools);
(3) using monolingual input and monolingual practices to achieve plurilingual competences (e.g. web-based training, blog);
(4) looking at language learning and CALL within non-monolingual populations.

One study permitted students to conduct a project on bilingualism. This study, therefore, would not, even with good will, be considered an example of MCALL. For the other studies, there was great range in how much emphasis was put on the multilingual aspect. For example, looking at category (c), one of these studies did so by taking a fully plurilingualism-informed perspective on CALL, while another study acknowledged plurilingual competences as a goal of language study, without this commitment noticeably influencing this study or the product.

It is to be expected that a label such as 'MCALL' might help bring together work that *actively* and *consciously* works on the interstices of multilingualism and CALL.

Introduction to This Volume

This volume intends to showcase work on multilingual CALL from a range of perspectives. Just looking at the technological diversity, the book features chat rooms and computer games, digital stories and ebook apps, online texts and telecollaboration via interactive whiteboards. In addition to productive language use, the receptive dimension (media as input) is taken into consideration by a range of chapters (Alvarez; Brunsmeier and Kolb; Buendgens-Kosten and Elsner; Elsner and Buendgens-Kosten).

While it is not untouched by the 'English problem' observed in CALL, that is the overrepresentation of English as the target language in CALL

(Sauro, 2016), several chapters focus on learning other languages than English, e.g. Pohl's chapter of Lower Sorbian as part of Russian foreign language instruction, Melo-Pfeifer on Romance languages or Alm on German, French, Japanese and Spanish. The actual diversity of languages is even larger when those languages that appear *with* English are considered (see especially Buendgens-Kosten and Elsner; Elsner and Buendgens-Kosten; Si'ilata). Meyer, Coyle and Schuck as well as Hallet go beyond looking at specific languages, extending the discussion to a wide range of genres, codes and multiliterate practices.

The chapters in this volume showcase learners from kindergarten to university, and settings from the classroom (Alvarez; Dausend; Pohl; Si'ilata; Cutrim Schmid) to after-school clubs (Brunsmeier and Kolb) and informal online practices (Alm). Learners in Europe, the United States (Alvarez), Australia (Alm) and New Zealand (Si'ilata) feature in the studies reported herein. Contributors include researchers as well as practitioners, who have written with both audiences in mind. Multilingual CALL requires multilingually aware and technologically savvy teachers, so two contributions look specifically at dimensions of teacher training (Si'ilata; Niesen).

The following overview will introduce the overall structure of the volume.

Multiliteracies and MCALL

In Chapter 1 of this volume, Wolfgang Hallet raises the concern that a multilingual change of pedagogies and teaching practices alone, will not lead to an eligible multilingual turn of minds, unless our understanding of 'languages' becomes a different one, too. Hallet argues that multilingualism is not only about a multiplicity of verbal languages in which individuals are proficient and which are used or co-present in discursive and social interaction. From his point of view, in digital environments in particular, the concept of multilingualism also includes symbolic languages and semiotic modes that engage in specific ways of meaning-making. Against this background, the author considers first, second and foreign languages as only three among many other semiotic resources and modes of making meaning. He therefore suggests an extension of our understanding of 'languages' beyond linguistic sign systems. As a conclusion, he points out the need to incorporate the acquisition of other, non-verbal literacies into language learning in order to equip learners with the symbolic resources that are required in multimodal acts of communication.

This broad concept of languages perfectly blends in with the pluriliteracies approach for teaching and learning (PTL) as introduced and described by Oliver Meyer, Do Coyle and Kevin Schuck in Chapter 2. The authors point out that 21st-century language environments first of all need to focus on plurimodal semiotics in order to prepare learners for a society in which digitalization increasingly dominates communication processes. With this, the authors indicate that digital media and educational technologies form an integral part of their envisioned learning environment. Second, the team of authors stresses that learning is most effective if it addresses topics that are meaningful to the learner. PTL is thus linked to a content and language integrated learning (CLIL) environment, which helps learners to develop subject-specific literacy in more than one language. The authors furthermore suggest that the integration of different genres and genre moves will help learners to develop the ability to express or verbalize subject-specific concepts or conceptual knowledge in an appropriate style. In a nutshell, the pluriliteracies approach intends to help learners become literate in content subjects and communicate knowledge across disciplines, cultures and languages in a wide variety of modes.

Multilingual texts

Learning in two (or more) languages is also one of the central themes of Chapter 3 of this volume. Sonja Brunsmeier and Annika Kolb focus on young primary students' reading processes while reading digital picture books in an extensive reading setting. The authors illustrate how digital books, as a combination of different modes, can facilitate the individual reading process, reinforce the understanding of a story and enhance the development of reading strategies. The authors report on some of the results of an action research project that looked at the children's strategies to individually and in pairs read and understand digital picture books. In this context, the authors identified the functions of the two languages and realized that the learners predominantly made use of two languages while working with the books: the target language (English) and the school language (German) with regard to understanding the stories, accomplishing post-reading tasks and discussing opinions about the digital picture books.

Related results were found in different, small-scale studies and one larger research study on the use of multilingual digital picture books as described by Daniela Elsner and Judith Buendgens-Kosten in Chapter 4. The authors illustrate that monolingual and plurilingual children readily make use of different languages on a receptive level if provided by the learning environment. Yet, the data show that learners have very individual ways of and reasons for using the different languages. Whereas for some learners switching multiple times between different input languages is more a matter of delight or identity comfort, for others the possibility to make use of different languages seems to serve as a valuable comprehension aid. Against this background, the authors recommend the use of multilingual digital picture books in primary school language classrooms as a contribution to a language- and technology-friendly learning environment.

The initiation of a language-friendly environment in primary schools is also one of the major goals of the project described by Henriette Dausend in Chapter 5. The author introduces the concept of transcurricular teaching, which provides principles for multilingual tasks that allow students to use all of their available languages in communicative situations in foreign language classrooms. Besides presenting examples of transcurricular tasks and materials, the author discusses whether and how digital media – especially tablets – can be used to initiate multilingual talk. On the basis of an exploratory study in primary classrooms, Dausend shows that learners are strongly motivated to use tablets to produce, record, edit and save multilingual talk. The author concludes that tablets are a useful medium to foster plurilingual competences in primary classrooms.

In Chapter 6, John Michael Alvarez moves from young learners to older learners, suggesting that the provision of texts in different languages leads to more output and better understanding. The author reports on a research study focusing on the use of native language texts in secondary school classrooms in California. Late-entry multilingual students read a text in the target language English and in their respective native language. The study clearly indicates that the provision of the native language texts increased the quantity and quality of classroom discourse and written production in English. Alvarez assumes that alternatively, advantaging these same learners with the capability to utilize productive language in their home language, can increase receptive target language development.

Even more languages are being offered to secondary school students on the language learning platform MElang-E, which is introduced by Judith Buendgens-Kosten and Daniela Elsner in Chapter 7. MElang-E is an online tool for multiple language learning that was inspired by serious games and developed within a project financed by the European Commission. Its target group are European teenage language learners (upper beginners and lower intermediate learners of English), as well as individuals interested in exploring multilingualism in Europe more generally. The authors describe how MElang-E provides plenty of opportunities to develop English communicative skills in a virtual setting, while also providing a first taste of languages such as German, French, Spanish, Catalan or Luxembourgish. It becomes obvious: the focus of the game lies in the exploration and enjoyment of different languages. The game exemplifies multiple language use as it occurs in the real, multilingual world, and thus caters to the development of language awareness.

Intercomprehension and CALL

In Chapter 8, Manuela Pohl introduces another promising way to stimulate polyglot communication among speakers of different mother tongues and raise language awareness through intercomprehension. The contribution offers an example of a task-based project in which students have to apply their previously gained knowledge in Russian in order to identify words and sentences in Lower Sorbian. The author shows how the application of different intercomprehensive strategies enables the secondary school learners to decode a Lower Sorbian street sign without any explicit knowledge of this language. In this context, Pohl also highlights the benefits of using digital technology for the creation of and work with intercomprehensive tasks.

In Chapter 9, Sílvia Melo-Pfeifer introduces another project focusing on the use of intercomprehension strategies: the Galanet project. The European project aimed at understanding the functioning of online interaction between speakers of different Romance languages. Students with different first languages (Catalan, French, Italian, Portuguese, Spanish and Romanian) were requested to use their own Romance language to collaborate on intercultural and multilingual online tasks with speakers of other languages. The results of the study, which show that students made use of a multitude of different languages (including non-Romance languages) in order to work on the tasks, give rise to the assumption that students' use of their entire linguistic repertoires is an act of multilingual identity performance and a sign of multiple affective belongings.

Multilingual online exchange and telecollaboration

In Chapter 10, Eulene Cutrim-Schmid reports on a school-based research project that investigated online communication between distant classes of young learners using English as a lingua franca. The project exploited the technical affordances of synchronous computer-mediated communication (CMC) between primary school learners in France and Germany using live audio/video and screen sharing in a task-based framework. The findings derived from video recordings, participant observation and interviews indicate that, even though the main focus of the project was the development of English skills for authentic communication, the project also created several opportunities for the development of pupils' plurilingual competence.

In Chapter 11, Antonie Alm moves from formal to informal learning environments. The author reports on a research project that investigated the self-reported L2 Facebook practices and writing strategies of advanced language learners (of German, French, Japanese and Spanish). The study shows that only a minority of language students use the social network for L2 practice/active use. Alm assumes that the majority of students are thus obviously not aware of the potential that Facebook (or other social networks) has for L2 practice, and thus simply do not make use of it. The author recommends that this reluctance with regard to the use of social networks for L2 practice should be taken into consideration when educators plan on integrating such tools in their classes.

MCALL and professional development of teachers

The important role educators play with regard to the establishment of multilingual environments is highlighted by Rae Si'ilata in Chapter 12. The author presents the results of a qualitative study conducted in Year 1 primary classrooms in South Auckland, Aotearoa New Zealand. The researcher investigated the work of teachers within a professional learning and development (PLD) pilot program that focused on the utilization of bilingual texts to support Samoan (Pacific) bilingual learners' English literacy development. The teachers combined the use of the bilingual texts with digital tools, including interactive whiteboards, digital sound files and student iPads to promote English language and literacy learning in English medium classrooms at school. The author asks the question, what enables teachers to change their (monolingual) beliefs and practices in relation to the use of heritage languages as resources for learning?

In the last chapter, Chapter 13, Heike Niesen looks at the value of video analyses for the professional development of future English as a foreign language/English as a second language (EFL/ESL) teachers at university. Based on research findings on how different types of teaching videos as well as video analyses settings foster mathematics and science teachers' professional development, the author of this contribution addresses the question whether these insights may be adapted to the field of foreign language teaching. More precisely, the question is raised in what ways several types and settings of teaching videos in computer-assisted learning environments contribute to the development of pre-service EFL teachers' ability to notice, analyze and act upon relevant classroom events in simulated multilingual classrooms. Niesen presents the results of a small-scale explorative study she conducted in two pre-service teacher seminars at Goethe University Frankfurt, which focused on multilingual learning and teaching processes. Although the majority of findings support the insights gained in former studies, subject-related specifics were detected by the author.

The volume ends with a contribution by Gabriela Meier, 'Learning in Multilingually and Digitally Mediated Spaces: The MCALL Approach', in which she draws together the different themes touched upon in this volume, situating them in the broader context of research and practice.

The editors of this book hope that this volume will achieve the goals outlined above.

Note

* Referred to as 'plurilingual', as contrasting with 'multilingual', by the CEFR (Council of Europe, 2011: 5f.).

References

Buendgens-Kosten, J. (2016) Building a multilingual niche: Code-choice and code-alternation at the Day of Multilingual Blogging. *Domínios de Lingu@gem* 10 (4), 1379–403.

Butzkamm, W. (1973) *Aufgeklärte Einsprachigkeit: Zur Entdogmatisierung der Methode im Fremdsprachenunterricht*. Heidelberg: Quelle & Meyer.

Conteh, J. and Meier, G. (eds) (2014) *The Multilingual Turn in Languages Education: Opportunity and Challenges*. Bristol: Multilingual Matters.

Cook, V. (2001) Using the first language in the classroom. *The Canadian Modern Language Review* 57 (3), 402–423.

Council of Europe (2011) *Common European Framework of Reference for Languages: Learning, Teaching, Assessment*. See http://www.coe.int/t/dg4/linguistic/Source/Framework_EN.pdf (accessed 5 April 2018).

Cummins, J. (2008) Teaching for transfer: Challenging the two solitudes assumption in bilingual education. In J. Cummins and N.H. Hornberger (eds) *Encyclopedia of Language and Education: Volume 5: Bilingual Education* (pp. 65–75). New York: Springer.

Eurydice (2017) Key data on teaching languages at school in Europe 2017. https://publications.europa.eu/en/publication-detail/-/publication/ff10cc21-aef9-11e7-837e-01aa75ed71a1/language-en/format-PDF

García, O. (2009) *Bilingual Education in the 21st Century. A Global Perspective*. Malden, MA: Wiley-Blackwell.

Gogolin, I. and Reich, H. (2001) Immigrant languages in federal Germany. In G. Extra and D. Gorter (eds) *The Other Languages of Europe: Demographic, Sociolinguistic and Educational Perspectives* (pp. 193–214). Clevedon: Multilingual Matters.

Howatt, A.P.R. (1984) *A History of English Language Teaching*. Oxford: Oxford University Press.

Königs, F.G. (2004) Mehrsprachigkeit: Von den Schwierigkeiten, einer guten Idee zum tatsächlichen Durchbruch zu verhelfen. In K.-R. Bausch, F.G. Königs and H.-J. Krumm (eds) *Mehrsprachigkeit im Fokus: Arbeitspapiere der 24. Frühjahrskonferenz zur Erforschung des Fremdsprachenunterrichts* (pp. 96–104).Tübingen: Narr.

Königs, F.G. (2015) Keine Angst vor der Muttersprache – vor den (anderen) Fremdsprachen aber auch nicht! Überlegungen zum Verhältnis von Einsprachigkeit und Zweisprachigkeit im Fremdsprachenunterricht. *Zeitschrift für Interkulturellen Fremdsprachenunterricht* 20 (2), 5–14.

Legenhausen, L. (1991) Code-switching in learners' discourse. *International Review of Applied Linguistics in Language Teaching* 29, 61–73.

May, S. (ed.) (2014) *The Multilingual Turn: Implications for SLA, TESOL, and Bilingual Education*. London: Routledge.

Sauro, S. (2016) Does CALL have an English problem? *Language Learning & Technology* 20 (3), 229–247.

Scott, V.M. (2010) *Double Talk: Deconstructing Monolingualism in Classroom Second Language Learning*. Boston, MA: Prentice Hall.

Sockett, G. (2014) *The Online Informal Learning of English*. Houndmills/New York: Palgrave Macmillan.

Weinreich, U. (1953) *Languages in Contact*. New York: Linguistic Circle.

Part 1
Multiliteracies and MCALL

1 The Multiple Languages of Digital Communication

Wolfgang Hallet

The Cultural Need to Communicate in Multiple Languages

The notion of multilingualism traditionally refers to a multiplicity of verbal languages in which individuals are proficient and which are used or co-present in discursive and social interaction. A large number of societal and cultural factors have led to a growing diversification of the languages in everyday communication and in almost all cultural domains. In light of more recent European and worldwide tendencies of a return to nation-state policies and nationalized thinking, the obvious needs to be restated: migration (forced and free) and globalization have made it almost impossible to communicate solely in the native language any longer. Jobs and employees move freely across Europe and other continents, and even smaller companies often operate globally or Europe-wide so that the world of work has clearly become multilingual. The same applies to public communication and the circulation of knowledge or content of all kind, and of popular cultural artifacts in particular. Media corporations operate globally; TV channels, the film industry, streaming portals and the world wide web in general have made it possible to communicate everything in almost any language globally, so that anyone who is proficient in the language of the content that they would like to access (a Spanish website, a French feature film or an American TV show, for example) is able to do so, no matter where they are located. The same applies to the domain of education and knowledge production. In many educational institutions, the national language is no longer the only medium of instruction and scientific knowledge; moreover, due to cultural multilingualism (as is the case in countries such as Switzerland, Northern Italy and Luxembourg) the education system as a whole is multilingual. Last but not least, people seek refuge across states and continents or decide to migrate, and people's personal lives have become more mobile. Travelling has become an almost natural part of people's private lives so that they experience the need to communicate in a foreign language in their own personal lives.

To summarize: the need to educate multilingual citizens (or 'multilingual subjects', as Claire Kramsch [2010] terms them) is not simply a pedagogically desirable goal, but it is a response to cultural developments represented by all of these processes of migratory, cultural and economic globalization and is therefore a pressing educational issue (Elsner *et al.*, 2013: 57). However, all of the processes sketched above are not only characterized by the use of different languages, often in the same communicative or institutional context. They have also produced, or at least go hand in hand with, new ways and modes to communicate. The internet has enhanced the spread of other symbolic languages, and visual languages (diagrammatic, photographic, filmic, etc.) in particular, and communication in general has become diversified in terms of the sign systems that are routinely used. This is why this chapter argues that the concept of language needs to be extended beyond the system of linguistic signs in order to account for the large number of other symbolic languages that are used in everyday communication, and in digital environments in particular. These other symbolic languages and semiotic modes can be considered languages in their own right that engage in specific ways of making meaning, either on their own or in combination with each other and the verbal language (multimodality). In a semiotic approach, the large potential and the chances that the use of linguistic and non-linguistic sign systems offer in multilingual environments and all processes of meaning-making needs to be investigated. In such an approach, second and foreign languages are conceived of as semiotic resources and modes of meaning-making, among a large range of other semiotic modes. One of the conclusions that will be addressed concerns the need to incorporate the acquisition of other non-verbal literacies into language learning in order to equip learners with the symbolic resources that are required in multimodal and multilingual acts of communication and develop their semiotic competence, or 'symbolic power' (Kramsch, 2010: 13–14). In that sense, all language learning is almost 'naturally' bound to be 'multilingual'.

Digital Communication: From 'Language' to 'Literacies'

In the domain of teaching and learning languages, communicating content between interlocutors in given situations and interactions is the core of the use of language and of all language learning. What, then, do we do with digital types and forms of communication that are inherent to the utterance itself? Examples of such digital communicative forms are the combination of a photograph and a small story on one of the instant messaging platforms (WhatsApp, Facebook, Instagram), an explainer video on a video platform, but also an electronic slide that may combine verbal text, an image and sound in a single 'text' (the slide).

Since the digital texts in these examples are quite distinct and generically different from each other (e.g. the digital story and the explanatory text), subsuming all of them under 'media' doesn't appear to be a particularly appropriate way of conceptualizing or categorizing them. In any case, it is not helpful in terms of a concept of language learning. On the other hand, as a result of its implementation in the federal educational standards for foreign languages, 'media' is a category and an explanatory framework that is widely used in pedagogical theories, and 'media competence' (*Medienkompetenz*) has become the most popular and widespread pedagogical concept in Germany on which everybody in the field draws as a standard rationale applied to (or imposed on) all aspects of foreign language learning (e.g. KMK, 2012: 22–23). However, 'media' is an extremely broad and abstract concept that can mean anything and everything: the feature film, the internet, the graphic novel, the tablet, the email, the smartphone, the photograph, the tweet – all of these are counted under media, although, obviously, the term encompasses a wide range of inconsistent categories. As the examples demonstrate, 'media' may refer to the artifact or 'text' as well as to the technical device or to the channel that carries the signs; it may refer to the hardware as well as the software; and it may denote a whole media system (e.g. 'the press') as well as a single learning device like the electronic dictionary. On the other hand, pen and paper ('old media', as it were) or the printed book don't really come to mind when the notion of 'media' is used, although they obviously are part of the ('old') media system. Most likely, no one would argue that reading a novel enhances 'media competence' – whereas a feature film is supposed to do so. That's why 'media competence' is not particularly apt to grasp the phenomena that one needs to focus upon in the contexts of teaching and learning languages.

To summarize: technologies in themselves do not 'naturally' affect or transform language learning processes and interactions, nor do they enhance them, unless this transformation is pedagogically conceptualized and put into practice. As David Buckingham (2009) argues:

> We need to move beyond the idea that technology has consequences in and of itself. There may indeed be great creative, educational and democratic potential here; but whether that potential is realized depends on how the technology is used, and on the social relationships that are constructed around it. We need to think creatively about the new forms of educational practice, and the new forms of community, which can make this happen. Technology in itself will not make children creative, nor will it motivate or enable them to learn. Children need to develop specific skills both in using software and hardware, and in more 'traditional' areas of literacy and artistic expression, if the potential is to be realized. (Buckingham, 2009: 138)

This critique of 'media' as a category and of computer or technology-oriented concepts in language learning is, of course, not meant to deny or ignore the valuable, often innovative proposals and contributions that have been made by them in the field of learning and teaching languages. On the contrary, historically and methodologically, they were the first and the most productive approaches that accounted for the role of what used to be (and sometimes is still) called 'the new media'. However, since digital technology is no longer one factor among others or a single phenomenon, but has instead become a whole, omnipresent dimension of everyday life that affects everybody's ways of thinking, communicating and doing, and society as a whole as well as the social lives of individuals, 'digitalization' must be reconceptualized as a dimension of school education. It is not a factor that is additional or external to acts of communication and to language learning. Rather, digitalization has become inherent to the use and acquisition of languages, no matter whether they are native, second or foreign: to a great extent, communication itself has taken on a digital form; a large number of communicative acts are digital themselves and occur in electronic environments. This is why digital acts of discourse and digital formats of communication – digital modes and genres, the digital languages – need to be taught and learned in the language classroom.

The emergence of new multimedia technologies, of the digitalization of communication and of the electronic hypertext in particular, has therefore made it most urgent to account for the combination of different symbolic forms in displays and environments in which 'meaning' can no longer be explained as resulting from the use of the natural human language alone. In digital communication, the contribution of other codes and sign systems such as sound and music, maps and diagrams, photographs and moving images, is most obvious and almost standard:

> Multimodal production is now a ubiquitous fact of representation and communication. That forces us urgently to develop precise tools requisite for the description and analysis of texts and semiotic entities of contemporary communication. (Kress, 2010: 102)

Therefore, theories not only of cultural semiosis and communication, but also of language learning and of multilingualism must explain and describe how meaning is made across (and simultaneously through) a variety of different semiotic systems, semiotic and generic modes (carried by different 'media' and placed in different medial environments, digital media among them), and how a combination of all of these modes and media is able to produce one integrated, or even coherent and more or less conventionalized meaning.

Multiliteracies pedagogy (The New London Group, 2000) has responded to both, the fundamental cultural changes delineated in the first section of this chapter, and the need for a new pedagogy in light of these sociocultural and economic changes. Therefore, the purpose of the multiliteracies pedagogy is twofold:

> First, we want to extend the idea and scope of literacy pedagogy to account for the context of our culturally and linguistically diverse and increasingly globalised societies; to account for the multifarious cultures that interrelate and the plurality of texts that circulate. Second, we argue that literacy pedagogy now must account for the burgeoning variety of text forms associated with information and multimedia technologies. (The New London Group, 2000: 9)

The fundamental cultural changes in communication, interaction and orientation as described by The New London Group (2000) can briefly be summarized as the global circulation of texts of all kinds (resulting in the pluralization and individualization of cultural, ethical or religious orientations), the enormous multiplication of the amount of data and information that is accessible (e.g. through online search tools), the acceleration of the distribution of information and texts (of all kinds) and the use and combination of a large variety of semiotic modes in single acts of representation and communication, be they visual, diagrammatic or cartographic or other languages (cf. Elsner & Viebrock, 2013; Etus, 2013: 36).

These social, cultural and communicative changes were partly, but not exclusively, caused by digitalization. In any case, this more or less sociological and cultural analysis urges us to develop an emancipatory pedagogical theory that attempts to define the competencies, abilities and skills that schools need to teach in order to educate young people for a self-determined life, and full and equal participation in all spheres of the societies in which they (will) live and work. Digital education [*digitale Bildung*] must therefore be conceived as part of a larger pedagogical framework that draws upon the social, cultural and societal changes, processes and conditions in which the young generation live and which they must be able to actively design and create ('designing social futures', The New London Group, 2000; also cf. BMBF, 2016: 6).

As the name suggests, the multiliteracies approach responds to the large variety of semiotic modes that are used in everyday and in online communication and the need to integrate the teaching and learning of these 'languages' into school education. As opposed to media- or technology-oriented concepts, multiliteracies pedagogy focuses upon the processes of meaning-making in communicative interaction. It addresses the various modes of communication and draws attention to the specificity of the respective sign system that is used in a communicative act. Sometimes, this occurs on its own, as in a photograph, but it may also occur in combination with other modes, as in the combination of language and images in a film or on TV. Accordingly, the multiliteracies approach articulates the need to educate the students' proficiency in a range of literacies (the 'languages' of the different sign systems) and their combination in communicative interaction. Although the multiliteracies approach was not designed for the foreign language classroom, the literacies concept points to the fact that an individual's capacity to 'pursue their happiness' and to participate fully in societal processes and cultural discourses depends largely on the ability to make meaning of signs; to acquire and share knowledge; to articulate thoughts, emotions and experiences; and to engage in all sorts of communicative interaction (being 'literate') in a large variety of sign systems, not least in a foreign language.

This is why in the English classroom, generally speaking, digital education must account for the digital dimension and the multisemiotic character of discourses in the foreign language and in the individual's cultural, political and social environment. School education needs to equip the students with digital competencies and multiple literacies (cf. Walker & White, 2013: 8–9). For the English classroom, this must be specified as digital and multiliteral discourse competence in the foreign language, which encompasses proficiency in a wide range of digital communicative formats across sign systems and languages (with a main focus on verbal language); their combination in a single act of communication (multimodality, as in electronic slides or online videos); the ability to engage in social and communicative practices in digital environments; and the ability to reflect critically upon their own and others' digital practices and ways of self-constitution, social interaction and sociality.

Multiple 'Languages': Semiotic Modes and Digital Genres

The notion of a multiplicity of literacies that schools and foreign language classrooms need to educate points to the need for a reconceptualization of the notion of 'language'. Literacy traditionally refers to the ability to read and write. If applied to other sign systems, they are obviously also regarded as 'languages' that serve to encode and decode meaning in a more or less conventionalized manner and are used in communicative interaction, acts of representation and meaning-making. In order to make this extension of the notion of language more convincing, it is helpful to briefly enquire in what sense various semiotic modes possess qualities that are traditionally assigned to languages. In social semiotics, the concept of multimodality is closely tied to a functional definition of the semiotic mode. The vast majority of modes can be regarded as utterances, i.e. textual or medial (generic) entities and meaning-making units in social interaction that produce three different types of meaning in a more or less conventionalized manner. According to Halliday's (2010: 29–31) metafunctional principles of communication (also cf. Etus, 2013: 36–37; Hallet, 2016: 32–35), these different functions of producing meaning are:

- the ideational function: a semiotic mode is able to produce, to carry and to communicate a message, or content, knowledge and experience;
- the interpersonal function: it is able to establish interpersonal constellations and social interaction, with clearly defined and mutually recognizable roles and parts of the respective participants;
- the textual function: it is a clearly bounded, coherent ensemble of signs that are arranged in a particular, more or less stable or conventionalized way (e.g. situatedness, revolving around an identifiable issue, having a 'center', or a beginning, middle and end for linear text; keeping proportions, developing or unfolding in an expected way and so forth).

What is important here: these criteria clearly apply to traditional linguistic texts, written or spoken. But they also apply to a lot of other ways of saying things or expressing and communicating meaning: the black and white wedding photograph, the interactive digital map, the online self-video and so forth. All of these utterances are considered to be texts that serve very specific communicative or signifying purposes in clearly defined and bounded social and cultural contexts, and they employ different sign systems through which they engage in acts of meaning-making. Of course, all of these modes are also tied to medial carriers or 'channels' that are employed in a given communicative situation or context, according to the purpose and the addressee(s) of an utterance.

If such modes are regarded as (and taught like) languages, they must also be characterized by communicative efficiency and a capacity to produce meaning in a way that is specific for a particular mode and distinct from other 'languages'. This distinct communicative capacity of a semiotic mode is called 'affordance' and is the deeper reason why maps or diagrams are employed in everyday communication, online and offline. A topographical map is a specific and, as a rule, more efficient way of displaying features of an area or region or piece of land that would otherwise, e.g. in the verbal language, be difficult (or very inefficient) to grasp and communicate. A color photograph of a family scene can communicate very complex content, e.g. rendering impressions of the persons who were present, a detailed representation of the setting, the mood and atmosphere and, maybe, even social relations or interactions. As against this, a verbal text produced for the same representational purposes would probably have to be endlessly long, but incomplete.

Apart from the communicative functions in everyday contexts (across different domains like the world of work or personal lives), semiotic modes also play an important role in shaping and representing scientific and disciplinary knowledge. Discipline-specific symbolic languages represent the specific epistemologies and forms of knowledge that are used and taught in content subjects, e.g. the formulae and symbols in mathematics or chemistry or the 'languages' of maps in geography. Therefore, teaching such 'languages' in language classrooms for the purpose of everyday communication also affects and enhances learning in monolingual or bilingual content-subject classrooms (or content and language integrated learning [CLIL]; for details cf. Hallet, 2016: 140–171). Like modes and genres in everyday communication, such subject-specific languages are characterized and defined by individual semantic elements – a 'vocabulary', as it were – like colors, graphic forms or conventionalized symbols, and also by complex codes, i.e. the 'grammars' that provide syntax and combination rules that allow complex content to be symbolized and communicated in specific semiotic forms. This is why content and CLIL classrooms are in themselves characterized by the use of multiple languages and why they offer paradigmatic experiences of plurilingual discourse, and learning and teaching (cf. Hallet, 2012 for details).

The functional use of semiotic modes in everyday communication and social interaction is only possible because they are 'a socially shaped and culturally given resource for making meaning in representation and communication' (Kress, 2010: 53) and 'used in recognisably stable ways as a means of articulating discourse' (Kress & van Leeuwen, 2001: 25). This feature of the stable, conventionalized meaning of modes paves the way to the language classroom since the most advanced form of conventionalized semiotic modes are the genres of everyday communication, e.g. the discursive genres of a handwritten letter, an email, a handwritten diary entry or a newspaper article or the multimodal genres of a brochure, a TV talk show or a music video clip in popular culture. But, there are also non-discursive genres like maps and plans of all sorts or diagrams, charts and photographs that are omnipresent in everyday communication and representation.

It is for this reason that the genre approach seems to be best suited if the teaching and learning of a range of semiotic modes is to be integrated into the language classroom. As the meta-communicative functions suggest, the genre approach regards texts as 'language in use' and the building blocks of cultural discourses, independent of their symbolic form or the combination of various modes in a single 'text' (as in the multimedia hypertext). The textual quality of an utterance, independent of the semiotic form, and the way it is embedded in the larger discourse make it possible to assign genres a curricular place in the language classroom and curriculum and to acquire them at the level of text. Generic learning cannot be described in detail here (cf. Hallet, 2016), but it is important to keep in mind that semiotic modes in the conventionalized form of genres show all features of a language. In particular, they

- are based on codes in terms of a more or less conventionalized meaning that is assigned to signs and a grammar that organizes the signs in a meaningful way;
- bear textual and generic features since the signs are organized in a consistent way that constitutes textual cohesion and coherence, i.e. a recognizable structure;
- possess a characteristic affordance, a specific way of producing meaning that is different from other languages and modes or a communicative advantage over them, e.g. real-time communication at a distance via instant messaging formats;
- respond to other utterances in a cultural discourse or they initiate or co-constitute it; this positioning in the discourse is not only an important dimension of the foreign language discourse competence, but it is the only way to produce meaning and to decide why a certain genre and mode is chosen and what its communicative advantages or capacities are;
- are often tied to a conventionalized purpose and context of communication and interaction that defines the style and register that is used, the type of sign system that is considered adequate (or inadequate, e.g. a private photograph in business communication) and the way in which it is rendered (e.g. electronic vs. 'real' mail).

With this focus on the function of a text in the context of a cultural discourse in mind, it turns out that 'discourse competence' as the overall dimension and principle of language learning can be (and must be) implemented at the level of the production of meaningful utterances. But the broad range of semiotic modes that are involved in meaning-making in cultural discourses also implies that discourse competence in the true sense cannot be accomplished if based on traditional language skills only, as suggested in the *Common European Framework of Reference for Languages* or in the German foreign language standards for the secondary and the upper secondary level. In any case, it is useful to apply the genre approach to digital communication, too, because, as in all fields of communication, proficiency in the most common generic forms of communication can be regarded as crucial in every language learning process.

In light of the critical remarks on the concept of 'media', it is important to remember once again that a genre is always co-defined by the medial or material carrier that is employed in the respective utterance (pen and paper, the chisel and stone, the electronic screen, etc.). Actually, the medial dimension is one of the communicative options that the use of a genre implies (e.g. sending a personal handwritten letter vs. a phone call vs. sending an email). The genre approach, therefore, does not ignore the presence and employment of media in acts of communication, but the medial dimension is embedded into other dimensions of the choice of a genre, like the social and cultural context and situation, the addressee(s), the outreach and the purpose of the utterance.

Acquiring and using digital genres implies definitions of and decisions on:

- the purpose and the digital format of the act of communication, presentation or representation that is most efficient or best-suited (an email letter, a tweet, a digital explainer video, an electronic slide);
- the type of electronic environment in which the text or the act of communication is placed (a university teaching and learning platform, a www chat forum, a video channel, etc.);
- the textual and generic digital format that is chosen, including the underlying cultural, linguistic and textual rules for form, structure, style and register.

The genre approach not only makes it possible to integrate other symbolic languages into language learning, but it also relates the use of digital genres in everyday communication to their non-digital 'relatives'. Digital storytelling would thus be part of the acquisition of a general narrative competence since narratives are the macro-genre that can be realized in different forms at the level of the textual utterance and in different modes (written, oral, multimodal and digital). Certain generic features of narratives like action and plot, causal effects and a transformation of the state of things between the beginning and the end can thus be acquired across modes, no matter whether they are written, photographic or digitally visual, whereas other features would be specific to one of the modes only, as, e.g. in the use of animated or moving images that may constitute a digital narrative.

Generic learning also develops an awareness of the type of contribution that one would like to make to a larger discourse. Alongside the Australian genre approach in the context of the Halliday school (Hallet, 2016: 68–72), three basic types of genre (macro-genres) that are particularly relevant and important, both in cultural communication and in school education, can be distinguished: narratives, expository (factual) texts and arguments (cf. Hallet, 2016: 77–86; the general genre matrix for foreign language learning on p. 78). Genre learning leads to conscious decision-making with regard to the genre of an utterance, its structural and textual features and its communicative affordance (cf. Hallet [2014] for digital oral communication).

The genre matrix in Figure 1.1 is a synopsis of the different types and modes of narratives in an attempt to define 'narrative' at the micro-level of genre (the second column to the left) and according to the mode that is employed at the level of the actual utterance, demonstrating how

macro genre	genre	oral mode	written mode	multimodal mode	digital mode
narratives	recount	**Talking to friends at school**: My practicum in Australia	**Written recount**: My practicum in Australia	**Portfolio:** My practicum in Australia	**Blog entry:** My practicum in Australia (a multimodal recount, text, photos etc.)
	story	**Phone call to my parents:** My friend's accident and helicopter rescue	**Written story:** My friend's accident and helicopter rescue	**A comic:** My friend's accident and helicopter rescue	**Social networks post, photos and text:** My friend's accident and helicopter rescue
	anecdote	**Talking to my boy/girlfriend:** An incident at the holiday camp	**A letter to my friend:** An incident at the holiday camp	**Photo album:** An incident at the holiday camp	**A slide show for my family:** An incident at the holiday camp
	exemplum	**Classroom presentation:** The story of the life of a pair of blue jeans	**A school magazine article:** The story of the life of a pair of blue jeans	**A flyer:** The story of the life of a pair of blue jeans	**Online presentation:** An illustrated flow chart: The story of the life of a pair of blue jeans
	vision	**Telling my parents:** The first three months after my final school exam	**A diary entry:** The first three months after my final school exam	**An illustrated scenario (maps etc.):** The first three months after my final school exam	**Chat forum contribution:** The first three months after my final school exam

Figure 1.1 A genre matrix for narrative texts (Hallet, 2016: 82)

the place of digital genres in cultural communication and in language education can be defined. As to the two columns on the right, it must be noted that digital genres are multimodal as a rule; but it makes sense to set the digital formats off against non-digital multimodal forms like the newspaper cartoon, the comic or the print poster (second column to the right). On the one hand, the matrix thus visualizes the affordances of different modes of narration, the different purposes or functions of narration and communication (e.g. recount vs. story) and the textual and structural differences between them. On the other hand, the matrix represents the commonalities, analogies and continuities between non-digital spoken or written narratives, non-digital multimodal forms (the cartoon, the map in a news story, etc.) and the respective digital narrative genres, e.g. the short online video, the online comic, including an online database or digital toolkit for the creation of panels, characters and speech or thought bubbles. Producing a small handwritten story can thus support the ability to produce a digital narrative, and vice versa: the conscious use or analysis of a video game may lead to a deeper understanding of narrative constituents like protagonist, perspective, setting and action, and of narration in general, and will thus contribute to the development of narrative competence.

The level of the genre in terms of the textual form and communicative function of an utterance is an appropriate way of integrating the acquisition of a multiplicity of literacies into language learning that correspond with the most important generic and semiotic modes of everyday communication as displayed in the genre matrix. It makes it possible to teach 'the languages' of semiotic modes by:

- teaching the specific semantic and communicative potential (and limits) of a range of semiotic modes (affordance);
- teaching the codes and grammars of non-alphabetic modes, e.g. the cultural and aesthetic codes that are employed and displayed in visual images (cf. Hallet, 2010 for details);
- the systematic training of the purposeful use of non-alphabetic 'languages' (sign systems), rather than occasional or accidental use in the production of meaningful utterances that are embedded in larger cultural discourses;
- defining the place and the specific affordances of the verbal language in multimodal designs and the affordances of the other semiotic modes;
- identifying the type of interrelatedness of the single semiotic modes and their contribution to the meaning of a coherent multimodal text or communicative act.

As complex as most of the generic forms in the matrix may appear to be, it is important to remember that all of them can be taught and produced at very early stages of language learning, albeit in basic form. A digital picture story (the digital mode in the matrix in Figure 1.1) may serve as an example. In order to introduce young language learners into visual storytelling and into the production of digital narratives, they can be asked to sequentialize a number of photographs, ready-made images from the internet, hand-drawn sketches or self-made comic panels in a digital slideshow in such a manner that they form a narrative, e.g. the story of an incident, an autobiographic episode or any other series of events or actions. The production of a picture story, fiction or non-fiction alike, not only requires and develops narrative competence based on the features of a good story (e.g. rising action, climax, falling action); it also relies on and enhances the learners' visual literacy, i.e. the production and selection of appropriate images (photos, drawings, etc.) according to the genre that they intend to produce. Furthermore, verbal narration must be added to the series of images, either as a complementary written text in the form of captions, possibly together with thought or speech bubbles in the manner of comic panels, or as a voice-over narrative in which the learner takes on the role of the narrator and presents the picture story. A sound and music track may complete the presentation of the story. Such a digital story becomes fully multimodal if all of the modal and communicative options delineated above (the sign systems or 'languages': images, written text, oral narration, sound) are integrated into the narrative. This integration is in itself yet another ability that must be trained and developed since it depends on the choices of and decisions on how all of these different 'languages' (sign systems) are adequately and appropriately combined.

This way, the story that is produced is a relatively complex artifact that makes use of almost all of the modes that are nowadays used in everyday internet communication, and in social networks in particular (Facebook, Instagram, etc.), which is largely dominated by visual communication and narration. The production of a digital multimodal picture story can also be regularly used and trained to prepare the competent production of digital videos that have become so popular in online communication. On the other hand, all of these modes are standard elements (applications) in today's personal computer or smartphone software, and the level and complexity of the individual ingredients (images, written or spoken text, etc.) can easily be adapted to the learners' stage of language learning and their proficiency in the foreign language.

Semiotic Translation

With regard to foreign language learning, there is one last, very important implication that needs to be mentioned since it must also be systematically developed in foreign language learning contexts and conceptualized in didactics: the role of semiotic translation in everyday communication and the importance of the competence to translate different semiotic modes into each other, and from and into the foreign language in particular (also cf. Hallet [2012] for the bilingual classroom). In everyday communication, translating or mediating between different sign systems is a standard practice and communicative routine: representing the content of a painting to someone who cannot see it in the words of the foreign language; turning the navigation that the electronic map offers into a verbal 'finding your way' description; interpreting a topographical map in terms of the features and structures that a landscape will probably show; translating a statistical diagram in a newspaper article into a verbal report – all of these are daily routines, both in everyday communication and in educational contexts. In the foreign language classroom, such acts of semiotic translation are particularly relevant because they are cognitively challenging in terms of comprehending and interpreting the information in non-verbal texts (making meaning of them); and they are highly relevant for the process of language learning itself since they rely on and can develop the linguistic and lexical repertoire that is required to adequately 'translate' (or 'mediate') the content and information of a non-verbal text into the foreign language.

Understood and practiced this way, the semiotic and generic approach turns out to possess the potential to develop almost to a full extent the semiotic and textual repertoire that language users should have at their disposal. They will thus be able to acquire the 'symbolic power' that Claire Kramsch may have in mind for the multilingual subject, but which she doesn't really spell out in terms of the whole range of semiotic modes that must be part of it. If the teaching and learning of English and of other foreign languages aims at young people's proficiency in all of the different types and modes of generic communication, including its digital variants, then discourse competence will not remain a buzzword; it will become a true and realistic goal.

References

BMBF (2016) – Bundesministerium für Forschung und Bildung (2016) *Bildungsoffensive für die digitale Wissensgesellschaft: Strategie des Bundesministeriums für Bildung und Forschung*. Berlin: BMBF.

Buckingham, D. (2009) New media, new childhoods? Children's changing cultural environment in the age of digital technology. In M.J. Kehily (ed.) *Introduction to Childhood Studies* (2nd edn; pp. 117–138). Maidenhead: Open University Press.

Elsner, D. and Viebrock, B. (2013) Developing multiliteracies in the 21st century: Motives for new approaches of teaching and learning languages. In D. Elsner, S. Helff and B. Viebrock (eds) *Films, Graphic Novels & Visuals: Developing Multiliteracies in Foreign Language Education – An Interdisciplinary Approach* (pp. 17–32). Zürich/Münster: LIT.

Elsner, D., Helff, S. and Viebrock, B. (eds) (2013) *Films, Graphic Novels and Visuals. Developing Multiliteracies in Foreign Language Education*. Zürich/Münster: LIT.

Etus, Ö. (2013) New realms of meaning making: Multimodal literacies in language classrooms. In D. Elsner, S. Helff and B. Viebrock (eds) *Films, Graphic Novels & Visuals: Developing Multiliteracies in Foreign Language Education – An Interdisciplinary Approach* (pp. 33–51). Zürich/Münster: LIT.

Hallet, W. (2010) Viewing cultures: Kulturelles Sehen und Bildverstehen im Fremdsprachenunterricht. In C. Hecke and C. Surkamp (eds) *Bilder im Fremdsprachenunterricht. Neue Ansätze, Kompetenzen und Methoden* (pp. 26–54). Tübingen: Narr.

Hallet, W. (2012) Semiotic translation and literacy learning in CLIL. In D. Marsh and O. Meyer (eds) *Quality Interfaces: Examining Evidence & Exploring Solutions in CLIL* (pp. 191–201). Eichstaett: Eichstaett Academic Press.

Hallet, W. (2014) Beyond speaking: Neue Mündlichkeiten. In E. Burwitz-Melzer, F.G. Königs and C. Riemer (eds) *Perspektiven der Mündlichkeit* (pp. 69–78). Tübingen: Narr.

Hallet, W. (2016) *Genres im fremdsprachlichen und bilingualen Unterricht: Formen und Muster der sprachlichen Interaktion*. Seelze: Klett Kallmeyer.

Halliday, M.A.K. (2010) *An Introduction to Functional Grammar*. London: Hodder Education.

KMK (2012) – Sekretariat der Ständigen Konferenz der Kultusminister der Länder in der Bundesrepublik Deutschland (ed.) (2012) Bildungsstandards für die fortgeführte Fremdsprache (Englisch/Französisch) für die Allgemeine Hochschulreife. Beschluss der Kultusministerkonferenz vom 18.10.2012. See http://www.kmk.org/fileadmin/veroeffentlichungen_beschluesse/2012/2012_10_18-Bildungsstandards-Fortgef-FS-Abi.pdf (accessed 10 October 2016).

Kramsch, C. (2010) *The Multilingual Subject: What Foreign Language Learners Say about Their Experience and Why It Matters*. Oxford: Oxford University Press.

Kress, G. (2010) *Multimodality: A Social Semiotic Approach to Contemporary Communication*. London/New York: Routledge.

Kress, G. and van Leeuwen, T. (2001) *Multimodal Discourse: The Modes and Media of Contemporary Communication*. London: Arnold.

The New London Group (2000) A pedagogy of multiliteracies. Designing social futures. In B. Cope and M. Kalantzis (eds) *Multiliteracies. Literacy Learning and the Design of Social Futures* (pp. 9–37). London/New York: Routledge.

Walker, A. and White, G. (2013) *Technology Enhanced Language Learning: Connecting Theory and Practice*. Oxford: Oxford University Press.

2 Learnscaping: Creating Next-Gen Learning Environments for Pluriliteracies Growth

Oliver Meyer, Do Coyle and Kevin Schuck

In this first section, we would like to make the case for pluriliteracies as an appropriate framework for mapping the broader goals of 21st-century plurilingual education involving critical thinking, knowledge creation, application and communication as well as social participation within and across individual subjects of schooling. We will argue that the processes of digitization and globalization have significantly impacted on the way we communicate and work and have not only raised the importance of literacies but also changed the very nature of literacies themselves. Next, we will present recent developments within the field of literacies research and demonstrate how these developments have influenced the Graz Group Pluriliteracies Framework for teaching and learning. In this chapter, we would like to expand the conceptual framework of a pluriliteracies approach to teaching for learning (PTL) to demonstrate how an overarching ecological approach to deeper learning must move beyond the cognitive domain and take account of the affective domain and integrate the use of digital media in the classroom. We make the case for a new paradigm where the creation of ecological learning environments for plurilingual education and practices are situated.

The Importance of Literacies as Key Competencies for Multilingual Societies

A recent high-level report on literacy stresses the paramount importance of literacy development for the future of Europe's workforce:

> Literacy is more essential than ever before. In societies dominated by the written word, it is a fundamental requirement for citizens of all ages in modern Europe. Literacy empowers the individual to develop capacities of reflection, critique and empathy, leading to a sense of self-efficacy, identity

> and full participation in society. (EU High Level Group of Experts on Literacy, 2012: 21)

Digitization is listed as one of the key reasons why literacy is gaining in importance as digital communication currently centers on the written word and is, in essence, changing the very nature of literacy:

> [...] the digital world requires higher-order problem solving skills. Reading print on paper and reading online share many core characteristics, but reading online demands a greater ability to evaluate information critically within the context of a seemingly infinite universe of available options. Likewise, there is an increasing need for the ability to extract and use knowledge from an ever-growing number of online resources. (EU High Level Group of Experts on Literacy, 2012: 23)

With an emphasis on the global economy and labor markets, demands are increasing for highly literate 'knowledge workers' who can apply 'theoretical and analytical knowledge acquired through formal education to develop new products or services' (Chiriac & Ghitiu-Bratescu, 2011: 15). According to Kale *et al.* (2011), economic success rests on the skills of these individual knowledge workers to transfer knowledge successfully through acquiring, assimilating and processing the constant stream of information in ways that are contextually relevant, meaningful and appropriate (Eppler & Burkhard, 2004).

The report further acknowledges that, taking account of global shifts, literacy has an increasingly multilingual dimension. Therefore, to prepare students adequately for the challenges described above and to help them become creative, responsible global citizens, there is a need for pedagogies that will promote the development of learners' pluriliterate repertories, enabling them to construct, critically analyze and communicate 'expert' knowledge adequately and successfully across cultures, languages and disciplines using a wide variety of modes.

Current developments in the fields of literacies: From multiliteracies to pluriliteracies; from general to disciplinary literacies

Gee (1989) defines literacy as command of secondary discourses and uses of languages. Based on the idea that literacies are not only related to different cultural contexts and social structures but are also embedded in different channels or multiple modes of communication, The New London Group (1996) proposed a multiliteracies pedagogy that focuses on how literacy practices have been influenced by local and global, social, cultural and technological change. Anstey (2002) suggests that an active and informed global citizen is one equipped with multiliterate skills and understanding. He defines a multiliterate person as flexible and strategic and able to understand and develop literacy practices using a range of texts and technologies in socially responsible ways and according to diverse social, cultural and linguistic demands.

Emphasizing the variability and interconnectedness of literacy practices and identities in various sociocultural contexts, the hybridity of literacy practices afforded by new technologies and the increasing interrelationship of semiotic systems, García *et al.* (2007) introduce the term *pluriliteracies* to capture the sociolinguistic realities of 21st-century plurilingual societies. Their pluriliteracies approach is dynamic and open to ways in which cultural contexts and social relations influence and impact literacy practices within and beyond schooling.

Shanahan and Shanahan (2008, 2012) have conceptualized literacy development as the process of moving from basic to intermediary to disciplinary literacies. They challenge the widely held assumption that knowledge can be accessed and built through a set of generalized study skills, that learning any kind of text is quasi-independent of the underlying subject matter and that basic reading skills automatically evolve into more advanced skills. Instead, Shanahan and Shanahan promote the idea of teaching disciplinary literacies that address the profound differences in the language used in various disciplines to construct and communicate knowledge and in ways different disciplines read and approach texts.

Drawing on research over the last decade, disciplinary or subject literacy is rapidly gaining attention on a global scale as evidenced, for example, by the work of Dobbs *et al.* (2016), Fang and Coatoam (2013), Gillis (2014), Jetton and Shanahan (2012), Schleppegrell (2004) and Weinburgh and Silva (2012). Within the European context, Beacco *et al.* (2015: 26) have applied the concept of *scientific literacy* to a school context, arguing for a generalized notion of *literacy for all subjects* as an indicator of quality education in general and, more specifically, to describe the broader goals of subject education. Scientific literacy has been defined as

> evolving combination of the science-related attitudes, skills, and knowledge students need in order to develop inquiry, problem-solving, and decision-making abilities, to become lifelong learners, and to maintain a sense of wonder about the world around them. (Council of Ministers of Education, Canada, 1997: 4)

Beacco *et al.* (2015: 27) identified six interdependent dimensions of scientific literacy that have fundamental implications for pedagogic approaches:

(1) Processing and acquiring subject knowledge and in-depth understanding of texts that deal with subject-matter issues.

(2) Negotiating the meaning of new knowledge items in relation to already existing ones.
(3) Reflecting on how a new insight developed and was acquired.
(4) Considering the validity and use of knowledge, applying it to other/ new contexts.
(5) Preparing for and participating in socio-scientific debates and the relevant discourses outside of school.
(6) Questioning critically the meaning and scope of rules or conventions, generalizing the acquired procedural knowledge and skills (as part of one's general education).

These implications raise challenging questions about how school learners access and participate effectively in these processes, to become equipped with the necessary skills and understanding essential for 'deeper' learning in the disciplines.

Deeper learning has been defined as 'the process through which an individual becomes capable of taking what was learned in one situation and applying it to a new situation' (National Research Council, 2012: SUM-4).

After a comprehensive review of the available research, the report concludes that such transfer of learning or, more specifically, 'specific transfer of general principles' (National Research Council, 2012: 4-3) is dependent on 'the way in which the individual and the community structures and organizes the intertwined knowledge and skills' (National Research Council, 2012: SUM-5). In other words, developing subject-specific literacies through mastering the specific ways of generating and communicating knowledge will lead to transferable knowledge and skills. Therefore, for deeper learning to be successful, it must be 'situated within, and emerge from, the practices in different settings and communities [...] with their own cultures, languages, tools and modes of discourse' (National Research Council, 2012).

Much of the work in developing subject literacies does not specifically take account of contexts where learners are using more than one language in their learning process. This presents an urgent need and provides an opportune forum for the Graz Group to draw on the work of García *et al.* (2007), Hornberger (2003) and The New London Group (1996), to develop a PTL. PTL promotes subject literacy development *in more than one language* as the key to deeper learning and the development of transferable skills. This approach focuses on helping learners become literate in content subjects and empowering them to successfully and appropriately communicate that knowledge across disciplines, cultures and languages in a wide variety of modes to become more creative and responsible global citizens (Meyer *et al.*, 2015a).

A pluriliteracies approach to teaching for learning

The pluriliteracies model in Figure 2.1 maps pluriliteracies development and illustrates how students can be mentored in the disciplines or subjects of schooling. It rests on a number of premises:

First, focusing on learning potential, we believe that knowledge acquisition is a process of meaning-making for understanding and acting in the world. All knowledge is constituted in semiotic systems with language as the most central (Mohan *et al.*, 2010). Since we live in an image-based and increasingly digital world where semiotics are multimodal and hybrid in nature, the term *pluriliteracies* not only accommodates learning and operating in more than one language, but it also encompasses the need for education to address plurimodal semiotics.

Second, subject-specific literacy develops with a growing ability to express or verbalize subject-specific concepts or conceptual knowledge in an appropriate style using the appropriate genre and genre moves for the specific purpose of communication. This process is languaging, i.e. using language(s) to mediate increasingly cognitively complex acts of thinking and understanding, i.e. 'the process of making meaning and shaping knowledge and experience through language' (Swain, 2006). Lantolf and Poehner (2014) propose that languaging is a prerequisite of transferable knowledge. Moreover, if we consider genres as goal-oriented, purposeful activities, then genres act as guiding principles along the knowledge path to a discipline. This is because genres can be matched to the four major activity domains of school subjects (doing,

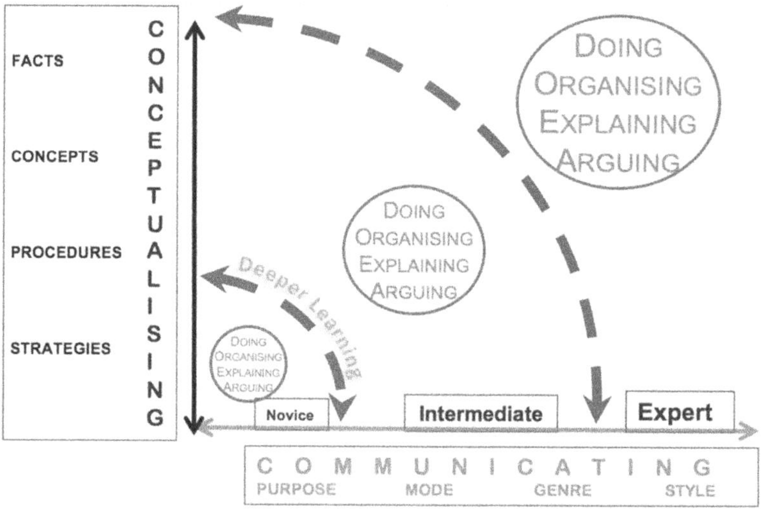

Figure 2.1 The Graz Group pluriliteracies model (Meyer *et al.*, 2015a)

organizing, explaining, arguing; see Table 2.1), which learners need to master in order to become literate. Genres can be broken down into smaller parts (i.e. genre moves, micro genres and/or cognitive discourse functions) and 'scaled' up or down in complexity according to the breadth of obligatory and optional genre moves, the depth of the content information provided in each of these moves and the quality of language use at the discourse, sentence and lexico-grammatical level (Byrnes, 2002; Hallet, 2016; Meyer *et al.*, 2017).

Third, considering the above, there are further pedagogic implications for effectively implementing the pluriliteracies model. Built

Table 2.1 Scientific processes, genres and modes

Scientific Processes	Genres	Purposes
doing things scientifically	• Experiments & Protocols	Instruct someone how to do things
	• Laboratory reports	Provide a recount of the method, as well as the results, discussions and conclusions.
	• Investigations	Set out the design and decisions behind students' attempts to behave scientifically
describing & organising the world scientifically	• Descriptions	Describe multiple aspects/features of a natural or physical phenomenon
	• Comparisons	Compare features of two or more physical phenomena
	• Compositions	Present (describe and or define) component parts of a physical phenomenon
	• Classifications	Present different types/classes of a phenomenon
explaining phenomena scientifically	**temporal explanations**	
	• sequential explanations	Explain physical phenomena by presenting the events producing the phenomena in chronological order
	non-temporal explanations	
	• factorial/consequential explanations	Explain the multiple factors/consequences that contribute to a particular event or phenomenon
	• theoretical explanations	Define and illustrate a theoretical principle
arguing scientifically	• Arguments	Persuade to agree with a particular point of view on an issue and some exhort the reader/listener to take action
	• Discussions	Present the case for more than one point of view

Source: Based on Polias (2016), adapted.

on the principle that all learners can successfully participate in working and constructing knowledge in a subject at an age-appropriate level (see Figure 2.1 and Table 2.1), classroom practices should scaffold meaningful practice activities and complex challenging tasks with appropriate feedback and feedforward if subject-specific skills are to be automatized and deeper learning is to occur (DeKeyser, 2007; Graz Group, 2015; Lyster, 2007).

In sum, according to our pluriliteracies model, pluriliterate 'experts' are increasingly sensitive to the social and cultural context and able to participate in meaningful social interactions across disciplines, cultures and languages by adapting their message and mode for specific purposes and audiences.

Success criteria for literacies learning: Adding the learner

While the theoretical underpinning and rationale for the pluriliteracies model presented and discussed in the previous section are based on current thinking and research by academics and educators, its interpretation, application and implementation is challenging. The model requires a radical review of classroom practices, which in turn have pedagogic implications for all teachers involved. Literacies development does not just happen, but needs to be planned for and consciously fostered in the content subject lessons. In order to support teachers as they mentor students' literacies development, the Graz Group, in collaboration with teachers and teacher educators, identified five fundamental core principles that inform the PTL approach (Meyer *et al.*, 2015b):

(1) Conceptualizing learning progression
(2) Focusing on the learner
(3) Languaging for understanding
(4) Realizing cultural embeddedness
(5) Rethinking scaffolding for learner development

It is not in the scope of this chapter to analyze each of these in depth, but key challenges that permeate the model focus on planning for the specificities of literacies development outlined above and on providing the appropriate materials and activities to help learners make progress along the knowledge pathway into a discipline.

However, as Walqui (2006) postulates, learning does not take place in a vacuum, but rather is embedded in a sociocultural milieu. He emphasizes the need not only to focus on cognitive development but also to take account of shared social practices that impact on learner engagement in learning. Student engagement can be defined as 'the capacity and inclination for students to take ownership of their past, present, and future educational experiences by enlisting their cognitive, behavioral, and emotional investment in learning' (NASBE, 2015: 8), which establishes the affective domain as a fundamental prerequisite of deeper learning.

Pietarinen *et al.* (2014) provide an excellent overview of research studies on the multidimensional construct of student engagement. Many studies promote learner 'investment' as an essential contributor to cognitive engagement, manifest in the quality of the relationships with teachers and peers. In a similar vein, we argue that emotional and cognitive engagement are both socially embedded and highly dependent on the quality of interaction manifested in the daily pedagogical practices adopted by teachers. This implies that affect and cognitive engagement are not individual attributes, but rather are socially constructed and re-constructed in everyday school interactions. This leads us to conclude that the school-related well-being of students can be understood as the key mediator that simultaneously enhances emotional engagement in school and the sense of cognitive engagement in studying various school subjects. Moreover, Morcom (2015) emphasizes the teacher's role in creating shared spaces, where students have a voice, described by Renshaw (2013) as an 'enabling condition' for scaffolding to encourage learner agency. He holds that learning with and from others is as much about building relationships as it is about mastering a specific skill.

While it is accepted and understood that emotional engagement is essential for learning, we argue that, unless the affective domain is directly and transparently linked to cognitive and language progression through growing appropriate conditions for learning, its full impact will not be realized. In other words, if pluriliteracies learning is to be successful, it needs to be situated in learning environments that connect desired learning outcomes and literacy development with the individual needs of an increasingly heterogeneous student body 'to support a safe, engaging learning climate where students can take risks, make mistakes and drive their own learning' (Parsi, 2015). Such environments need to be designed in such a way that they can act as a 'third space' or a 'zone of transformation' (Pane, 2009) that 'merges the "first space" of people's home, community, and peer networks with "second space" of the discourses they encounter in more formalized institutions [...]' (Moje, 2004: 41) in order to 'challenge, destabilize and expand literacy practices that are typically valued in school' (Moje, 2004: 44). We will return to the implications of and for learning environments in the final section of this chapter.

The Digital Dimension

> While it is possible to teach for deeper learning without technology, it is hard to imagine how our schools will scale up such instruction without support from digital tools and media. (Dede, 2014: 4)

In this section, we would like to argue that in line with recent technological and sociocultural trends, creating the learning environments described previously is increasingly reliant on educational technology because of its potential to combine/blend traditional and non-traditional face-to-face and authentic learning activities to promote student voice and agency and call for new pedagogies that are

> more reflective of engagement, proactively support structural steps to both personalize student learning and engage parents and communities in that learning and preparing educators to support a safe, engaging learning climate where students can take risks, make mistakes and drive their own learning. (Parsi, 2015)

Rapid technological developments are changing the ways we live our lives in terms of work and leisure. Yet, in educational settings, the role of technology is lagging behind especially regarding its impact on the quality of learning. Throughout the last two decades, the potential of technology has shifted from teaching students how to use digital tools to using tools to support the development of cognitive and creative skills, and currently where

> the focus is squarely on learning, not tools. [...] students still need to be proficient in foundational technology skills, but that's not the end. It's the means to an end where the expectation is that students will use technology when appropriate to take charge of their own learning. (ISTE, 2016b: Pos 100/1109)

Dede (2014: 7) echoes these thoughts when he states that the focus of educational technology has turned from 'artificial intelligence to amplifying the intelligence of teachers and students'. He calls for teaching strategies and principles that are geared toward deeper learning and which integrate the use of information and communication technology (ICT) because 'technology as a catalyst is effective only when used to enable learning with richer content, more powerful pedagogy, more valid assessments, and links between in- and out-of-classroom learning' (Dede, 2014: 6).

As the web has increasingly become more pervasive and interactive and characterized by features such as 'tagging, social networks and user-created taxonomies of content called "folksonomies"' (Borland, 2007), it is clear that Web 3.0 enabled by the convergence of several technology trends (such as ubiquitous connectivity, network computing, open technologies, open identity as well as semantic web technologies) (Spivack, 2007) will further impact formal and informal learning. The question remains when and how will the integration of digital literacies into classroom learning become a reality?

The 2016 edition of the International Society for Technology in Education (ISTE, 2016a) Standards lists seven key areas of digital literacies along with indicators and age bands to guide the development of skills and competencies needed to engage and thrive in a connected, digital world. These are listed below since we believe that developing digital literacies is fundamental to becoming a pluriliterate citizen and goes far beyond the narrow interpretation of 'using computers in the classroom':

(1) Empowered Learner: Students leverage technology to take an active role in choosing, achieving and demonstrating competency in their learning goals, informed by the learning sciences.
(2) Digital Citizen: Students recognize the rights, responsibilities and opportunities of living, learning and working in an interconnected digital world, and they act and model in ways that are safe, legal and ethical.
(3) Knowledge Constructor: Students critically curate a variety of resources using digital tools to construct knowledge, produce creative artifacts and make meaningful learning experiences for themselves and others.
(4) Innovative Designer: Students use a variety of technologies within a design process to identify and solve problems by creating new, useful or imaginative solutions.
(5) Computational Thinker: Students develop and employ strategies for understanding and solving problems in ways that leverage the power of technological methods to develop and test solutions.
(6) Creative Communicator: Students communicate clearly and express themselves creatively for a variety of purposes using the platforms, tools, styles, formats and digital media appropriate to their goals.
(7) Global Collaborator: Students use digital tools to broaden their perspectives and enrich their learning by collaborating with others and working effectively in teams both locally and globally.

We believe that educational technology has the potential to provide teachers and learners with an array of tools that – when used appropriately – have the potential to transform learning.

Transforming learning involves personalizing the learning experience, promoting joint knowledge construction through collaborative learning tools, broadening access to learning through online environments and learning management systems as well as providing tools that support learners as creators.

Dede (2014) goes further in suggesting the need to explore virtual worlds and gaming (simulations and augmented reality) to enhance student motivation and engagement by providing them with learning opportunities familiar to their out-of-school world.

Ultimately, the transformative potential of digital tools lies in their ability to establish connections between what Brown and Thomas (in Dede, 2014: 4) call 'learning about', which is the more traditional sense of school-based learning; 'learning to do', which is often represented in formal education through problem-based and project-based pedagogies; and 'learning to be' or 'becoming', which is currently centered in informal learning, fundamentally about identity formation, and generative for deep engagement as well as the formation of intrapersonal and interpersonal skills. This position leads to a more integrated and holistic view of learning and it focuses attention on optimizing spaces so that using appropriate digital tools is normalized and digital literacies are core. In the pluriliteracies model, digital literacies form a subcategory of subject-specific literacies. Digital literacies develop as learners apply subject-specific skills and strategies to critically decode or encode digital text or work through digital channels, i.e. they use digital modes to build and share knowledge.

Throughout this chapter, the need to transform learning is constantly reiterated and we acknowledge that such claims are extensively acknowledged yet complex to put into practice. A reluctance to embrace the rapidly changing nature and potential of the digital world is matched by a paucity of appropriate digital tools available to learners in the formal settings. Integrating digital technology into schools is currently problematic and often associated with social and economic issues. Moreover, much of the literature on educational technology and digital literacies is devoid of content, focusing more on the 'how' of learning rather than on learning trajectories, specific outcomes, skills and competencies. Therefore, it would appear imperative to make the connection between digital technologies and classroom learning better understood and embraced by more educators through disseminating examples of current practices.

In the next section, we will argue that framing PTL within a deeper learning paradigm offers a trajectory for the integration of digital media because it provides practitioners with theory-based criteria to discern the specific added value of its use or application.

A Paradigm Shift: Moving from Traditional Teaching Spaces to Learnscapes

Given some of the radical rethinking required to transform classroom practices that support the growth of PTL, creating appropriate conditions for learning and understanding the underlying principles upon which PTL is built, is challenging and complex. It cannot easily be translated into a series of 'quick fix' plans since a more 'organic' understanding of learning is emphasized to encourage learners, with support from their teachers, to develop the knowledge, skills and attitudes as well as the confidence needed to become increasingly pluriliterate. Throughout this chapter, two aspects have emerged as being fundamental but which have not yet been overtly linked to the PTL model: the affective domain and digital literacies. In both the academic and professional literature, these are well documented yet often remain as separate strands. In the PTL, we are suggesting that creating optimal affective conditions for learning is at the core of the model and that modes of learning involving digital technologies (starting with those technologies that are by no means 'new' but poorly understood as learning tools) are integral to deeper learning. In essence, the notion of creating safe 'integrated learning spaces' is fundamental to developing and sustaining a pluriliterate approach to learning. In this way, our understanding of 'integration' as 'learning spaces', which is contentious and unresolved in content and language integrated learning developments (Nikula *et al.*, 2016) is at the core of the pluriliteracies model.

Learnscapes: Integrated learning spaces for PTL

To sum up what we have stated so far, providing students with opportunities to successfully engage in all the dimensions of subject learning necessary for the successful acquisition of pluriliteracies requires learning environments that engage learners on multiple levels by

- encouraging student buy-in and rewarding long-term commitment;
- providing challenging complex tasks to allow students to (co-) construct and share/communicate knowledge and understanding as well as promoting the use of subject-specific skills and strategies and adding complementary controlled practice/focus-on-form activities to systematically support the automatization of those skills;
- promoting learner agency and creativity.

We have also made the case that digital media and educational technologies must form an integral part of a deeper learning environment because of their potential to significantly increase learner engagement by establishing deeper connections between learners and their learning environment through processes of customization and individualization. Web 3.0 and its associated technologies make it possible to customize elements considered to be highly indicative of successful subject and language learning (Becker *et al.*, 2016; Dede, 2014; Hallet, 2012; Hattie & Yates, 2013; Kapp, 2014; Lantolf & Poehner, 2014; Lyster, 2007; Meyer, 2010; Ortega, 2008; Ritchhart *et al.*, 2011) and thus respond to the different needs of individual learners. Table 2.2 is by no means comprehensive but exemplifies the added value that the use of educational technology promises. It indicates the kind of deliberate and evidence-based modifications needed if learning environments are to succeed as spaces for making learning deeper, more engaging, highly individualized and transparent.

Table 2.2 Added value of educational technologies

Elements of learning environment	Added value of ICT	Sample application
(Co-)Constructing knowledge	Making input/content more immersive	Google Street View, Aurasma, Earth AR, Star Walk, Power of Minus Ten, Ibooks author, book widgets
	Matching language level of input/content material and skill level of learner	newsela.com, newsinlevels.com
	Providing tools to make thinking/conceptual development visible	Cmaptools, Ideament, Explain Everything
Online support	Online dictionaries etc.	visual.merriam-webster.com, macmillandictionary.com, visuwords.com, ozdic.com, words-to-use.com
Practice	Personalized/joint practice of lexical element	vocabulary.com, vocapp.com, quizlet.com
Sharing knowledge	Enabling and managing learner collaboration beyond the classroom	schoolastic.com, edmodo.com, etc., mindmeister.com, padlet.com
	Increasing authenticity of learning outcomes/products	Blogs, Wikis, boomwriter
Promoting autonomy	Using e-portfolios for student work	Seesaw, eBackpack
Motivating students	Gamifying the classroom	Classcraft
Feedback and reflection	Creating back-channels and using exit tickets	Socratic, Quizlet, Kahoot, Poll Everywhere

Clearly, the integration of digital tools will not only require a new technological infrastructure but will also have to empower teachers to make better use of instructional strategies, especially if the goal is 'to help all students, not just an elite few to reach mastery of ambitious standards' (Dede, 2014: 1).

Educational technology blogger Gerstein (2013) argues that the evolution from Web 1.0 to Web 3.0 could be used as a metaphor to demonstrate how education should be evolving to accommodate the rapid change in technology, related learning outcomes, student needs and community expectations. The implications for formal teaching and learning contexts are exceedingly challenging as set out in Table 2.3.

The following scenario showcases how some of the above-mentioned digital platforms, applications and tools can be used to create ecologies for deeper learning by promoting pluriliteracies development within an education 3.0 paradigm:

(1) **Doing:** Learners are tasked to do research on a current topic (i.e. political developments in the United States, Brexit, North Korea, etc.) using *newsela.com*. This multilanguage news platform offers

Table 2.3 From Education 1.0 to Education 3.0

	Education 1.0	Education 2.0	Education 3.0
Meaning is...	dictated	socially constructed	socially constructed and contextually reinvented
Technology is...	confiscated at the classroom door (digital refugees)	cautiously adopted (digital immigrants)	everywhere (ambient, digital universe)
Teaching is done...	teacher to student	teacher to student and student to student	teacher to student student to student student to teacher people-technology-people (co-constructivism)
Learning is taking place...	in a building (brick)	in a building or online (brick and click)	Everywhere
Hard- and soft-ware in schools are...	purchased at great cost and ignored	open source and available at lower cost	available at low cost and are used purposively

Source: Gerstein (2013) (Licensed under a Creative Commons – Attribution License).

learners the ability to adjust the difficulty of the chosen text to their specific reading level. In-built comprehension quizzes provide instant feedback to the learners and inform teachers on their learners' reading skills development.

By touching a word they don't understand, language learners will be shown a definition, explanation, image as well as an audio recording of the actual word by the onboard dictionaries of their mobile devices. Throughout, learners are encouraged to record words/phrases/collocations that they may not understand or find noteworthy, and use them to create interactive flashcards on *quizlet*, which not only offers different kinds of gamified practice/learning activities and games but also allows them to share their flashcards with their teachers and peers. The learners may then move on to do further research using *perspecs*. This app curates news articles from a variety of resources to offer three different perspectives (pro, neutral, con) on every topic presented.

In multilingual settings, students may analyze how the topic is reported on in different countries. This is not only an excellent and authentic opportunity for translanguaging activities. Such comparisons also provide an intercultural perspective on the issue/topic.

(2) **Organizing/Explaining:** To deepen their understanding and in order to make their own learning visual, learners might then continue to create a digital concept map on the topic of their research using *cmaptools*. In contrast to mind mapping, concept maps require users to label the connections between individual facts or keys terms and thus

support the formation and internalization of conceptual knowledge. Sharing and comparing their digital concept maps with other learners not only serves to visualize their understanding but also offers an incentive to language their understanding and to correct conceptual misunderstandings/misrepresentations.

(3) **Arguing:** Next, students will be asked to communicate and demonstrate their understanding of the topic by turning their concept maps into a full-blown 'text' in a genre and mode (oral, written) of their choosing using an app that best suits their text/product and needs. The first draft of their learning outcome/product (i.e. the video, the cartoon, the blogpost, etc.) will be uploaded to their password-protected learning platforms such as *edmodo* or *scholastic* and reviewed by their peers who use lexis and collocation tools such as *ozdic.com* or *words-to-use.com*. The corrected drafts will then be uploaded and sent to their teachers before being published in their personal digital portfolio, on a classroom blog, website or *padlet*.

Situating PTL within an education 3.0 paradigm requires rethinking the way we traditionally conceive formal learning and learning spaces and it forces us to bridge the gap between formal and informal learning because deeper learning rests in great part on student engagement. Engagement is fluid yet dynamic, societally driven yet highly individual. It cannot be promoted or sustained by traditional one-size-fits-all approaches to teaching and learning.

Instead, we propose further investigation into the potential of integrated, hybrid spaces where educational technologies are used along with traditional and transformative teaching methods to personalize learning experience and to bridge formal and informal learning. We suggest that this will increase student engagement (cognitive, social, behavioral) and promote deeper learning and agency. To make the ecological underpinning of the new paradigm transparent, we will refer to these integrated learning spaces as *learnscapes*.

Learnscaping: Designing Ecosystems for PTL

The design, guidance and supervision of learnscapes require alternative approaches to teaching and learning that call on a wide range of competences. Learnscaping requires re-conceptualizing how we grow shared safe plurilingual learning spaces that normalize digital learning and seek to provide engaging opportunities promoting learning based on increasingly challenging subject understanding enabled by individual language progression – that is all the components brought together into a learning or knowledge ecology. Many educators, however, are ill-equipped for the challenges of teaching and mentoring digital age learning. The ISTE (2008, 2017) lists five key competence areas for teachers and corresponding performance indicators:

(1) Facilitate and inspire student learning and creativity.
(2) Design and develop digital age learning experiences and assessments.
(3) Model digital age work and learning.
(4) Promote and model digital citizenship and responsibility.
(5) Engage in professional growth and leadership.

Yet, in identifying the five competences, development and progression in each is dependent on the growth of the others, which requires both holistic and detailed planning, mentoring and consideration of the interweaving strands conceptualized as an ecosystem. Conceptualizing learnscapes as spatial constructs allows us to highlight elements that have been neglected in pedagogic discourse: despite their hybridity, such spaces follow certain architectural principles regarding layout and interaction, which may prove detrimental or conducive to deeper learning and the way that knowledge is constructed and shared.

Thus, having made the case for theoretically driven change, the next stage is to gather evidence of PTL in ways that will build confidence and provide examples to encourage learnscaping beyond pioneers. A focus not only on teaching practices but also on teacher education is critical. Case studies are ongoing and currently being collated.

One example, from master's practitioners studying Theories of Practice at the University of Aberdeen involves the use of iPads as integrated learning spaces where video teacher feedback is airdropped to individual learners. Developing a range of 'walk-up-and-use' digital tools to enable teachers and students to simultaneously engage in analyzing the depth of their learning is transparently connecting ownership of learning with knowledge building (Coyle, 2013). Another example, funded by the German national ministry of science and education (BMBF: Qualitätsoffensive Lehrerbildung/Towards Quality in Teacher Training 2016–2019) involves the redesigning of a joint master's program at the University of Mainz (English Didactics and Educational Sciences) to equip students (teachers) with a range of competences needed to design, grow and evaluate pluriliteracies learnscapes.

Interestingly, the authors' critical evaluation of the digital learning materials/ibooks produced so far, indicates that focusing on the development of materials and tasks as well as on digital applications/apps alone does not guarantee the successful creation of high-quality learnscapes: it is becoming increasingly clear that the question of how integral elements of such learning spaces are presented/arranged and how they interact with each other to form an organic whole might be of equal importance as the development of those elements/tasks themselves. In other words, students need to critically reflect on the ecological architecture and design of those integrated environments and act accordingly.

To conclude, in order to promote deeper learning across subjects, cultures and languages, teachers need not only familiarize themselves with the elements of PTL but also learn about the architectural/design principles that govern integrated learning environments or learnscapes. They need to learn what Jahnke and Norberg (2013) call 'digital didactics' to understand the rules that govern the 'new normalcy' of digital learning spaces and the ecological infrastructure that determines their growth.

References

Beacco, J.-C., Fleming, M., Goullier, F., Thürmann, E. and Vollmer, H. (2015) The language dimension in all subjects. *A Handbook for Curriculum Development and Teacher Training*. Strasbourg: Council of Europe. See www.coe.int/t/dg4/linguistic/Source/Handbook-Scol_final_EN.pdf (accessed 5 April 2018).

Becker, C., Blell, G. and Rössler, A. (eds) (2016) *Web 2.0 und Komplexe Kompetenzaufgaben im Fremdsprachenunterricht*. Frankfurt: Peter Lang.

Borland, J. (2007) New technologies will make online search more intelligent – and may even lead to a 'Web 3.0'. See https://www.technologyreview.com/s/407401/a-smarter-web/ (accessed 5 April 2018).

Bull, G. and Anstey, M. (2007) What's so different about multiliteracies? See http://www.curriculum.edu.au/leader/whats_so_different_about_multiliteracies,18881.html (accessed 5 April 2018).

Byrnes, H. (2002) Towards academic-level foreign language abilities: Reconsidering foundational assumptions, expanding pedagogical options. In B.L. Leaver and B. Shektman (eds) *Developing Professional-Level Language Proficiency* (pp. 34–58). Cambridge: Cambridge University Press.

Chiriac, S.E. and Ghitiu-Bratescu, A. (2011) Linking globalisation, sustainable development and knowledge transfer: A network based approach. *Journal of Doctoral Research in Economics* 3 (1), 12–22.

Council of Ministers of Education, Canada (CMEC) (1997) *Common Framework of Science Learning Outcomes K to 12: Pan-Canadian Protocol for Collaboration on School Curriculum for Use by Curriculum Developers*. Toronto, ON: CMEC.

Coyle, D. (2013) Listening to learners: An investigation into 'successful learning' across CLIL contexts. *International Journal of Bilingual Education and Bilingualism* 16 (3), 244–266.

Dede, C. (2014) The role of digital technologies in deeper learning. In R. Heller, R.E. Wolfe and A. Steinberg (eds) *Students at the Center: Deeper Learning Research Series*. Boston, MA: Jobs for the Future. See http://www.jff.org/sites/default/files/publications/materials/The-Role-of-Digital-Technologies-in-Deeper-Learning-120114.pdf (accessed 5 April 2018).

DeKeyser, R. (2007) *Practice in a Second Language: Perspectives from Applied Linguistics and Cognitive Psychology*. New York: Cambridge University Press.

Dobbs, C.L., Ippolito, J.C. and Charner-Laird, M. (2016) Layering intermediate and disciplinary literacy work: Lessons learned from a secondary social studies teacher team. *Journal of Adolescent and Adult Literacy* 60 (2), 131–139.

Eppler, M.J. and Burkhard, R.A. (2004) Knowledge Visualization: Towards a New Discipline and its Fields of Application. ICA Working Paper 2/2004. Institute for Corporate Communication, Università della Svizzera italiana.

EU High Level Group of Experts on Literacy (2012) Final Report. Luxembourg: Publications Office of the European Union. See https://ec.europa.eu/epale/en/resource-centre/content/eu-high-level-group-literacy-report (accessed April 5, 2018).

Fang, Z., and Coatoam, S. (2013) Disciplinary literacy: What you want to know about it. *Journal of Adolescent & Adult Literacy* 56 (8), 627–632.

García, O., Bartlett, L. and Kleifgen, J.A. (2007) From biliteracy to pluriliteracies. In P. Auer and L. Wei (eds) *Handbook of Applied Linguistics, Vol. 5: Multilingualism* (pp. 207–228). Berlin: Mouton-De Gruyter.

Gee, J.P. (1989) What is literacy? *Journal of Education* 171, 18–25.

Gerstein, J. (2013) Education 3.0 and the Pedagogy (Andragogy, Heutagogy) of Mobile Learning. *User Generated Education*, blog. See https://usergeneratededucation.wordpress.com/2013/05/13/education-3-0-and-the-pedagogy-andragogy-heutagogy-of-mobile-learning/ (accessed April 5, 2018).

Gillis, V. (2014) Disciplinary literacy: Adapt not adopt. *Journal of Adolescent & Adult Literacy* 57 (8), 614–623.

Graz Group (2015) The Graz Group model: Mapping pluriliteracies development. *A Pluriliteracies Approach to Teaching for Learning*. European Centre for Modern Languages. See https://pluriliteracies.ecml.at/Portals/54/publications/pluriliteracies-Putting-a-pluriliteracies-approach-into-practice.pdf access date: April 5, 2018.

Hallet, W. (2012) *Kompetenzaufgaben im Englischunterricht: Grundlagen und Unterrichtsbeispiele*. Seelze: Klett/Kallmeyer.

Hallet, W. (2016) *Genres im Fremdsprachlichen und Bilingualen Unterricht: Formen und Muster der Sprachlichen Interaktion*. Seelze: Klett/Kallmeyer.

Hattie, J. and Yates, G. (2013) *Visible Learning and the Science of How We Learn*. London: Routledge.

Hornberger, N. (2003) *Continua of Biliteracy: An Ecological Framework for Educational Policy, Research and Practice in Multilingual Settings*. Clevedon: Multilingual Matters.

ISTE (2008, 2017) The ISTE Standards for Teachers. International Society for Technology in Education. See http://www.iste.org/standards/standards/standards-for-teachers (accessed 5 April 2018).

ISTE (2016a) The 2016 ISTE Standards for Students. International Society for Technology in Education. See https://www.iste.org/standards/standards/for-students-2016 (accessed 5 April 2018).

ISTE (2016b) 2016 ISTE Standards for Students (ebook). International Society for Technology in Education. See https://www.iste.org/resources/product?ID=4073&ChildProduct=4074 (accessed 5 April 2018).

Jahnke, I. and Norberg, A. (2013) Digital Didactics: Scaffolding a New Normality of Learning. In *Open Education 2030 – Contributions to the JRC-IPTS Call for Vision Papers. Part III: Higher Education* (pp. 129–134). See http://blogs.ec.europa.eu/openeducation2030/category/vision-papers/higher-education/ (accessed 5 April 2018).

Jetton, T.L. and Shanahan, C. (eds) (2012) *Adolescent Literacy in the Academic Disciplines: General Principles and Practical Strategies*. New York: Guilford.

Kale, D., Little, S. and Hinton, M. (2011) Reconfiguration of knowledge management practices in new product development: The case of the Indian pharmaceutical industry. In K.A. Grant (ed.) *Case Studies in Knowledge Management Research* (pp. 102–119). Reading: Academic Publishing International Ltd.

Kapp, K. (2014) *The Gamification of Learning and Instruction Fieldbook: Ideas into Practice*. San Francisco, CA: Wiley.

Lantolf, J.P, and Poehner, M.E. (2014) *Sociocultural Theory and the Pedagogical Imperative in L2 Education: Vygotskian Praxis and the Research/Practice Divide*. New York: Routledge.

Lyster, R. (2007) *Learning and Teaching Languages through Content: A Counterbalanced Approach*. Philadelphia, PA: John Benjamins.

Meyer, O. (2010) Towards quality-CLIL: Successful planning and teaching strategies. *Puls* 33, 11–29.

Meyer, O., Coyle, D., Halbach, A., Schuck, K. and Ting, T. (2015a) A pluriliteracies approach to content and language integrated learning: Mapping learner progressions in knowledge construction and meaning-making. *Language, Culture, and Curriculum* 28 (1), 41–57.

Meyer, O., Coyle, D. and Halbach, C. (2015b) A pluriliteracies approach to teaching for learning: Putting a pluriliteracies approach into practice. European Centre for Modern Languages. See https://pluriliteracies.ecml.at/Portals/54/publications/pluriliteracies-Putting-a-pluriliteracies-approach-into-practice.pdf (accessed 5 April 2018).

Meyer, O. and Coyle, D. (2017) Pluriliteracies Teaching for Learning: conceptualizing progression for deeper learning in literacies development. *European Journal of Applied Linguistics*, 5/2, 199–222.

Mohan, B., Leung, C. and Slater, T. (2010) Assessing language and content: A functional perspective. In A. Paran and S. Lies (eds) *Testing the Untestable in Language Education* (pp. 217–240). Bristol: Multilingual Matters.

Moje, E.B. (2004) Powerful spaces: Tracing the out-of-school literacy spaces of Latino/a youth. In K. Leander and M. Sheehy (eds) *Spatializing Literacy Research and Practice* (pp. 15–38). New York: Peter Lang.

Morcom, V. (2015) Scaffolding social and emotional learning within 'shared affective spaces' to reduce bullying: A sociocultural perspective. *Learning, Culture and Social Interaction* 6, 77–86.

NASBE Study Group on Student Engagement (2015) A State of Engagement. Alexandria, VA: National Association of State Boards of Education. See http://www.nasbe.org/wp-content/uploads/StudentEngagementStudyGroupReport_March-2015_FINAL.pdf access date: April 5, 2018

National Research Council (2012) *Education for Life and Work: Developing Transferable Knowledge and Skills in the 21st Century*. Committee on Defining Deeper Learning and 21st Century Skills, J.W. Pellegrino and M.L. Hilton, Editors. Board on Testing and Assessment and Board on Science Education, Division of Behavioral and Social Sciences and Education. Washington, DC: The National Academies Press.

Nikula, T., Dafouz, E., Moore, P. and Smit, U. (eds) (2016) *Conceptualising Integration in CLIL and Multilingual Education*. Bristol: Multilingual Matters.

Ortega, L. (2008) *Understanding Second Language Acquisition*. London: Routledge.

Pane, D.M. (2009) Third space: Blended teaching and learning. *Journal of the Research Center for Educational Technology (RCET)* 5 (1), 64–92.

Parsi, A. (2015) Student engagement's three variables: Emotion, behavior, cognition. *Getting Smart*, blog. See http://gettingsmart.com/2015/03/student-engagements-three-variables-emotion-behavior-cognition/ (accessed 5 April 2018).

Pietarinen, J., Soini, T. and Pyhältö, K. (2014) Students' emotional and cognitive engagement as the determinants of well-being and achievement in school. *International Journal of Educational Research* 67, 40–51.

Polias, J. (2016) *Apprenticing Students into Science: Doing, Talking, and Writing Scientifically*. Melbourne: Lexis Education.

Renshaw, P. (2013) The social cultural and emotional dimensions of scaffolding. *Learning, Culture and Social Interaction* 2, 56–60.

Ritchhart, R., Church, M. and Morrison, K. (2011) *Making Thinking Visible: How to Promote Engagement, Understanding, and Independence for All Learners.* San Francisco, CA: Wiley.

Schleppegrell, M.J. (2004) *The Language of Schooling: A Functional Linguistics Perspective.* Mahwah, NJ: Erlbaum.

Shanahan, T. and Shanahan, C. (2008) Teaching disciplinary literacy to adolescents: Rethinking content-area literacy. *Harvard Educational Review* 78 (1), 40–59.

Shanahan, T. and Shanahan, C. (2012) What is disciplinary literacy and why does it matter? *Top Lang Disorders* 32 (1), 7–18.

Spivack, N. (2007) Web 3.0: The Third Generation Web is Coming. https://lifeboat.com/ex/web.3.0 (accessed 5 April 2018).

Swain, M. (2006) Languaging, agency and collaboration in advanced language proficiency. In H. Byrnes (ed.) *Advanced Language Learning: The Contribution of Halliday and Vygotsky* (pp. 95–108). London: Continuum.

The New London Group (Cazden, C., Cope, B., Fairclough, N., Gee, J., Kalantzis, M., Kress, G., Luke, A., Luke, C., Michaels, S. and Nakata, M.) (1996) A pedagogy of multiliteracies: Designing social futures. *Harvard Educational Review* 66 (1), 60.

Walqui, A. (2006) Scaffolding instruction for English language learners: A conceptual framework. *The International Journal of Bilingual Education and Bilingualism* 9 (2), 159–180.

Weinburgh, M.H and Silva, C. (2012) An instructional theory for English language learners: The 5R model for enhancing academic language development in inquiry-based science. In B.J. Irby, G. Brown and R. Lara-Alecio (eds) and J. Koch (sect. ed.) *Handbook of Educational Theories* (pp. 293–304). Charlotte, NC: Information Age Publishing Inc.

Part 2
Multilingual Texts

3 'I like the character, weil er so richtig funny ist': Reading Story Apps in the Primary EFL Classroom

Sonja Brunsmeier and Annika Kolb

New Media – New Texts: Story Apps in the Primary EFL Classroom

Picture books play an important role in childhood education and have long been seen as a very valuable resource particularly for early foreign language learning (Cameron, 2001: 123ff.; Legutke *et al.*, 2009: 72ff.; Mourão, 2015). Over the last few decades, the rapid development of technologies has brought about new picture book formats. Picture books are now produced as story apps for electronic devices (e.g. tablets, mobile phones, computers), thereby 'expanding to include auditory, tactile, and performative dimensions' (Al-Yaqout & Nikolajeva, 2015: 1). In addition, these story apps offer interactive features that ask readers to take part in the story, fulfil tasks, solve problems and even choose characters, settings or specific story paths. A number of features make story apps particularly interesting for foreign language learners. For example, learners can choose their preferred mode of reading (e.g. 'read to me' or 'read by myself') and can navigate the reading process (e.g. thumbnail images to go forward/backward, pause, re-read words/sentences [passages]). There is also language and comprehension support (e.g. word and/or paragraph highlighting, animations, music and sounds) (Bircher, 2012; Cahill & McGill-Franzen, 2013). The multimodal nature of story apps influences children's emergent literacy development (Bus *et al.*, 2015: 79; Sargeant, 2015) and presents opportunities for different approaches to using literature in the primary English as a foreign language (EFL) classroom.

Picture books have often been presented by the teacher in a storytelling scenario (e.g. Brewster & Ellis, 2012: 186–202). This setting means that it is the teacher who reads the story to the children as a class. The interactive features and supportive elements of story apps allow children to read the stories on their own. For the primary EFL classroom, this could create new opportunities to develop young learners' reading competencies in the foreign language (Frisch, 2015; Kolb, 2012). Nevertheless, few research studies have been carried out in this area and little is known about the individual reading processes of children and the strategies they employ to understand the stories.

One interesting aspect in this regard is the learners' choice of language in collaborative reading scenarios. First studies (e.g. projects LIKE, MuViT and MElang-E, see Buendgens-Kosten & Elsner, Elsner & Buendgens-Kosten, this volume) focusing on the role and function of different languages in the EFL classroom show that beginners employ diverse patterns of code-switching, for example to satisfy their curiosity and clarify understanding (Buendgens-Kosten, 2015; Elsner *et al.*, 2014). In the plurilingual classroom, the concept of translanguaging (García & Wei, 2014) is a potentially useful strategy. Canagarajah (2011: 401) defines it as 'the ability of multilingual speakers to shuttle between languages, treating the diverse languages that form their repertoire as an integrated system'. The underlying belief is that using the first language (L1) or another known language is a useful tool in teaching a foreign language in general (López Corcoll & González-Davies, 2016: 68). Investigations are beginning to look at how effective bridging between languages can be fostered to assist the reading process in a foreign language.

This chapter presents an ongoing research project on story apps in the primary EFL classroom in an extensive reading setting. Following an action research approach, the study uses classroom videos, student products and learner interviews to look at the children's strategies for reading and understanding story apps on their own. A focus of the project is the learners' choice of language. Key questions include to what extent, in which situations and for what purpose do the children use the target language (English) and the school language (German) when they try to understand the stories, complete post-reading activities and discuss their opinions about the stories?

Research Context and Research Design

The 'English Book Club' is a voluntary afternoon programme that takes place once a week (60 minutes) for third and fourth graders (8–10 year olds) at a German primary school. Overall, 29 children, who were then divided into two groups, registered for this extra-curricular offer and hence took part in this study. The children who attend the 'English Book Club' all speak German fluently with some children speaking an L1 other than German at home. They have been learning English since Grade 1 with two English lessons a week, the target level by the end of primary school is A1 (Council of Europe, 2001). The classroom language in the English lessons is usually English; the teacher encourages the children to use the target language as much as possible, for example by giving prompts, providing chunks and structures and establishing routines and rituals. In an extensive reading setting, the children are offered a variety of picture books and story apps. They choose the books they want to read – in most cases with a partner. Each story app is accompanied by pre- and post-reading activities that focus on aspects of the content and language of the story apps. Further, a story map activity asks the children to note down key points related to the story app (e.g. summary of the content, author, setting and characters). Finally, the children are asked for their opinion on the story.

The qualitative research design follows a classroom action research approach (Burns, 2010). To find out how children read story apps on their own and which language they use in the reading process with a partner, two research cycles have been conducted so far (see Figure 3.1).

The study uses a variety of data collection methods to gain insight into the reading processes from different perspectives. Video recordings are used to document how the children proceed when reading the story apps on their own. Using a micro-ethnographic approach that focuses on patterns of interactions between protagonists in a specific setting, the videos try to capture the ongoing interactions in the classroom. Twice during the school year, the children are interviewed about their reading experience. Interviews are used because they 'allow [one] (...) to probe beneath the surface of things' (Richards, 2009: 183). The interviews shed

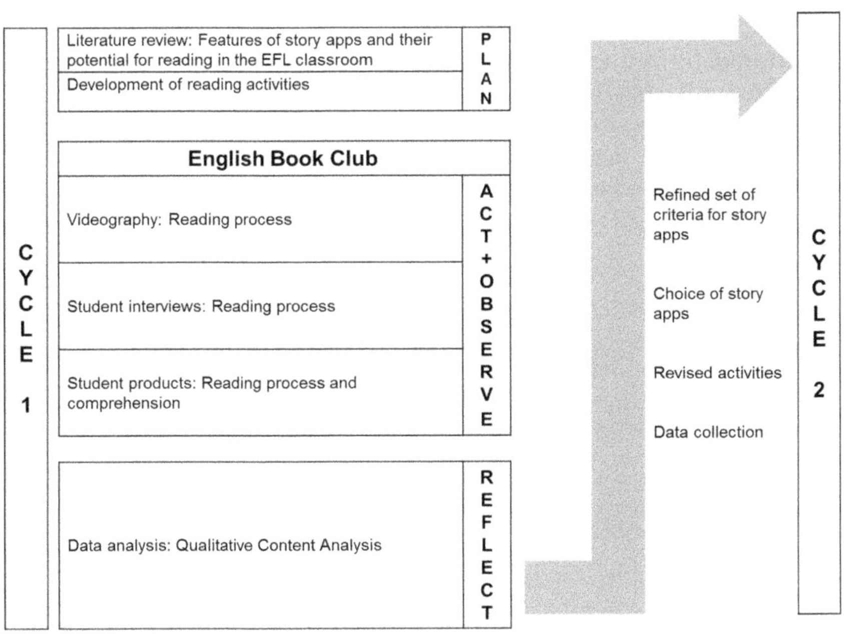

Figure 3.1 Research design

light on the students' perspectives and experience of the reading processes. The students' worksheets are also looked at to see how successful they are in completing the pre- and post-reading activities as well as to read the opinions they note about the story apps.

The video recordings, the student interviews and the students' worksheets are analysed using the structured qualitative content analysis (Mayring, 2014) to identify patterns in the data. Whereas the transcripts of the interviews are used for categorisation, the video material is categorised as such, which allows for the identification of interesting sequences that are then transcribed.

Preliminary Results

First results with regard to the learners' choice of language (i.e. use of the target language [English] and the school language [German]) can be presented in three areas: (1) understanding the story apps, (2) completing post-reading activities and (3) discussing the story apps.

Understanding story apps

The videos provide insight into the students' reading processes. During the reading process, the learners' choice of language is relevant when they (a) communicate with their partner(s) (see Table 3.1) and (b) show individual reactions to the story (see Table 3.2).

Understanding story apps: Communicating with partner(s)

Almost all students decided to read the story apps with a partner. Table 3.1 provides an overview of language choices when the children communicate with their partner(s).

The children's conversations with their partner show that they mix the foreign language and the language of schooling (German) when they speak

Table 3.1 Understanding story apps (language choices and functions)

Communicating with the partner(s)	Learners ...	Language choice tends to be ...	The function of language is to ...
Content	clarify global understanding.	German (other than inserting key words in English).	check understanding.
	share opinions.	German.	get meaning across.
Management	organise the reading process.	German.	organise aspects around the reading of the texts, allowing the children to focus on the content of the story.
	navigate the app.	German (non-verbal actions for demonstrations).	get most out of the story.

Table 3.2 Individual reactions (language choices and functions)

Individual reactions	Learners ...	Language choice tends to be ...	The function of language is to ...
Using language playfully	repeat words from the story.	English.	make meaning from the text and become a player in the story.
	imitate sounds.	English.	experiment with the foreign language.
Reading	read sentences from the screen aloud.	English.	practice pronunciation.
	re-read words/sentences ('read to me' function).	English.	understand the content.
Participating in and co-creating the story	react to prompts and do/ complete activities.	non-verbal and English.	proceed in the story.

about the content of the stories. The school language is used when the students clarify their global understanding of the story, but 'key words' from the stories are inserted in the foreign language.

J: (...) *go to the museum*. (J writes down the storypath on his worksheet.)
P: Nein, wir machen / [No, we are doing.][1]
J: Doch, wir gehen zum Museum. [Yes, we are going to the museum.]
P: Nein, wir machen etwas anderes. Wir machen das doch mit den Spielsachen. (unv.). [No, we are doing something else. We are doing this, with the toys. (inaudible).]
P: (reads aloud from the worksheet) (...) *purple* Dino. (J and P look at one another.) Wir waren gar nicht beim *purple* Dino. [We did not go to the 'purple' dinosaur.]
J: Wir waren beim *orange* Dino – bei dem orangenen Dino. [We went to the 'orange' dinosaur – to the orange dinosaur.]
P: Ja, bei diesem anderen. [Yes, to the other one.]
J: Ja, *orange* Dino. [Yes, the 'orange' dinosaur.]
P: *Purple* waren wir aber auch noch – bei diesem Großen, wo wir standen. [We also saw the 'purple' – this big one, where we were standing.]
J: Ja, aber das war doch nicht im *toy store*. [Yes, but this wasn't in the 'toy store'.]
P: Ja * doch * wir müssen das, wo wir beim *toy store* (waren). [Yes* yes* we have to put down the one we saw in the 'toy store'.] (Corrects it on his worksheet.)
J: Ja, eben, das war der Orangene. Gelb war * Ja, doch, *orange*. Orange. [Yes, because this was the orange one. Yellow was * Yes, yes, 'orange'. Orange.]

Every now and then while reading the story apps, the children also share their opinions with their partner(s). This comprises evaluative and emotional comments as well as revising predictions made before reading the actual story, which are communicated in the language of schooling (German).

N: Geile Rutsche. [Cool slide.]
(F and N are reading the first slides of the app.)
F: Hä, das ist doch eine Rutsche?! [Isn't this a slide?!] (Looks at the pre-task on his worksheet.)
N: Ja. *2Sek.* Was hast du gedacht? [Yes. *2sec * What did you think?]
F: Was anderes. [Something else.]
N: Achso. [I see.]
F: Dann muss ich jetzt alles wegradieren. [Then I have to erase everything.] (Changes his answer in the pre-task.)

Management includes organising the joint reading process. This means that the children explicitly discuss how to proceed during the while-reading phase. To deal with these issues, the children opt for the German language, allowing them to keep their attention focused on actually understanding the story apps.

P: Du hast schon zweimal, jetzt darf ich drücken. [You pressed it twice, now it is my turn.]
(N opens the app 'Dino Boy'.)
F: Warte kurz. * Noch nicht. Ich muss noch schreiben. [Wait. * Not yet. I still have to write.] (N starts the app 'Dino Boy'.)
F: Mach leiser. [Turn it down.]

In addition, the children figure out how to navigate the app. German is used to explore and explain how to work with the story apps. Quite often, these explanations are accompanied by actions. This means that the children demonstrate to their partner(s) how different features of the app can be used best.

P: Warte! * Halt! * Stopp. * Wir müssen doch zurück. [Wait! * Hold on! * Stop. We have to go back.] (P and N are touching repeatedly the arrow to get back to the previous pages.)
N: So, dann kannst du halt hier immer etwas antippen. [So, then you can always press something here.] (N shows F on the iPad what he means.)

Understanding story apps: Individual reactions

While reading the story apps, the children show different individual reactions to the stories. Table 3.2 gives an overview of these. Several situations were observed in which the children pick up individual words and repeat them. This shows how attentively they follow the content of the story and again supports the impression that they are very eager to make meaning from the text. At different points in the story, the children read a few words with the narrator. Not only do they read along with the narrator but they also read parts of the app's title out loud to themselves. In addition, other students were observed reading along silently, which is apparent from their lips moving as they articulate the words. Some also read aloud by repeating expressions that different characters say.

It was also noted that the children imitate sounds from the story apps. This indicates that they really enjoy reading the stories and shows their open attitude towards learning English as well as their emotional involvement.

(**Narrator of the app:** A roller coaster car has so many ups and way too many downs. Not to mention the clack clackity clack clack.)
E: Clack clackity clack clack (laughs).

Some learners read sentences aloud from the screen allowing them to practice their pronunciation. This aspect is also reflected in the interviews as this example shows.

I: Ist noch irgendwas anders? [Is there something else that is different?]
S: Ja, man kann, wenn man ein Wort nicht versteht, nicht verstanden hat, nochmal drauf drücken und dann sagt er es nochmal. [Yes you can, if you don't understand a word, have not understood it, press on it again and then he says it again.]

This feature of audio narration ('read to me'), which allows children to listen to words, sentences and/or passages again, is very much appreciated since the children can read and listen to the text more than once. Re-reading serves as a comprehension strategy that assists the understanding of the story apps.

The story apps include activities that allow the children to become participants and co-creators of the story. At various points during the reading process, the children react to prompts and feel directly addressed by the narrator of the story as in this example:

(**Narrator of the app:** Shall he [Dino Boy] try the toy store, the playground or the museum?)
J: Toy store! Toy store!

Having these choices of setting or characters gives the readers the feeling that they are co-creating the story. This feeling is enhanced by a wide range of activities in which they are asked to become players in the story and perform actions that are necessary for the plot. These activities often require non-verbal actions from the children (e.g. tapping objects/characters, swiping, tilting). Completing these activities in the while-reading phase proves that the children must have understood the text and shows the depth with which they dive into the stories. 'The word/image counterpoint, essential in any picture book, requires the user's action, providing them with stronger agency. Tapping, touching and tracing become embodied actions to reading and viewing that enhances the user's affective engagement' (Al-Yaqout & Nikolajeva, 2015: 5).

B: Wenn ihr jetzt die normalen Bilderbücher, die wir ja zuerst gelesen haben, mit den digitalen Bilderbüchern auf den iPads vergleicht. Was konntet ihr denn auf den iPads alles machen, was ihr im Bilderbuch nicht konntet? (…) [When you now compare the normal picture books, that we read at first, with the story apps: what were you able to do with the iPads that you could not do with the picture books? (...)]

L: Zum Beispiel bei 'The three little pigs' musste man dann auf Holz zum Beispiel drücken und dann bauen sie ein Haus. Und auf die Figuren kann man auch tippen, dann sagen die halt was. [For example with 'The three little pigs' you had to, for example, press on the wood and then they would build a house. And you can also press on the characters, then they would say something.]

Completing post-reading activities

When working on the post-reading activities, the learners' choice of language is (a) influenced by features of these activities (see Table 3.3) and becomes further observable when they (b) talk to their partner(s) (see Table 3.4) and (c) show individual reactions (see Table 3.5).

Completing post-reading activities: Features

The design of the post-reading activities seems to greatly influence which language the learners use to do them (see Table 3.3). In activities that either explicitly integrate the linguistic level and/or encourage detailed engagement with the text, the children mostly try to use the foreign language (see Figure 3.2).

As well as requiring learners to note down key points (e.g. author, setting and characters) about the story apps, the story map activity requires

Table 3.3 Design features (language choices and functions)

Activities that focused on (the) …	Language choice tends to be …
Linguistic level	English.
Global understanding	German or English.
Creative reactions to the text	German and/or English.

them to write a summary of the story. In this way, the students' global understanding of the story is checked. Depending on their individual ability and personal preferences, the children opt for either one of the two languages (see Figure 3.3).

Some activities encourage the children to record their ideas in English, for instance, activities that leave room for subjective and creative reactions to the texts and activities that are closely linked to the language used in the stories and/or provide language support (e.g. examples, words) (see Figure 3.4).

Completing post-reading activities: Talking to partner

The majority of the children decide to work together on the post-reading activities. Table 3.4 provides an overview of languages choices when the children talk to their partner(s). The children often discuss and/or compare their solutions to the activities with each other. Before they actually write down their answers, they discuss possible ideas. Depending on the type of activity, this leads to a review of the reading process (e.g. talking about the content of the app) or to collecting and brainstorming ideas to do activities that call for subjective and creative reactions to the text. Once the children have completed the activity, some of them compare their results. They either want to check whether their answer is correct or are curious to hear about the creative ideas of the other(s).

Table 3.4 Talking to the partner(s) (language choices and functions)

Talking to the partner(s)	Learners ...	Language choice tends to be ...
Discussing and comparing solutions	collect and discuss possible answers before they write them down.	a mix of English and German.
	compare what they have written down afterwards.	a mix of English and German.
Asking for help	complete the activities together.	German (in addition to inserting key words in English).
Focus on form	check how to spell words.	German.

Table 3.5 Individual reactions (language choices and functions)

Individual reactions	Learners ...	Language choice tends to be ...	The function of language is to ...
Reading aloud	read task instructions and/or sentences aloud.	English.	clarify activities and/or contents.
Use key words	use words that were central to the plot or that they knew before.	English.	show knowledge (content and language wise).
Talking to oneself	verbalise what they are working on.	German.	organise the working process.
Translating sentences	translate sentences.		ensure understanding.

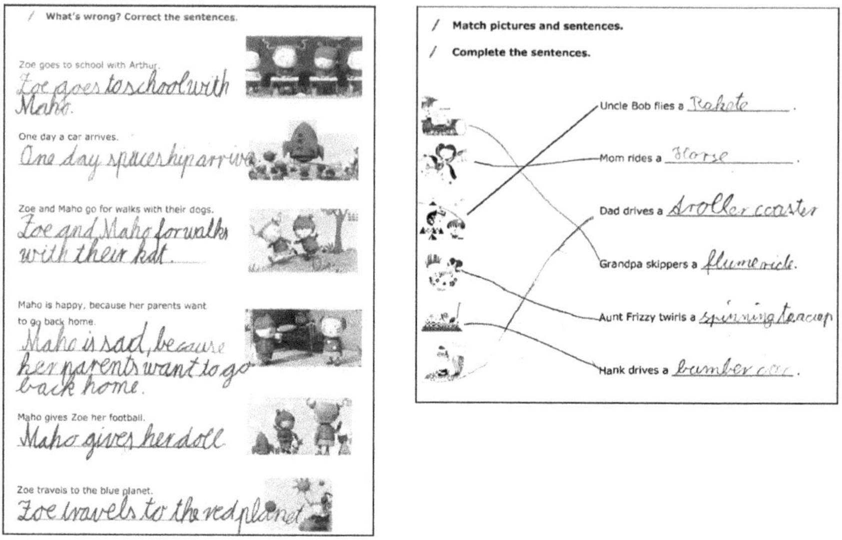

Figure 3.2 Activities that integrate the linguistic level and/or encourage detailed engagement with the text

N: Was schreiben wir jetzt bei 'This is the story'? [What shall we write down for 'This is the story'?]

P: Eine Familie, die sich um seinen Sohn ver(unv.). [A family who is (inaudible) about their son.] (F and N laugh.)

N: Gute Idee. [Good idea.] (Starts to write.)

F: Was? * Eine? [What? * A?]

N: Familie. [Family.]

P: Familie. [Family.]
(N and P speak slowly together and write down what they say on their worksheet: A family who ...)

P: Was ist das? [What is that?] (Looks at J.'s worksheet.)

J: A train with a ghost.

P: * Oh * a train! (Corrects his own entry on the worksheet.)
(...)

J: Also, wie unsere eigene Kreation aussieht. [So, what our own creation looks like.] (Translates the next task, where the students can create their own creature (→ Figure 3.4). P and J use the app to get some inspiration.)

P: Ich habe unten gemacht, ne? [I did the lower half, right?]

J: Ja. [Yes.]

P: Oder mach/ soll ich/ [Or I do/ should I/]
(P and J continue to use the app for inspiration.)

J: Hier ist es doch. [Here it is.]

P: Machst du das? [Are you going to do this one?]

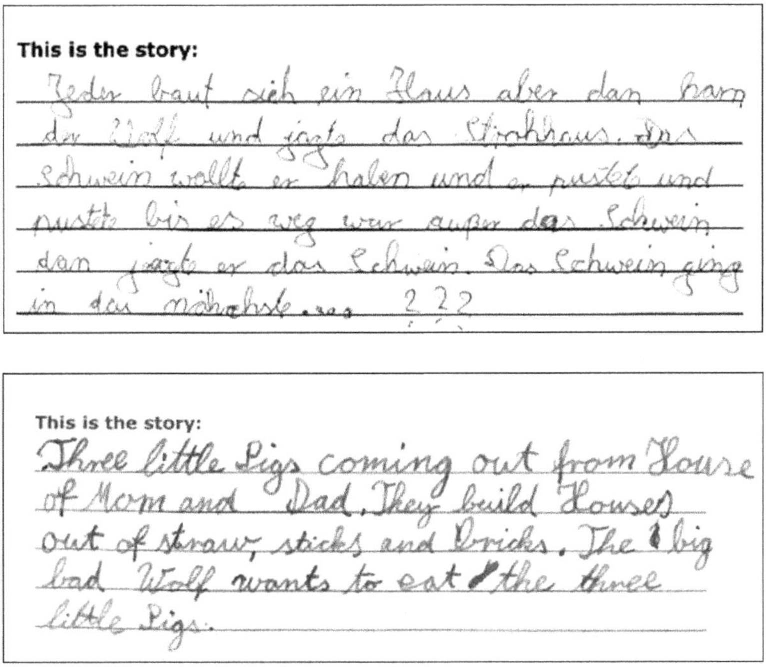
This is the story:
Jeder baut sich ein Haus aber dan kam
der Wolf und jagte das Strohhaus. Das
Schwein wollt er holen und er pustet und
pustete bis es weg war aber das Schwein
dan jagte er das Schwein. Das Schwein ging
in das nächste... ???

This is the story:
Three little Pigs coming out from House
of Mom and Dad. They build Houses
out of straw, sticks and bricks. The big
bad Wolf wants to eat the three
little Pigs.

Figure 3.3 Summaries of the story apps (language choice based on individual preferences and abilities)

J: Ja. [Yes.]
P: Dann mache ich das andere. [Then I'll do the other one.]

During the process of working on the activities, questions arise and the children ask each other for help to complete the activities.

(P and N do the post-task on the worksheet 'The Three Little Pigs'. Here they have to fill in the gaps with keywords and match the sentence with the right picture.)
P: Was kommt da jetzt hin? [What is supposed to be there?] (Looks at N's worksheet.)
N: Schau mal, das da [Look, this one here.] (First points to the word on his worksheet and then to the matching gap on P's worksheet.)

The children are eager to write down their answers correctly. A focus on form – initiated by the children – often becomes observable with regard to spelling.

P: Wie schreibt man *boat* auf Englisch? [P: How do you spell *boat* in English?]
C: Und eigentlich klein jetzt? [And usually with a small letter?]

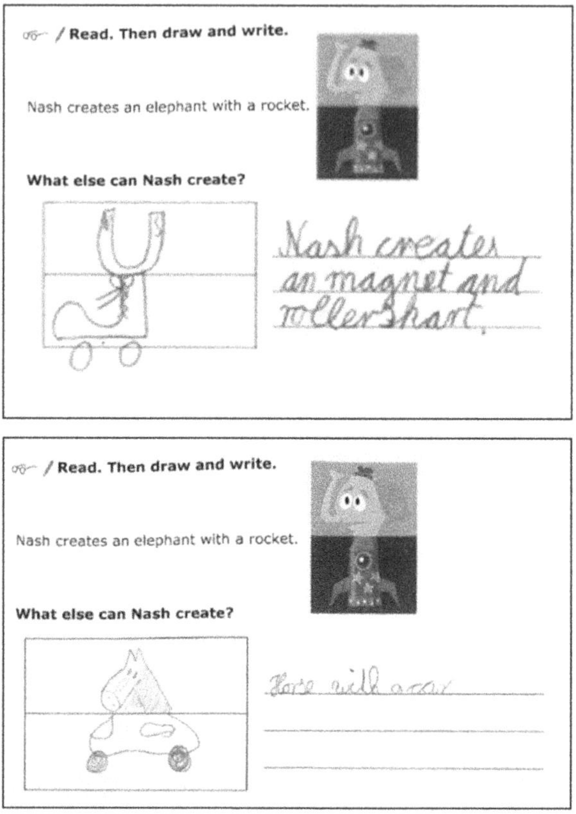

Figure 3.4 Activities that leave room for subjective and creative reactions

L: Nein, am Satzanfang immer groß. [No, at the beginning of a sentence you always have to use a capital letter.]
C: Groß. Auch im Englischen? [A capital letter. Also in English?]
L: Ja. [Yes.]

Completing post-reading activities: Individual reactions

While completing the post-reading activities, the learners show different individual reactions. Table 3.5 offers an overview of these. Reading the task instructions and/or sentences from the worksheets out loud serves two major purposes. Firstly, it helps the children to better understand what is required of them. Secondly, reading out loud also aids the organisation of pair work – indicating which activity needs to be worked on next and/or what needs to be clarified.

Inserting key words in English is a frequently used practice. Most of the key words used are either central to the plot of the story or words that the children already know (e.g. characters such as the 'big bad wolf' in the story app. 'The Three Little Pigs', places like 'playground', objects like 'window' or colours like 'yellow'). These English key words are naturally combined with the language of schooling.

By talking to themselves, the learners verbalise what they are working on. In this way, they organise their own working process and allow their partner(s) to follow them.

P: Hier muss das doch irgendwo sein. [It has to be here, somewhere.] (P is looking for a particular word on the slide and is therefore looking through the app.)

P: Wir brauchen jetzt noch das eine. Wo ist noch eine Lücke frei. Ne * Ne [Now we just need this one. Where is there a free gap. No * No. *] (Looks on his worksheet for the last free gap.) * Ah da. * Der Wolf * da weiß ich wo das ist. [Ah there * The wolf * this, I know where it is.] (Looks for the slide on the iPad.)

Children translate sentences to clarify their content.

Discussing story apps

At the end of each reading phase, the children are asked for their opinions. They individually note these on their worksheets and are invited to share them with the class during circle time at the end of each weekly English Book Club (see Table 3.6).

Discussing opinions about story apps

On the final page of the material, the children are always asked to rate the story app and add reasons for their personal opinions. These activities offer a lot of pre-structured language that is meant to encourage them to express their opinions in English. Depending on the children's ability and personal preferences they either use English or German (see Figure 3.5).

Discussing opinions about story apps: Discussion circle

At the end of each weekly English Book Club session, the children have circle time to report to their classmates which story app they read and share and discuss their opinions with them. This phase is led by the English Book

Table 3.6 Discussing opinions about the story apps (language choices and functions)

Discussing opinions about story apps	Learners ...	Language choice tends to be ...	The function of language is to ...
Worksheet	note their opinions in a written form.	a mix of English and German.	get meaning across.
Discussion circle	share and discuss their opinions with their classmates.	a mix of English and German.	get meaning across.

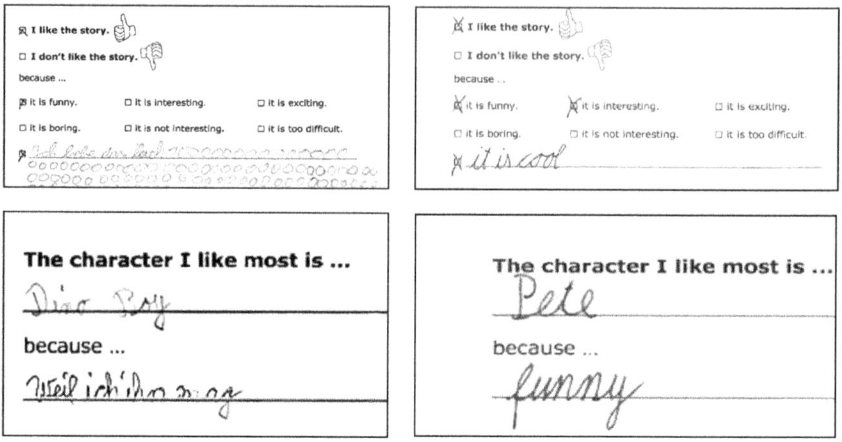

Figure 3.5 Rating the story app and providing reasons for personal opinions

Club instructor, who encourages the children to speak as much English as possible. As the transcripts reveal, the teacher's individual language support and the task support offered (e.g. cards with sentence beginnings) help the children to use the foreign language. Since the children's main goal is to get their meaning across, they also mix languages to share their opinions and reasons for these with the group.

N: (reads his sentence from the paper ribbon) I like the story very much.
T: Aha! And why do you like the story very much?
N: * It is funny and * interesting.
T: Okay. Thank you very much.
T: You would like to start, D?
D: I read 'Smelly Peter'. * I like the story very, very, very much.
T: Wow, this sounds like a really good story. Why do you like the story?
D: Ähm * weil es da um Erbsen geht, um beans. Also andere * [Uhm * because it is about peas, about 'beans'. Also other*.]
S: Erbsen. [Peas.] (D nods in confirmation.)
T: And what happens in the story?
D: Ähm * Peter wird entführt. He it is funny and exc/ * exciting. [Uhm * Peter is kidnapped. 'He it is funny and exc/ * exciting.']
T: Okay, thank you for you presentation. Well done.

Summary and Discussion

The preliminary results allow one to draw first conclusions regarding the use of languages. When understanding the story apps, completing post-reading activities and discussing the story apps, the learners' choice of language seems to be influenced by (a) individual factors, (b) the addressees (their partner[s]), (c) the interactive features of the story apps as well as

(d) the activities the children work on. The target language (English), the language of schooling (German) and a 'language mix' serve different functions (see Figure 3.6).

(a) To what extent learners use the foreign language probably depends on individual factors like motivation, interest and their level of ability. With regard to these factors, the teacher's knowledge of her/his students is important so that she/he can offer individual support (e.g. modelling of tasks, dictionaries, corrective feedback). Nevertheless, if children use the language of schooling with their partner while reading the story apps, it does not necessarily mean they are not interested in the story or are reluctant to use the foreign language. Instead, talking in the language of schooling to each other is a strategy that allows the students to check their understanding, clarify words in the story and/or share opinions about the plot, for example. This means that use of the language of schooling supports the reading process. German was used on a meta-level for organisational matters (e.g. organising the reading process, focus on form, clarification requests). Using the language of schooling (German) for organisational matters meant the young learners could devote more attention to following the stories and doing the activities in the target language (English).
(b) The majority of the children decided to read the story apps with another student. This partner played an important role in exploring

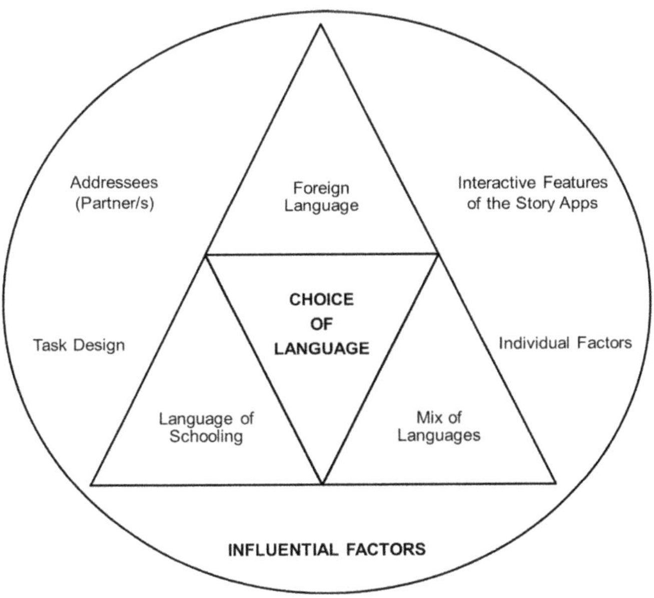

Figure 3.6 Factors that influence the learners' choice of language

and communicating about the story app: the children used the German language in the pre-reading phase to organise the reading process (e.g. who reads/clicks when and what). While reading the story app, evaluative and emotional comments were shared with the partner(s) in the language of schooling. In the post-reading phase, languages were mixed to discuss possible solutions, ask each other for help and write the answers correctly, for example.

(c) The students used several of the interactive features of the story apps (e.g. audio narration, task completion) for comprehension purposes, while the fact that they were animated (e.g. sounds, music, animations) helped them to remain focused on the stories. Throughout the reading processes, the children mixed the use of the foreign language and the language of schooling. This indicates their willingness and openness to use the foreign language. The learners also show what they can already do. Overall, a high level of motivation to understand the story apps in the foreign language could be observed.

(d) The design of the activities influenced the students' language choice. Activities that focused on the linguistic level tended to encourage the use of the foreign language. To complete these activities, children worked very closely with the story apps (e.g. skimming and scanning through the slides). In this way, the story apps provided language input. When fully engaged with the text, some children were also able to complete activities that invited subjective and individual reactions to the story in the foreign language.

These results show that both languages play an important role in the individual reading processes of the children. They are in line with the growing awareness that a monolingual approach to foreign language learning that tries to prevent children from using other languages than the target language for fear of negative transfer, too little exposure to the target language and a lack of effort on part of the learners to use the target language does not use learners' full potential (Hall & Cook, 2012; López Corcoll & Gonzalez-Davies, 2016).

The data show that the children use as much German as necessary, but also as much English as they possibly can; they use whatever linguistic resources they have at their disposal. The different languages tend to fulfil different functions. Whereas German is the language of choice to organise pair work, manage the reading process as well as talk about language on a meta-level, English literally 'comes into play' when the children get involved in the story, show emotional reactions to the text and participate as players and co-creators of the story. They also use the English language to display their developing linguistic competences, for example, when they insert key words in English in German statements or try to talk about what they like about the stories during circle time in English.

These results suggest several consequences for the classroom: it is possible to approach challenging content and complex tasks in the primary classroom. When material is personally relevant for students, they can complete complex tasks such as reading stories in English on their own if one allows them to draw on their full range of resources, an idea that is also promoted by the translanguaging approach (García & Wei, 2014; López Corcoll & Gonzalez-Davies, 2016). Further research is needed to find out how the use of students' L1 (including cases where this is not the language of schooling) can be integrated effectively in learning to read in a foreign language. Since many story apps also allow readers to choose a variety of languages, further studies could explore how children with an L1 other than German might use this feature. Research could also investigate how young learners can be supported so that they use their different languages effectively.

Story apps seem to be especially suitable for independent reading since the interactive features support the learners' understanding and prompt them to use the target language spontaneously and in conversations with their partners to some extent. Activities that are intended to support the reading process of story apps should explicitly integrate the linguistic level if the use of English is to be fostered. If children can rely too much on the illustrations and animations to figure out the plot and do the post-reading activities, they will not engage as much in target language use. Further research could look deeper into how the reading process is affected by the integration of multimodal elements in the texts and how the interplay between the different elements can effectively promote language learning.

Note

(1) In the transcripts from the students' videos, square brackets are used to give the English translation of the children's comments in German. Within these, words in quotation marks show that these words were used in English by the children. In the original German texts, these words are marked in italics. * indicates short pauses.

References

Al-Yaqout, G. and Nikolajeva, M. (2015) Re-conceptualising picturebook theory in the digital age. *Nordic Journal of ChildLit Aesthetics* 6. See http://www.childlitaesthetics.net/index.php/blft/article/view/26971 (accessed 9 April 2018).

Bircher, K. (2012) What makes a good picture book app? *The Horn Book Magazine*, 72–78.

Brewster, J. and Ellis, G. (2012) *The Primary English Teacher's Guide*. Harlow: Penguin English Guides.

Buendgens-Kosten, J. (2015) Multilingual CALL: More than just translation drills? *eLearning Papers* 45, 43–46.

Burns, A. (2010) *Doing Action Research in English Language Teaching. A Guide for Practitioners*. New York: Routledge.

Bus, A.G., Takacs, Z.K. and Kegel, C.A.T. (2015) Affordances and limitations of electronic storybooks for young children's emergent literacy. *Developmental Review* 35, 79–97.

Cahill, M. and McGill-Franzen, A. (2013) Selecting 'app'ealing and 'app'ropriate book apps for beginning readers. *The Reading Teacher* 1 (67), 30–39.

Cameron, L. (2001) *Teaching Languages to Young Learners*. Cambridge: Cambridge University Press.

Canagarajah, S. (2011) Codemeshing in academic writing: Identifying teachable strategies of translanguaging. *The Modern Language Journal* 95 (3), 401–417.

Council of Europe (2001) *Common European Framework of Reference for Languages: Learning, teaching, assessment*. Cambridge: Cambridge University Press.

Elsner, D., Buendgens-Kosten, J. and Hardy, I. (2014) Awareness of multilingual resources: EFL primary students' receptive and productive code-switching during collaborative reading. In J. Enever, E. Lindgren and S. Ivanov (eds) *Conference Proceedings from Early Language Learning: Theory and Practice 2014* (pp. 41–49). Umea: Umea University.

Frisch, S. (2015) Eckpunkte einer theoretisch und empirisch basierten Lesedidaktik für den Englischunterricht in der Grundschule. In M. Kötter and J. Rymarczyk (eds) *Englischunterricht auf der Primarstufe: Neue Forschungen – weitere Entwicklungen* (pp. 15–34). Frankfurt: Lang.

García, O. and Wei, L. (2014) *Translanguaging: Language, Bilingualism and Education*. New York: Macmillan.

Hall, G. and Cook, G. (2012) Own-language use in language teaching and learning. *Language Teaching* 45 (3), 271–330.

Kolb, A. (2012) Extensive reading of picturebooks in primary EFL. In J. Bland and C. Lütge (eds) *Children's Literature in Second Language Education* (pp. 33–43). London: Bloomsbury.

Legutke, M.K., Müller-Hartmann, A. and Schocker-von Ditfurth, M. (2009) *Teaching English in the Primary School*. Stuttgart: Klett.

López Corcoll, C. and González-Davies, M. (2016) Switching codes in the plurilingual classroom. *ELT Journal* 70 (1), 67–77.

Mayring, P. (2014) Qualitative content analysis: theoretical foundation, basic procedures and software solution. See http://nbn-resolving.de/urn:nbn:de:0168-ssoar-395173 (accessed 23 October 2016).

Mourão, S. (2015) The potential of picturebooks with young learners. In J. Bland (ed.) *Teaching English to Young Learners Critical Issues in Language Teaching with 3–12 Year Olds* (pp. 199–217). London: Bloomsbury.

Richards, K. (2009) Interviews. In J. Heigham and R.A. Croker (eds) *Qualitative Research in Applied Linguistics: A Practical Introduction* (pp. 182–199). Basingstoke: Palgrave Macmillan.

Sargeant, B. (2015) What is an ebook? What is a book app? And why should we care? An analysis of contemporary digital picture books. *Children's Literature in Education* 4 (46), 454–466.

References: Story apps

Dino Boy (3037). See https://itunes.apple.com/us/app/dinoboy-adventures/id455138887?mt=8

My Dad Drives a Roller Coaster Car (Crab Hill Press LLC). See https://itunes.apple.com/de/app/my-dad-drives-roller-coaster/id428268576?mt=8

Nash Smasher (Crab Hill Press LLC). See https://itunes.apple.com/us/app/nash-smasher!-for-ipad/id405340373?mt=8

The Three Little Pigs (Nosy Crow). See https://itunes.apple.com/de/app/three-little-pigs-by-nosy/id418543664?mt=8

Zoe's Green Planet (Square Igloo).

4 Awareness of Multilingual Resources: EFL Primary Students' Receptive Code-Switching during Collaborative Reading

Daniela Elsner and Judith Buendgens-Kosten

I'm Scat the Cat and with *my* hat, *I'm* going to change *my* colors just like that!

Traditional rhyme, author unknown

Introduction

Children all over the world learning languages love the rhyme about Scat the Cat. Many picture book artists have illustrated Scat in a variety of colourful and rich environments, and textbook authors have built a story around the big black cat for its use in language classrooms. What is most fascinating about Scat is the fact that he can easily adapt to his environment, simply by changing his colour. So, when Scat sits in a beautiful lush green meadow, he changes his colour from black into bright green, unifying him with the plants and the flowers he is surrounded by. When Scat relaxes on top of a pail of oranges, he changes his colour into orange, so that he harmoniously blends in with the fruit. However, Scat never drops his initial colour when changing it to another one. Anytime he wants to be a black cat again, he can choose to do so, and he does in the end.

Just like Scat the Cat, many people in our society adapt to their surroundings. However, they do not change their colours to do so, but their languages. The Special Eurobarometer 386 (European Commission, 2012) shows that Europeans recurrently use different languages when watching movies or TV shows, when listening to the radio or using the internet, or while travelling. And even though it is not possible to determine an exact number of bilingual and plurilingual speakers worldwide, we know that one of every five 5- to 17-year-olds in the United States is bilingual (García & Flores, 2014: 149). The Eurobarometer indicates that the majority of Europeans (54%) are able to communicate in at least one additional language, and about a quarter are able to hold a conversation in more than two languages (García & Flores, 2014). Overall, we may assume that for most people in the world it has become a daily routine to frequently change their language as their private or professional lives in a multilingual world afford them to do so.

This 'multilingual turn' in our society has also led to a multilingual turn in schools (Conteh & Meier, 2014; May, 2014). Unlike 20 years ago, when the monolingual child was assumed the norm in European classrooms, today's classrooms unite more and more learners with several languages and language varieties. In Germany alone, 99,472 school-age immigrants were integrated into the German school system in 2014 (German Federal Office of Statistics, 2016). Many more are expected within the next few years; most of them will not speak the school language but the languages of the country of their origin.

According to the Special Eurobarometer of 2012, most Europeans agree that 'all languages spoken within the EU should be treated equally', and that the 'improvement of language skills should be a policy priority' (European Commission, 2012: 119). Hence, teachers now stand in the front line when it comes to creating a 'language-friendly environment' in which 'different languages are heard and seen (...), speakers of all languages feel welcome and language learning is encouraged' (European Commission, 2008).

Without a doubt, it is a challenging task to develop feasible concepts for such multilingual learning environments. Thus, feasible suggestions for an integrative multilingual approach making active use of students' plurilingual competencies are hard to find, both in theory and in practice; for an overview of different attempts see Lohe and Elsner (2014) as well as Conteh and Meyer (2014).

The MuViT project (Elsner, 2011), as briefly described in the following passages of this chapter, was one of the first European attempts to integrate different languages into primary language classrooms by following a multiliteracies pedagogy approach (Elsner *et al.*, 2007; Elsner & Wildemann, 2013). Mostly in line with the pedagogical idea of translanguaging, as defined by e.g. García and Sylvan (2011) or García and Wei (2014), the MuViT learning environment affords students to actively make use of (their) different linguistic repertoires. To be more precise, the core of MuViT are multimodal, digital storybooks in five different languages (German, Spanish, Turkish, Russian, English), including several tasks that ask for language comparisons, linguistic reflections, code-switching and translations.

The developmental phase of the project (2010–2012) has been followed by different smaller projects and one larger research study (LIKE) focusing on a variety of questions linked to the use of the multilingual software application in an English as a foreign language (EFL) context. In this chapter, we will elaborate on these projects.

We will, moreover, discuss the outcomes of a qualitative analysis of eight students' receptive code-switching activities when working with one multilingual, multimodal digital storybook from the MuViT software in pairs. The data illustrate the different approaches students' make use of when working with multilingual media in mono- and multilingual co-learning situations.

The text will end with implications for the implementation of multilingual computer assisted language learning (CALL) through the use of multilingual and multimodal digital storybooks in primary schools.

The European project MuViT: Developing and investigating multilingual virtual talking books for primary language learners

The developmental phase of the EU-funded Comenius-Project 'MuViT' (Multilingual Virtual Talking Books) ran between 2010 and 2012 (Elsner, 2011; https://web.archive.org/web/20160404075740/http://www.mu-vit.eu/).Against the background of rapid cultural, linguistic and technological changes, especially in European schools, the following question challenged a group of researchers from five different countries: How can new technologies be exploited best for the creation of multilingual learning environments for learners in primary schools?

As the majority of teachers are not able to speak all of the languages their students speak, a language-friendly environment that includes and challenges learners of different language backgrounds requires multilingual media/technology. However, technological tools need to be easily applicable to teachers and students, and their usage needs to match the learning goals and principles of each classroom.

Having this in mind, the project group worked out a concept for the use of multilingual digital storybooks in primary classrooms. The main achievement was a software application, the MuViT Player, which includes six multimodal, multicodal and digital picture storybooks in English, German, Russian, Spanish and Turkish. The illustrated stories are read out by native speakers, and a simultaneous highlighting function (similar to karaoke) is available in which words are visually marked at the moment they are spoken. Children can switch between languages on any given page and at all times, simply by clicking on one of six flag symbols provided on each page (Russian is available both in Cyrillic and in Latin script). Two pages of vocabulary introduction precede each story in order to facilitate comprehension of the following stories. Subsequent to the work with the storybooks, text comprehension exercises and language awareness activities follow. Through these, children become aware of differences and similarities between their native language(s), the school language and the target language English, and become sensitised to various languages.

MuViT offers students the opportunity to *actively* switch their *input* language on a receptive level, which – in standard classroom situations – is not possible as the teacher as the main input provider (with the exception of peer learning situations) decides on the input language in conversations and tasks.

We define this self-directed change of the input language as receptive code-switching (Elsner & Lohe, 2013). Unlike prior definitions of receptive code-switching, which describe receptive code-switching as a reaction to the productive code-switching of another person (e.g. Nemoianu, 1980; Quintero & Rummel, 1998), we believe that receptive code-switching is moreover an active and self-driven choice of language input. However, receptive code-switching in this sense relies on the use of multilingual media. In order to enable learners to choose the language of their choice when reading and/or listening, the medium needs to include multiple language versions of one text, which can be switched by the reader with relatively little effort.

Through the (digital) opportunity for receptive code-switching, MuViT wants to support learners with different language backgrounds in their reading processes in the foreign language English. Learners whose home language is not the school language but one of the other languages provided in MuViT, get the chance to read the stories in all of the languages they currently use. Yet, the multilingual stories also intend to arouse students' interest and curiosity for new languages and support learners in their foreign language learning processes (which is usually English), regardless of whether they are mono- or plurilingual. The MuViT website also offers the MuViT authoring tool, which allows users to write and upload their own multilingual storybooks (Lohe *et al.*, 2014).

In a nutshell, dealing with the numerous languages offered by the digital storybooks should on the one hand help to improve the status of minority languages, and on the other hand raise students' language awareness of and in different languages, including modern foreign languages, the school language and heritage languages. With this, MuViT blends in with the idea of translanguaging as defined by García (2009):

> Translanguaging is the act performed by bilinguals and multilinguals of accessing different linguistic features of various modes of what are described as autonomous languages, in order to maximize communicative potential. It is an approach to bilingualism and multilingualism practices of bilinguals and multilinguals that are readily observable in order to make sense of their multilingual worlds. (García, 2009)

Yet, the pedagogical aims of MuViT go even beyond this concept, as the MuViT application not only affords bilinguals and multilinguals the opportunity to make use of the various linguistic features and modes to cater to the languages they already know, but it also invites monolingual learners to translanguage in order to learn (about) modern foreign and less popular languages as well as about their similarities and differences. In MuViT, users can use a language they have no command of, alongside languages they are learning and languages they are fluent in. When working with MuViT, monolinguals, bilinguals and plurilinguals are similar in at least one regard: in MuViT, all learners find at least one language they know, but also many others that are new to them. In this way, MuViT creates opportunities for translanguaging practices for all students within the classroom, regardless of their linguistic background. For some, it can be a normal way to engage with the languages in their lives. For others, it can be a format through which they can acquire new linguistic and meta-linguistic competencies.

Research on the use of MuViT in EFL classrooms

Unlike the majority of research studies in the field of multilingual pedagogy, which tend to look at multilingual approaches to language learning through the lens of the second/the school language (for an overview see May, 2014 or Conteh & Meier, 2014), our research, which is connected to the use of the MuViT software application in schools, is dedicated to multilingual CALL in the context of foreign language classrooms.

The majority of European learners start learning a foreign language, mostly English, in school when they are between 6 and 8 years old. For students with a bilingual or plurilingual language background, this means that with the beginning of these lessons they start learning a third or even a fourth language. This field of research – sometimes referred to as tertiary language learning – has not experienced much attention up to this point (for an overview see Jessner, 2008). One of its central questions is how does the prior knowledge of two or more languages impact individual foreign language learning processes in school contexts? Looking at the rather diverging results of the corresponding research studies, we need to admit that a clear answer to this question is still missing.

Whereas a few studies show that plurilingual learners can benefit from their multiple language (learning) knowledge in further language learning (e.g. Goebel *et al.*, 2011; Jessner, 2008), others find negative effects of plurilingualism regarding the development of specific competencies such as listening, reading or writing in English as a third language (Elsner, 2007; Groot-Wilken *et al*,. 2007; Wilden & Porsch, 2015). A third group of findings shows that there seem to be no significant differences between mono- and plurilingual learners when it comes to foreign language learning in education settings (e.g. Özdemir, 2006; Sanders & Meijers, 1995; van Gelderen *et al.*, 2003).

Searching for reasons for these conflicting results, we can see that most of the studies do not take all of the factors that impact the language learning success of plurilingual learners into consideration (e.g. language proficiency, social and socio-linguistic factors, status/prestige of the language, linguistic distance, etc.; for details see Elsner [2015]).

What we can agree on at this point, is the fact that plurilinguals possess specific linguistic resources that monolinguals do not have. Whether or not these resources can be used effectively with regard to further language learning or whether these linguistic resources may hinder learners in their learning processes depends on many factors and circumstances of the individual and the individual situation. Yet, we are convinced that multilingual affordances within the language classroom are supportive of both mono- and multilingual learners when learning foreign languages (see also Elsner *et al.*, 2015). How useful MuViT would be for foreign language learners with different language backgrounds was and still is being investigated in different smaller and larger research projects that will be looked at in the following.

Research on MuViT: Results of university students' investigations

After the release of the MuViT software, different smaller exploratory research projects were initiated by PhD students and by master students in the context of their final theses for their first state examination (which equals a Master in Education). The studies presented here were conducted under the supervision of Daniela Elsner and/or Ilonca Hardy at the University of Frankfurt. They were published in a book edited by Daniela Elsner and Viviane Lohe in 2014 (for additional student projects supervised by Anja Wildemann at the University Koblenz Landau, see Wildemann and Fornol [2015]).

Jasmin Krumm (2014) investigated 'Receptive Code Switching Behavior of Mono- and Multilingual Learners While Reading in the Foreign Language English'. In a quasi-experimental study with 32 children ages 9–11, Krumm examined whether differences could be found in the receptive code-switching behaviour of mono- and multilingual learners reading a multilingual storybook in the foreign language (either using a multilingual version or an English-only version of the story). Krumm found that first of all the switching behaviour of the mono- and plurilingual students did not differ significantly in terms of frequency. The observations and log file protocols showed that both groups of learners made use of the switch-language option, and that all of the students predominantly switched between two languages only, English as their first foreign language and German as their school language. The other language versions, Russian, Turkish and Spanish, were scarcely used during reading phases. Moreover, the pre- and post-test assessing reading fluency and vocabulary gain showed that there were no significant differences between students who worked with the multilingual storybooks and those who worked with the English-only version of the books. At the same time, Krumm found that for reading fluency, the students who used the English-only version of the books showed slightly better results. Yet, it needs to be said that the study focused on a very small number of learners, and the results thus need to be treated with caution.

In another study, Creutz (2014) focused on the 'Effects of EFL Primary School Learners' Self- Concepts on their Performance during Cooperative Tasks' when working with the MuViT stories with a partner. Using questionnaires, tests and observations, Creutz found that a higher self-concept with regard to students' performance in EFL led to significantly less switches to the learners' school and/or native language German. In other words – the better the learners perceived their own language skills in the foreign language to be, the less they tended to switch to other languages.

In her project, Heier (2014) examined possible differences between children with German as their first language and German as a second language when working with one of the MuViT stories and corresponding guided reading tasks. Twenty-four children worked in pairs with a partner of the same mono- or bilingual language background. The author used pre- and post-tests to assess vocabulary improvement and reading comprehension. Heier used log file data and video recordings of dyad interactions to study receptive and productive code-switching. Heier found, just like Krumm (2014), that the children did not make much use (neither receptively nor productively) of the other languages besides English or German, even if one of their first languages was Turkish, which is a language offered in the software application. However, Heier also found that the Turkish-German children were more interested in the different language versions of the stories and worked more creatively with the multilingual books.

In her PhD research project, Viviane Lohe looks at the development of pupils' language awareness through the use of multilingual virtual talking books (Lohe, 2018). The results of the pilot study give reasons to assume that language awareness on a cognitive and an affective level can be enhanced with the digital multilingual material, as students readily worked with the storybooks over a longer period, started to compare languages and spotted differences and similarities between languages they already knew and those that they had not been familiar with before (see Lohe & Elsner, 2013). Yet, Lohe presumes that a deliberate approach to the use of the multilingual digital stories is necessary in order to maintain students' motivation over a longer period, and to ensure a sustainable improvement of students' language awareness.

Regardless of their different research foci, the authors of all of the above studies pointed out that the participating children, no matter whether they were monolingual, bilingual or plurilingual, were extremely motivated to use the digital storybooks. All of the learners in these studies made use of different language versions of the storybooks, when they were offered to them. However, the learners did not necessarily switch into all of the provided languages with the same degree of interest or the same frequency.

What none of the studies took a closer look at, though, were the purposes of the learners who switched languages on a receptive as well as on a productive level when working with a partner. The rather small studies were also not able to explain what impact multilingual and multimodal learning situations with multilingual digital storybooks has on young learners' development in the foreign language English. These questions are at the centre of the research project LIKE, which will be elaborated on in the next section.

MuViT research: Negotiation of meaning and code-switching in collaborative settings

A larger-scale research project, called LIKE, focusing on the use of the MuViT software application in foreign language classrooms began in 2013. The acronym LIKE (Bedeutung der **LI** [Türkisch] und L2 [Deutsch] für die Entwicklung **k**ommunikativer Kompetenz in der L3 [Englisch] bei mehrsprachigen Schülerinnen und Schülern [Role of the L1 (Turkish) and L2 (German) for the development of communicative competence in the L3 (English) for plurilingual learners]) stands for an interdisciplinary research project investigating the potential of the L1/L2 for contributing to the development of communicative competence in the foreign language English for diverse language learners. More explicitly, the study focuses on the relationship between the salience of use of multilingual resources and the development of communicative competence (vocabulary development, text comprehension) in the English language.

The LIKE research environment offers pupils aged 9–12 years a reduced trilingual version (English, Turkish, German) and a reduced monolingual version (English) of one of the MuViT picture-audio storybooks called *Ruben and the Magic Stones* (see Figure 4.1). Learners can read the story on their own or activate an audio version by pressing the play button on each page (25 pages in total, including 4 pages with prompts to summarise, talk or reflect about the story). Just like in the other storybooks, the languages of the program can be switched on at any page by clicking on one of the

Figure 4.1 Screenshot of MuViT as adapted for LIKE (trilingual version)

flags in the upper left corner. Unlike the original version, no 'karaoke' highlighting function is provided, nor are the vocabulary introductions and the language awareness/comprehension test exercises available in the original version.

Children (total n = 118) work together in three different language dyad constellations: monolingual German/German pairs; mixed pairs with one monolingual-German and one bilingual Turkish/German child; and pairs with two bilingual (Turkish/German) children. Following a quasi-experimental 2 × 3 design, the experimental group is offered the trilingual version of the stories, whereas the control group is only offered the monolingual English version of the story.

In this way, the LIKE study offers the learners in the experimental group an environment that allows learners to switch languages on a productive and on a receptive level, whereas learners in the control group do not get the opportunity to switch their languages on a receptive level.

The LIKE study seeks to answer the following two central questions:

(1) How do different settings (regarding multilingual/monolingual materials, different dyad compositions) impact vocabulary learning and text comprehension in EFL?
(2) What roles do L1 and L2 play in multilingual and multimodal settings?

In order to answer these questions, we investigate the receptive and productive CS activities of the learners, their negotiation processes and the relationship between those aspects and the development of vocabulary learning and story comprehension. Overall, we believe that a maximum of affordances of multilingual language use has a positive impact on pupils' learning processes in English. For details concerning the full research questions and hypotheses underlying this study, see Elsner *et al.* (2014).

Reasons for and Types of Receptive Code-Switching: A Qualitative Analysis

In this chapter, we look at students' receptive code-switching activities, focusing on four dyads (eight learners) from the pilot study during their collaborative work with the computer program. We will discuss how and why mono- and plurilingual students in different peer constellations make use of the different languages offered by the learning environment.

We will discuss the following questions:

(1) How do monolingual (German) and bilingual/plurilingual (Turkish-German+X) students who work with a trilingual digital picture story (Turkish, German English) make use of the languages offered by the medium?
(2) What are their reasons for switching the languages within the computer program?

Sample

The data discussed in this chapter are taken from the LIKE pilot study. These were collected at the beginning of fifth year of a high school (with children previously having two years of EFL with two hours per week). A total of 24 children were investigated within 12 dyads, of which 18 children/9 dyads worked with the trilingual treatment. For the analysis of students' receptive code-switching behaviour, we focus on four dyads (eight learners) only (see Table 4.1).

Table 4.1 Overview of the four dyads

Name of dyad	Sex	Language combination	Treatment
Manul	F	German	Trilingual
	F	German German and Turkish	Trilingual
Caracal	M F	German and Persian and Kurdish and Turkish[a] German	Trilingual
Puma	F F	German German	Trilingual
Leopard	M M	German and Turkish German and Turkish	Trilingual

[a] The boy had not mentioned his Turkish language skills in the pre-test, but later on switched to Turkish when communicating with his partner.

Research setting

Participants were divided into dyads and a short information-gap activity was initiated to establish a communicative focus. Students then moved on to laptops in the same dyad constellation, in order to work with the modified MuViT version of *Ruben and the Magic Stones*, which had already been installed and opened up for the students. The children were given a brief introduction to the use of the software and how to work with the stories. The dyads working with the trilingual tool were asked to start with the English version of the story, but were told to also make use of the German or Turkish version if they wanted to. Integrated prompts and communicative tasks stimulated a holistic and comprehension-oriented processing of the story. The work with MuViT was recorded via webcam and screen capturing (both including audio). An integrated protocols function (log file) kept track of all receptive languages switches. After the work with MuViT, the children completed two post-tests.

In the following, we will describe the receptive code-switching behaviour of Manul, Caracal, Puma and Leopard, four dyads of the pilot study, using quantitative data generated through the log files and qualitative data (transcription of the conversation the children had with their partner during the work with the story, which was recorded by screencast videos), to show distinctions between receptive code-switching patterns that are not visible from the log file analysis alone. We chose these four dyads because they demonstrate well the breadth of different approaches the learners demonstrated when working with the story.

Receptive code-switching during collaborative work with MuViT: Results of the log file analysis

In a first step, we counted and compared the number and frequency of page views of each dyad. Figure 4.2 visualises the dyads' interactions with the story as a linear, temporal process. Each box visualises one page view, starting from the first page (bottom) to the last (top). The colour of the box gives information about the selected language (black: English, striped grey: German, white: Turkish). Information about the pages accessed was available, but has not been included in the graphic. The size of the boxes has no meaning, it is an artefact of the visualisation technique, reflecting the number of pages viewed (more pages viewed resulted in a smaller box).

Figure 4.2 shows that Manul read the story exclusively in English whereas Caracal looked at each page in German and in English as well as at a few pages in Turkish. Puma and Leopard showed frequent switches into one (or both) non-English languages. At the same time, Caracal made far fewer switches between languages than Puma and Leopard. Just on

Figure 4.2 Visualisation page views per language of the four dyads

the basis of the log file analysis, we can say that there are (at least) three patterns of receptive code-switching behaviour: not switching languages; switching languages rarely and maintaining the switch for multiple page views (macro switches); and switching frequently between languages, maintaining each switch for a short number of pages only (micro-switches). For a more technical description of macro and micro switches, see Bündgens-Kosten and Elsner (2014). In the following section, we will attempt to differentiate the code-switching behaviour even further, by including the video data (screen cast videos) in our analysis.

Screencast analysis

The analysis of the log files shows how the use of multilingual resources may differ from dyad to dyad. The transcripts of three selected receptive code-switching episodes allow us to further elaborate on the differences between Puma and Leopard.[1]

Excerpt I (Puma)

[**MuViT:**	Page 6 (Englisch) is open]
MuViT:	Did you understand everything? If not: Ask your partner for help. [Switch to page 7]
CHILD 1:	Mach das mal auf Deutsch (.) geh zurück und mach's auf Deutsch wenn wir's nicht verstanden haben (...)[[Do it in German (.). go back and do it in German if we haven't understood this (...)]] [Switch to page 6, change to German] [CHILD 1 reads text aloud] Hast du alles verstanden / wenn nein bitte deinen Partner um Hilfe (.) [[Have you understood everything/ if not ask your partner for help (.)]] okay doch wir haben alles verstanden oder / [Switch to English] oder hast du was nicht verstanden / [[OK, yes we have understood everything, right / [Switch to English] or is there something you did not understand /]]
CHILD 2:	Ich hab was ver (.) ich hab alles verstanden also er geht zur Schule und er hat ein roten Stein gefunden [[I have underst... something (.) I have understood everything well he goes to school and he has found a red stone]]
CHILD 1:	Ja und er stellt sich vor was er damit machen könnte [[Yes and he imagines what he could do with it]] [Switch to page 5]
CHILD 2:	Ja er könnte Bauarbeiter werden [[Yes, he could become a builder]]
CHILD 1:	Ja genau [[yes exactly]] [Switch to page 6, 7]

This passage shows the first code-switching episode of this dyad. For the first five pages, the learners only viewed, read and listened in English. On page six, they get the prompt to reassure with their partner if both of them have understood the story so far. This dyad seems to ignore the prompt at first and simply moves on to page 7 in English. By the time they realise that there is no further information about the prompt, one of the girls directs the other to go back one page and switch into the German language: 'Mach das mal auf Deutsch (.) geh zurück und mach's auf

Deutsch wenn wir's nicht verstanden haben (...)' [[Do it in German (.). go back and do it in German if we haven't understood this]]. When reading the prompt in German, they obviously understand what they have to do, as they start discussing the story in German. Having done this, they immediately switch back again into English. Another, similar switch follows when the children reach page 7.

The second excerpt is similar in structure.

Excerpt II (Puma)

[**MuViT:**	Page 7 (Englisch) is open]
MuViT:	The stone sparkles. Suddenly Ruben is in the middle of diggers and trailers.
CHILD 2:	Diggers / was heißt das diggers / diggers /[[Diggers / what does it mean diggers / diggers/]]
CHILD 1:	Mach das mal jetzt auf Deutsch [[Make it German now]] [Switch to German]
MuViT:	Der Stein funkelt. [[The stone sparkles]]
CHILD 2:	*Diggers* Bagger [Switch to English] [[Diggers Bagger[German word for *digger*]]]
MuViT:	The stone sparkles. Suddenly [Switch to page 8]
CHILD 2:	Mann oh ich bin so doof [unverständlich] [[Man oh I'm so stupid]]

In Excerpt II, one specific word – *diggers* – is not understood by the learners. *Diggers* was likely to catch the attention of the learners as it was included in the vocabulary pre-test. The question 'Diggers / was heißt das diggers / diggers /' /[[Diggers / what does it mean diggers / diggers/]] by Child 1, which Child 2 seems unable to answer, results in Child 2 asking for a receptive code-switch. In other words, the receptive code-switching itself has a function within a negotiation of meaning sequence ('non-understanding routine', Varonis & Gass, 1985). The learners switch from English to German and correctly identify the German equivalent for *diggers* (*Bagger*). The problem seems to be solved, the children switch back to English.

It becomes obvious that the Puma dyad performs receptive code-switching in order to understand a section of the text, or a specific word. Both types of code-switching are frequently spotted during the dyad's reading process. Yet, this strategy does not always lead to an optimal outcome. The data expose examples of children switching into another language in order to look up a word; however, due to syntactic differences between the languages, a false word is being identified as the equivalent, without the children noticing this (for an example, see Bündgens-Kosten *et al.*, 2016). Receptive code-switching provides for the opportunity to identify an equivalent word from the parallel text, but does not guarantee success.

Not all instances of receptive code-switching take place in negotiation of meaning sequences though. The dyad 'Leopard' provides examples for this alternative approach to receptive code-switching. The dyad switched to Turkish right at the start – even before any instructions could be given by the experimenters, indicating their strong motivation to use their home language in school (compared to the other 12 dyads in the pilot study, this dyad also shows the greatest quantity of Turkish page views). Only after an experimenter explains to them 'You can start in English and then if you want to change to Turkish you can change' do they engage with the English text.

The following passage (Excerpt III) is taken from the middle of the story, and demonstrates another, distinct language switching behaviour.

Excerpt III (Leopard)
[Page 9 is open in English]

MuViT:	Ruben can't hold on to the pipe. [Switch to German] Ruben kann das Rohr [Switch to English] Ruben can't hold [children laugh] on to the [Switch to German] Ruben kann [Switch to English] Ruben can't hold on to the pipe. It falls on his foot. 'I wish I were at school!'
CHILD 1:	Mach ma Türkisch [[Make it Turkish]] [Switch to Turkish]
MuViT:	Ruben boruyu tutamaz. Boru ayaginin üzerine düser. [[Ruben can't hold on to the pipe. It falls on his foot.]]
CHILDREN:	[laugh]
MuViT:	Ruben can't [Switch to page 10]

Even though many switches can be detected in this scene, it remains unclear why these switches occur. The only reaction that can be observed is the laughter of the children. Laughing, however, can have a multitude of meanings and is therefore hard to interpret. In combination with the language switches from English to German to English to Turkish, it could be an indicator for a strong motivation to switch the languages, and therefore an indicator for a strong interest in different languages: the children could be indicating their pleasure with the different language versions. But laughing could also mean amusement, sparked by the different speakers and the different sounds of the languages. What is clear though, is that this dyad's switches do not seem to be connected to any concerns related to comprehension.

Leopard exhibits a switching pattern that on the surface, looking only at the log file data, reminds one of the code-switching patterns of Puma.

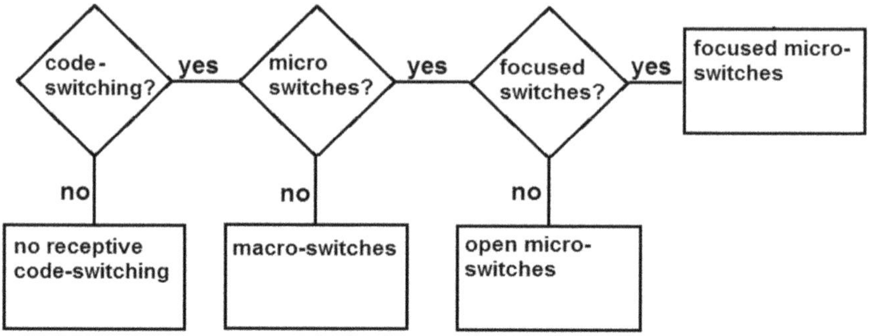

Figure 4.3 Types of receptive code-switching behaviour

Nevertheless, the motivation for and the purpose of frequent switching seems to clearly differ between the dyads.

On the one hand, we find switches that are motivated by concerns about comprehension. We will refer to this kind of receptive code-switching as *focused receptive code-switching.* Switches that seem to occur for non-comprehension-related reasons, and that are clearly connected with curiosity, amusement, fun or playfulness, we refer to as *open receptive code-switching.* A focused code-switch has been successful when the children engaging in it feel they have settled the comprehension issue they had experienced. An open switch, on the other hand, does not need to 'achieve' anything. If the learners had fun, and their curiosity has been satisfied, the open switch fulfilled its function.

As the motivations of children are not visible *per se*, the distinction between focused switches and open switches relies on what is established conversationally. If the children remain silent throughout, a receptive code-switch can neither be identified as focused nor as open switch. Figure 4.3 illustrates the different types of receptive code-switching described so far.

Conclusion

In this chapter, we introduced the multilingual digital picture book application 'MuViT' as a useful resource for multilingual learning environments, especially for foreign language classrooms. Digital storybooks in different languages allow learners to use the different languages they have at their disposal while developing literacy in a foreign language.

A number of research projects on the use of MuViT show that monolingual and plurilingual children make use of the different languages afforded by their digital surrounding. Yet, in our analysis, we could see that learners have very individual ways of and reasons for using the different languages. Whereas for some learners receptive language choice is more a matter of delight or identity comfort, for others the possibility to read or listen to other languages while working in a foreign language seems to be a welcomed aid.

Even though parallel research in LIKE (see Bündgens-Kosten *et al.*, 2016) has shown that not all types of receptive code-switching are immediately helpful with regard to language learning (e.g. when the learners look up a word in another language, but choose the wrong one due to different syntax systems), we believe that multilingual digital books, as one out of many possibilities including receptive and productive code-switching practices in the EFL classroom, are valuable tools within a multilingual pedagogy approach. From an EFL perspective, we believe that multilingual learning environments should provide different languages for learners, without losing track of subject-specific goals (e.g. the development of communicative competencies in the foreign language English). For us, the optimal multilingual environment entails multiple affordances of multiple receptive and productive language use, both for mono- and plurilingual learners.

Note

(1) Translations to English have been added in [[double brackets]].

References

Bündgens-Kosten, J. and Elsner, D. (2014) Rezeptives Code-Switching ein- und mehrsprachiger Lerner/innen in multilingualen Settings. *Fremdsprachen Lehren und Lernen* 42 (2), 56–73.

Bündgens-Kosten, J., Elsner, D. and Hardy, I. (2016) Videoanalyse ein- und mehrsprachiger Lerner/innen bei der computerbasierten Textarbeit: Die Rolle von Code-Switching und Negotiation im frühen Englischunterricht. In U. Rauin, M. Herrle and T. Engartner (eds) *Videoanalysen in der Unterrichtsforschung. Methodische Vorgehensweisen und Anwendungsbeispiele.* Weinheim: Beltz Juventa 225–241.

Conteh, J. and Meier, G. (eds) (2014) *The Multilingual Turn in Languages Education: Opportunities and Challenges.* Bristol: Multilingual Matters.

Creutz, M.A. (2014) Effekte von Selbstkonzepten auf die Bearbeitung kooperativer Lernaufgaben im Englischen der Grundschule. In D. Elsner and V. Lohe (eds) *Multimodalität und Fremdsprachenlernen* (Vol. 5). Aachen: Shaker 55–81.

Elsner, D. (2007) *Hörverstehen im Englischunterricht der Grundschule. Ein Leistungsvergleich zwischen Kindern mit deutscher Muttersprache und Deutsch als Zweitsprache.* Frankfurt am Main: Peter Lang.

Elsner, D. (2011) Developing multiliteracies, plurilingual awareness & critical thinking in the primary language classroom with multilingual virtual talking books. *Encuentro Journal* 20/2011-12, 1–12. See http://www.encuentrojournal.org/textcit.php?textdisplay=427 (accessed 23 March 2017).

Elsner, D. (2015) Inklusion von Herkunftssprachen: Mehrsprachigkeit als Herausforderung und Chance. In C. Bongartz and A. Rohde (eds) *Inklusion im Englischunterricht* (pp. 71–94). Frankfurt am Main: Peter Lang.

Elsner, D. and Lohe, V. (2013) Fostering Multilingualism with Computer-Based Multilingual Storybooks: The European Comenius Project MuViT. Presentation at the WorldCall

Conference Glasgow. See https://prezi.com/pbjnxpu-ybnj/fostering-multilingualism-with-computer-based-multilingual-storybooks-the-european-comenius-project-muvit/ (accessed 25 September 2016).

Elsner, D. and Wildemann, A. (2013) Multiliteracies entwickeln: Das europäische Projekt MuViT. *Journal of the Hasan Ali Yücel Faculty of Education* 10 (1), 1–20.

Elsner, D., Küster, L. and Viebrock, B. (eds) (2007) *Fremdsprachenkompetenzen für ein wachsendes Europa: Das Leitziel 'Multiliteralität'*. Frankfurt am Main: Peter Lang.

Elsner, D., Buendgens-Kosten, J. and Hardy, I. (2014) Awareness of multilingual resources: EFL primary students' receptive and productive code-switching during collaborative reading. In J. Enever, E. Lindgren and S. Ivanov (eds) *Conference Proceedings from Early Language Learning: Theory and Practice* (pp. 41–49). Umea: Umea University.

Elsner, D., Bündgens-Kosten, J. and Hardy, I. (2015) Affordanzen und Nutzung mehrsprachiger Lernumgebungen: erste Ergebnisse aus der Pilotierung zum Forschungsprojekt LIKE. In M. Kötter and J. Rymarczyk (eds) *Englischunterricht auf der Primarstufe: Neue Forschungen – weitere Entwicklungen* (pp. 35–57). Frankfurt am Main: Peter Lang.

European Commission (2008) Multilingualism: An asset for Europe and a shared commitment. Communication from the Commission to the Council, the European Parliament, The Council. The European and Social Committee of the Regions. COM (2008) 566 final. Brussels. See http://eur-lex.europa.eu/legal-content/EN/ALL/?uri=CELEX%3A52008DC0566 (accessed 23 March 2017).

European Commission (2012) Special Eurobarometer 386: Europeans and their languages. See http://ec.europa.eu/public_opinion/archives/ebs/ebs_386_en.pdf (accessed 18 September 2016).

García, O. (2009) *Bilingual Education in the 21st Century: A Global Perspective*. New York: Blackwell/Wiley.

García, O. and Sylvan, C.E. (2011) Pedagogies and practices in multilingual classrooms: Singularities in pluralities. *The Modern Language Journal* 95 (3), 385–400.

García, O. and Flores, N. (2014) Multilingualism and Common Core State Standards in the United States. In S. May (ed.) *The Multilingual Turn: Implications for SLA, TESOL, and Bilingual Education* (pp. 147–166). London: Routledge.

García, O. and Li, W. (2014) *Translanguaging: Language, Bilingualism and Education*. New York: Palgrave Macmillan.

German Federal Office of Statistics (Statistisches Bundesamt). See https://www.destatis.de/DE/Startseite.html (accessed 23 March 2017).

Goebel, K., Rauch, D. and Vieluf, S. (2011) Leistungsbedingungen und Leistungsergebnisse von Schülerinnen und Schülern türkischer, russischer und polnischer Herkunftssprachen. *Zeitschrift für Interkulturellen Fremdsprachenunterricht* 16 (2), 50–65.

Groot-Wilken, B., Engel, G. and Thürmann, E. (2007) Listening and Reading Comprehension: Erste Ergebnisse einer Studie zu Englisch ab Klasse 3 an nordrhein-westfälischen Grundschulen. *Forum Schule 1*. See http://www.grundschulverband.de/fileadmin/aktuell/Gaby_Engel_STS_Soest.pdf

Heier, L. (2014) Bearbeitungsprozesse einer textbasierten Lernaufgabe im Englischen: Ein Vergleich zwischen Kindern mit und ohne Migrationshintergrund. In D. Elsner and V. Lohe (eds) *Multimodalität und Fremdsprachenlernen* (Vol. 5). Aachen: Shaker 83–104.

Jessner, U. (2008) Teaching third languages: Findings, trends, challenges. *Language Teaching* 41 (1), 15–56.

Krumm, J. (2014) Rezeptives Codeswitching-Verhalten von ein- und mehrsprachigen Lernern beim Leseprozess in der Fremdsprache Englisch. In D. Elsner and V. Lohe (eds) *Multimodalität und Fremdsprachenlernen* (Vol. 5). Aachen: Shaker 11–30.

Lohe, V. (2018) *Die Entwicklung von Language Awareness bei Grundschulkindern durch mehrsprachige digitale Bilderbücher. Eine quasi-experimentelle Untersuchung zum Einsatz von MuViT in mehrsprachigen Lernumgebungen*. Tübingen: Narr.

Lohe, V. and Elsner, D. (2014) Developing language awareness in primary school children with multilingual virtual talking books: First results of the pilot study. *International Journal of Computer Assisted Language Learning and Teaching* 4 (4), 30–47.

Lohe, V., Armbrust, L. and Elsner, D. (2014) The MuViT authoring tool: Fostering communicative competences of young language learners. *Babylonia* 3, 21–27.

May, S. (ed.) (2014) *The Multilingual Turn: Implications for SLA, TESOL, and Bilingual Education*. London: Routledge.

Nemoianu, A.M. (1980) *The Boat's Gonna Leave: A Study of Children Learning a Second Language from Conversations with Other Children*. Amsterdam: J. Benjamins.

Özdemir, B. (2006) Bilinguale Kinder im Englischunterricht. In M. Pienemann, J. Keßler and E. Roos (eds) *Englischerwerb in der Grundschule* (pp. 110–121). Paderborn: Schöningh.

Quintero, E.P. and Rummel, M.K. (1998) *American Voices: Webs of Diversity*. Upper Saddle River, NJ: Merrill.

Sanders, M. and Meijers, G. (1995) English as L3 in the elementary school. *International Review for Applied Linguistics* 107–108, 59–78.

Van Gelderen, A., Schoonen, R., de Glopper, K., Hulstijn, J., Snellings, P. and Simis, A. (2003) Roles of linguistic knowledge, metacognitive knowledge and processing speed in L3, L2 and L1 reading comprehension. *International Journal of Bilingualism* 7 (1), 7–25.

Varonis, E. and Gass, S.M. (1985) Non-native/non-native conversations: A model for negotiation of meaning. *Applied Linguistics* 6 (1), 71–90.

Wildemann, A. and Fornol, S. (eds) (2015) *Sprachliches und mediales Lernen in der Grundschule*. Aachen: Shaker Verlag.

Wilden, E. and Porsch, R. (2015) Die Hör- und Leseverstehensleistungen im Fach Englisch von Kindern am Ende der Grundschulzeit unter besonderer Berücksichtigung von lebensweltlicher Ein- und Mehrsprachigkeit. In M. Kötter and J. Rymarczyk (eds) *Englischunterricht auf der Primarstufe: Neue Forschungen – weitere Entwicklungen* (pp. 59–80). Frankfurt am Main: Peter Lang.

5 This is How I Say It! Discourse with Tablets among Multilingual Learners

Henriette Dausend

Introduction

Diversity and heterogeneity are major key words in current educational debates. This chapter asks how learners with differing language competences can benefit from the given language diversity in class. It introduces a model of transcurricular teaching, which provides principles for multilingual tasks that allow pupils to use all of their language competences. It further discusses whether digital media – especially tablets – constitute a suitable means for initiating multilingual talk in transcurricular tasks and considers to what extent tablets can enable pupils to produce, record, edit and save multilingual talk, thus helping them to foster language competences in multilingual educational settings.

Diversity in Educational Contexts

'Heterogeneity' has become a key term in school education. Heterogeneity is commonly defined via differences that describe social groups or individuals (Gomolla, 2009: 22; Haß, 2006: 251; Sturm, 2013: 14ff.). These differences, or inhomogeneities as they are referred to in the original Greek understanding, should always be seen in perspective (Sturm, 2013: 15). The description of difference is therefore dependent on the respective personal, cultural, social and organisational context. Differences are socially constructed, solely concerned with individual factors (e.g. age, gender, milieu affiliation) and limited in time (Gomolla, 2009: 22).

In the context of foreign language teaching, learners' linguistic differences are considered primarily relevant factors and are discussed as such. Besides factors like age, gender, intelligence, motivation, learning styles and strategies, language aptitude, interests, needs and self-concept, other factors such as work ethic and social, cultural and linguistic backgrounds are likewise crucial (Haß, 2006: 250). In dealing with heterogeneity, it is thus advisable to treat difference and diversity as a normal condition and resource in the classroom (Gomolla, 2009: 21). Consequently, the question arises how linguistic diversity can be exploited for foreign language learning processes and how teaching can live up to it. For the teaching of foreign languages, the following question is derived from this claim: how should language be dealt with in heterogeneous learning contexts? The focus regarding this matter is on all of the following: the target language, the school and – if different from the previously mentioned – the family language of the pupils. All of the pupils' languages matter since existing language skills and the language competences that need to be acquired have a mutual influence on each other (Hufeisen, 2011: 267f.; Siebert-Ott, 2010: 152f.) Just as the linguistic environment is characterised by the pupils and their milieu affiliation, so too the pupils themselves are characterised by the school as an organisation milieu (Nohl, 2010: 206). Language is a central aspect of schooling (Lütje-Klose, 2004: 51), and it is necessary to discuss how different linguistic competences should be dealt with in foreign language teaching.

Diversity in Foreign Language Learning

The objective of English lessons is to promote foreign language discourse competence. This competence is described by the core curricula of the German federal states as a pro-active negotiation of meaning (Dausend, 2014: 40ff.). Accordingly, competences are to be understood as a conglomerate of abilities and skills, knowledge, opinions and attitudes (Weinert, 2001: 27f.). Competences develop as long-term dispositions over time when pupils use language in meaningful interactions. The overall goal is that the pupils are enabled to fully participate in society as well as to shape their own lives in a self-determined manner (Hallet, 2011: 30). Therefore, complex competences are needed that combine skills like listening, speaking, reading and writing with attitudes, knowledge, experiences and motivations, allowing the learner to participate in negotiation processes across linguistic and cultural borders (Bonnet & Breidbach, 2013: 33f.; Hallet, 2011: 36). The term 'discourse' emphasises both the negotiation processes between individuals and the use of skills such as 'saying/writing/listening/reading/viewing' (Gee, 1990: 142).

In order to further describe the nature of such discourses, and thus to be able to make statements about competences, it is necessary to figure out which factors characterise social discourses today. In the past decade, two particular developments have been observed that are crucial for the teaching context: both technological developments and increasing social diversity have led to an explosion of new communication contexts and modalities. Digital communication and globalisation change the way pupils interact and learn (Anstey & Bull, 2006: 19ff.). Especially the foreign language classroom can take advantage of the increasing complexity and multimodality of communication among people of different languages and cultures. As Cope and Kalantzis (2000: 19) state '[...] students will need to acquire the skills, strategies, and practices they need for work and leisure; active citizenship; participation in social, cultural, and community activities; and personal growth'.

With reference to the plurilingual backgrounds of learners, it should be considered

- to what extent language competences are present within the learning group;
- in which way those competences are applied by the pupils to participate in discourse;
- to what extent competences and discourses should be promoted;
- to what extent the use of the learners' language resources can be used for acquiring the foreign language.

Thus, the principles of teaching should be selected in such a way that they seize upon the character of the discourses (Bach & Breidbach, 2009: 286ff.; The New London Group, 2000: 10ff.). English lessons need to offer pupils the opportunity to apply and expand their linguistic knowledge as well as their cultural competences and knowledge, abilities and skills, opinions and attitudes.

The Notion of Transcurricular Teaching

Language competences can be developed if pupils use language in meaningful discourse. This use of language is influenced by the language competences that pupils already possess. These competences depend on the social and educational background of the pupils. In order to build on the pupils' pre-knowledge, teachers should take into account all of the pupils' languages and cultures (Dausend, 2015: 72ff.). Even if these are very different in diverse classrooms, the competences have to be respected and made use of in the lessons (Rösler, 2013: 156). Teachers are asked to initiate situations for discourse in which pupils might use the target language as well as their other language competences. Such teaching sessions take advantage of the linguistic and cultural competences when pupils negotiate meaning with the help of all their language potential – as they would do in situations outside the classroom as well.

This concept is embraced by the approach of transcurricular teaching, which promotes meaningful classroom discourses by means of teaching content. The notion of transcurricular learning helps to create these discursive learning situations. It provides information on how foreign language teaching should be implemented to enable phases of discursive speech. Individual and meaningful learning experiences are created when all the linguistic and cultural resources of the pupils are used in order to negotiate meaning. Therefore, relevant and predefined content is used to operationalise competences (Bär, 2013: 99f.). Such content should be oriented towards both the curricula and the interests and needs of the pupils. One point of orientation should always be pupils' living environment. In doing so, pedagogically meaningful content can be related to the needs and the previous experiences of the pupils. Doing so, transcurricular learning offers a bridge between the competences and content of different subject areas (overview in Dausend, 2014: 132ff.). Topics such as 'me and my family' can be established in parallel lessons, e.g. in English, social studies and art. Doing so, learners have the opportunity to report about their families and friends in the school and the target language during a whole set of lessons. A network of languages and content even provides the opportunity to overcome the linguistic allocations of the subjects. The target language and even the family language can be used if it appears appropriate in the respective situations. Such a learning environment can point out the meaning and the value of multilingualism as a norm rather than an exception in linguistically heterogeneous groups.

However, for a long time there has been the question of how an integration of the learners' languages can be implemented when the focus is on the foreign language and only individual learners exhibit competences in a specific language system. A possible answer can be found in the increasing digitalisation and globalisation of communication. The technical development of smartphones and tablets has enabled learners to independently explore transcurricular learning spaces, although this may happen mostly outside the school context. It is the communication settings that are constantly changing and developing through the interplay of increasingly powerful technology and the use of this technology by people (Dezuanni *et al.*, 2015: 7; Gattenhof & Dezuanni, 2015a: 31). The integration of tablets in teaching thus comes as a logical consequence. This is because the school is asked to engage in various modes of social communication if it endeavours to fulfil its task of preparing young people for a self-determined life. Furthermore, tablets are presented as a means that allow for self-regulated and action-oriented learning (Kirch, 2014: 50f.). Learners might include experiences of out-of-school discourse situations and extend their competences in using mobile devices that support the learning process. The multilingualism of private discourses could therefore be mirrored in the learning environment of the school by the pupils using their mobile devices for discourses. The possibilities provided by tablets for realising transcurricular teaching and language learning processes are illustrated in the following section.

Using Tablets in Transcurricular Teaching

Tablets offer many possibilities for foreign language learning as well as for multilingual discourses. Their size, lightness, mobility and the possibility to use the internet allow for individual and mobile access to the digital world providing a major linguistic input (Dezuanni *et al.*, 2015: 1). Tablets can help to initiate approaches such as transcurricular teaching as the mobile devices provide opportunities for speech production and discursive processes, which still remain a challenge for both pupils and teachers. 'Promoting oral production in the target language in a classroom seems something of a challenge' (Müller-Hartmann & Schocker-v. Ditfurth, 2009: 61). But in order to create discursive situations and to better exploit the language potential of learners (e.g. Engel *et al.*, 2009; Roos, 2007), tablets can enable self-regulated learning tasks. In those tasks, pupils are asked to use all their language competences when receiving or producing texts, audios, videos, books, comics, etc. 'The [tablet] can enable young children to create and share digital content that focuses on art forms and cross-curricular learning [...]' (Gattenhof & Dezuanni, 2015a: 30). It is especially story-making apps that offer pupils opportunities to develop their own stories and implement them linguistically (Gattenhof & Dezuanni, 2015b: 88; Kucirkova *et al.*, 2014: 174). Two examples are outlined in the following.

With the app Puppet Pals, a digital role play is created in which learners are able to select or create characters and backgrounds. They move their characters in front of different backgrounds according to the story they have developed. All their statements are simultaneously recorded by the app via a microphone integrated in the tablet. In this way, a synchronous recording of movements and language is created, which does not require any further processing. The Book Creator is another more complex example than Puppet Pals as it works with fewer predefined settings. It offers the chance to create a personal digital book in which texts, images, videos, colours and shapes are joined together.

The use of these productive apps in the classroom allows for the inclusion of speech while creating stories, journals and role plays. Creating stories helps pupils transfer personal experiences into a language product, building on existing competences and incorporating personal interests (Gattenhof & Dezuanni, 2015b: 97). In order to express themselves, they can use all their linguistic and cultural competences in order to develop storylines and implement them in a linguistically and visually appealing way. In the context of transcurricular learning, an app like Puppet Pals complements the idea of classic role plays when negotiation processes emerge among the members of a learning group. For the joint work with story-making apps, Falloon and Khoo (2014) found an added communicative value. They showed that pupils negotiated meaning when they had to agree on content and design, to define or defend their personal ideas, and to find compromises.

> It was apparent that the open nature of these apps, combined with the greater public work space affordances of the device, at least potentially could provide students with powerful environments supportive of critical but collaborative content development, as gauged by increased exploratory talk. (Falloon & Khoo, 2014: 27)

Story-making apps provide a chance for pupils to practice their discourse competence. Kirsch (2012) was able to point out that working with language collaboratively supports language competence, self-esteem and positive attitude towards other languages. In her research, children used the tablet to retell stories and to record these retellings. Kirsch (2012: 47f.) found that the mentioned positive effects derived from the possibility for the pupils to structure their language use by themselves, from listening to their own voices and from intensive interaction with their group members. For use in multilingual groups, working with story-making apps might motivate the learners to negotiate meaning regardless of the language category. Besides the school and target language, they may experiment with language and include competences related to their family language. As pupils need to create a final product in the target language, using other languages during the preparation and production of the story can support the negotiation processes as well as meta-linguistic insights into language.

For learning a foreign language, the language product the learners deal with is central as well. In the case of story-making apps, teachers have access to the language products of the students and get insight into their communicative competence. This enables teachers to determine the competence level of the pupils and to use it for both individual feedback and evaluation. Since the pupils act in a realistic language situation during the recording, it can be assumed that they make spontaneous linguistic mistakes, which can be diagnosed and analysed by the teacher within the product.

For English lessons in the German school context, however, no research results exist so far on how and for what purpose pupils use production-oriented apps in class. In order to be able to formulate statements about the possibilities that tablets offer from an empirical point of view, the project 'Teaching English with Tablets' (TET) was started in 2014. In the following, the research questions and design as well as first results are presented.

Research on Tablets in Transcurricular Teaching

The study 'Teaching English with Tablets' is being conducted by the Institute for English Teaching Methodology at Chemnitz University of Technology. The aim of the investigation is to describe the application of language competences while working with story-making apps in foreign language classes. Based on language production tasks, the research questions of the current study cycle are divided into one major and three minor questions:

- Which possibilities are offered by tablets for discursive negotiation processes in English lessons?
  (1) How do pupils interact when working on language production tasks with tablets during English classes?
  (2) How does the language use of pupils develop in language production group work phases?
  (3) Which attitudes do pupils and teachers show towards the benefit of tablets in language production group work phases?

Design of the study 'Teaching English with Tablets'

The study 'Teaching English with Tablets' offers explorative access to the use of tablets in the field of foreign language teaching. The language use of learners is investigated during learning tasks in which pupils work collaboratively with story-making apps (Kleemann *et al.*, 2013: 19). The work in teacher–researcher tandems allows for the linking of practical conditions and theoretical assumptions. It establishes cycles of action, observation, reflection and new action ideas in the sense of action research (Altrichter & Posch, 2007: 17). The teachers reflect on the work with tablets and generate new possibilities for implementation. The researchers accompany the teacher in this complex process as experts in research and learners at the same time. In this way, researchers also take on the role of the teacher in the TET study when they train the teachers in dealing with the tablets. In addition, the phases of joint lesson planning promote the interaction of teaching–learning processes between teachers and researchers since different kinds of expertise are brought together to develop a practicable teaching scenario. Together they analyse the usability of tablets in teaching languages and develop methods for successful implementation in the long run. An exploratory approach of slowly moving forward is realised in the context of action research. That way, data are collected and evaluated in order to subsequently make theoretical generalisations (Kleemann *et al.*, 2013: 25). Consequently, the findings are directly mirrored onto the presuppositions so that possible modifications lead to changes in further research cycles.

The selection of the participating teachers depends on criteria that qualify them for intensive cooperation such as

- interest in the use of digital media, in particular tablets, during English lessons;
- provision of information to the pupils' parents as well as advertisement of the project in school;

- willingness to participate in a six-hour training session;
- active participation in a planning discussion (60 minutes) at Chemnitz University;
- approval of being filmed during class and of being interviewed afterwards;
- support by school management.

In order to establish a teaching situation that is as realistic as possible, the work with the tablets is integrated by teachers in their regular lessons.

First data set of the study 'Teaching English with Tablets'

The first research cycle was performed between January and December 2015. During these eight months, it was possible to work with 7 teachers from five schools in the area of Chemnitz and a total of 145 pupils. The teachers attended training on the use of tablets in language teaching in January. Subsequently, each teacher prepared lessons in which the tablets were used for language production tasks together with a researcher. The tasks were based on the upcoming teaching content of each class and were modified according to the individual language competences of the different age groups:

- Grade 1 ($n = 18$): Retell the story using the app Our Story.
- Grade 2 ($n = 23$): Create a role play with Puppet Pals (topic: weather).
- Grade 3 ($n = 25$): Create a digital book with the Book Creator (topic: spring).
- Grade 4 ($n = 19$): Create a digital book with the Book Creator (topic: the ugly duckling); create a role play with Puppet Pals (free choice of topic).
- Grade 4 ($n = 24$): Create a digital book with the Book Creator (topic: hobbies).
- Grade 5 (school for children with specific needs, $n = 11$): Create a role play with Puppet Pals (topic: Christmas).
- Grade 7 (secondary school, $n = 25$): Create a role play with Puppet Pals (topic: Christmas).

All tasks were done by the pupils within a period of 90–225 minutes on one or more days. All pupils were supposed to create their stories using the English language as a main tool. All pupils used one of the three story-making apps: Book Creator (Red Jumper Limited, 2014), Puppet Pals (Polished Play 2012) and Our Story (The Open University, 2011) (see Table 5.1).

All pupils worked in pairs. In each class, four pairs were randomly selected (according to the explorative design of the study) to be recorded (audio and/or video) during the planning and the recording of the stories.

Table 5.1 Description of the functions of the apps Book Creator, Puppet Pals and Our Story

App	Description	Competence
Book Creator	Create your own books and layouts and send them in digital form. Insert text, images, audio and video files. Storage of the product.	To develop a script for a book and implement it. To arrange spoken and written texts. To combine voice recordings with visualisations and writing.
Puppet Pals	Create a digital role play with animated characters and recordings in your own language in real time. Storage of the product.	To develop a storyline and to implement it dialogically. To produce own speech to the movements of the characters and the storyline. Dialogic talk in real time.
Our Story	Create your own story. Align images, and leave a voice recording for each image.	Develop a storyline. Choose images and assign them to text. Talk to the pictures.

Additionally, pupils of different classes were further assessed via personal interviews (Grade 2, $n = 9$; Grade 4, $n = 13$; Grade 5, school for children with specific needs, $n = 11$) or questionnaires (Grade 7, $n = 23$). So far, all interviews as well as a large part of the video and audio data have been evaluated. First, video and audio data were approached with few pre-assumptions in order to see how far English had been used during the pupils' group work. Doing so, all assumptions were derived from the data themselves (Flick, 2014: 124ff; Strauss & Corbin, 1996: 43). In order to get a good overview, the data were divided into phases of language use, and labelled using MAXQDA (Version 11).

Secondly, all interviews were transcribed (Kuckartz, 2012: 136) and analysed according to Mayring (2015). The interviewees' answers were checked along the topics of the interview questions. From these, categories were created for detailed analysis. The questionnaires have not yet been included in the pool of data as the ongoing project aims to collect more questionnaires. The results of the first cycle will now be used to adjust the research organisation, data collection and the observation focus in a second cycle.

Results of the first data set of the study 'Teaching English with Tablets'

The first research cycle asks for possibilities that tablets offer for discursive negotiation processes in English lessons. The audio and video recordings of individual groups give first insights into how language is used during the working processes. In order to gain an overview of as many different purposes in language use as possible, all findings were collected independently of the age group (see Table 5.2). Most of the operations listed in Table 5.2 could be found within all age groups. Obviously,

Table 5.2 Different language use situations of the L1 German, L2 English and Lx

	L1 German	L2 English	Lx
Organisational issues	• Discuss task • Assign partners • Discuss the chronological sequence • Clarify technical issues		
Structural planning of the text	• Negotiate the plot • Select characters/ settings • Plan scenes	• Suggest text parts • Put text parts together • Practice texts • Write texts/take notes • Create titles	• Compare vocabulary (French/English)
Recording of the role plays	• Code-switching	• Recording of the texts	• Recording of the text (Russian) • Dialogues (Russian)
Reflection of the recording	• Evaluate recording	• View recordings	
Meta-linguistic references	• Assess language of the partners • Clarify words		

Source: Dausend and Nickel (2017).

differences occurred in the quality and quantity of the foreign language used according to the different language levels of pupils from Grades 1 to 7.

Generally, as most of the learners have German as a first language (L1), all groups used both the L1 German and the second language (L2) English for different purposes. Even the first grades tried to include several English words and phrases. German was mainly used for organisational clarification. Hence, the pupils used their competences in German to clarify tasks, to discuss information on the timing of their work and to talk about the technical conditions. Moreover, the learners applied German during the structural planning of their stories, negotiating the plot, planning the sequence of the scenes and selecting the characters and backgrounds in German. They further used German for meta-linguistic talk, giving feedback to the English pronunciation of a classmate in German or clarifying English terms by discussing them in German. German was also partially present during the recordings as single words or a German stress was used. However, the recordings of the stories the pupils produced were mainly in English. In order to create the story, the pupils from Grade 2 onwards used English when they suggested narrative text fragments and titles for the story. Together they developed a narrative text and practiced it in the target language. Some groups (starting even in Grade 2) also used their knowledge of the written language by taking notes of their narrative texts. The stories were recorded and also listened to in English. Some groups prepared multiple versions of their stories.

Observations showed that the pupils used a variety of languages even if the task was to create a story in English. Especially, the special need fifth graders showed a high variety in language use. Some even incorporated their family languages (German or others) in the language product, at times switching between languages. This insight into individual code-switching shows that some participants tend to use all language competences they have to express themselves. They negotiate meaning as wished for in transcurricular/multilingual teaching situations. These observations are consistent with the teachers' statements ($n = 5$), which were gathered in an informal interview after each tablet session. They considered the textual creativity of the language products as well as the motivation of the learners to be positive. Even the use of the German language during group work is seen as a helpful step to create a complex story and to transfer it into English. The teachers mentioned that they did not expect the pupils to produce as much English as they did. They were surprised at how freely the pupils used the English language. In addition, observations show that pupils also used other languages than English or German. The recordings of the preparation phase show two seventh graders comparing English and French words (without this being part of the task). In the fifth grade of a school for children with specific needs, there are phases in which a pair of pupils switches to Russian during the recording. In this case, both pupils draw on their family language, Russian. In the following interview, it became clear that this language change was not intentional, but happened unconsciously. Hereinafter, the preliminary results are used to provide first answers to the research questions.

Discussion of the Results

The objective of the study 'Teaching English with Tablets' is to describe which possibilities are offered by tablets for discursive negotiation processes in the sense of transcurricular teaching.

Working with tablets in general

Observations of teaching situations as well as feedback by the teachers indicate that the majority of the pupils work with the tablet in a very concentrated way. But there are phases in which the pupils do not focus on the tasks and work with Puppet Pals while having another self-selected focus. The pupils do not focus on the tasks in these self-determined working phases but are able to create an English-speaking story with Puppet Pals despite the distraction. Furthermore, a review of the products shows that all groups achieved a result in the target language English within the intended time. Therefore, the question arises: what function those phases of self-determined work have for the discursive behaviour of the learners and the use of their languages. There is a need to clarify why these phases emerge, what relevance the 'focus on things beside the actual tasks' has for the pupils and how they influence the work process and the negotiation processes (see also Buendgens-Kosten, 2015; Bündgens-Kosten & Elsner, 2014). But even if the learners do not engage in the task at times, they nevertheless indicate similar work steps in the interview. They mention such aspects as defining the topic of the plot or scene, proposing text fragments or dialogue, creating text, practicing text and recording to be important. It can be assumed that the design and functions of the app support the work process as well as the given task. This observation points out that creating stories with the tablet asks for good lesson planning in which features of the app and the task are coordinated. A learning task that offers possibilities for language discourse is still needed. The existing features of apps do not cater for language activities without appropriate tasks. Individual scaffolding can provide a support system necessary for the primary level that enables self-organised working with the app.

The initiation of discourse

Data show that learners negotiate meaning when creating and recording stories with the tablet. Video and audio sequences give insight into how diverse the negotiation processes are. Additionally, statements of the pupils indicate that they communicated with each other intensively. The majority of the pupils could name and describe processes during the interviews in which they negotiated meaning. The intensity of the discourses among the pupils becomes obvious in those statements that are critical of the partner or group work, addressing conflicts as well as solutions for solving these. Especially in the lower grades, these conflicts mainly take place in the family language. Even if the English language is neglected within conflicts, it underlines how flexibly language is used. Pupils seem to use the language they feel is most appropriate for the situation. This competence of choosing languages might have a positive effect on a general discursive competence. A look at the higher grades shows that the use of English is increasing but also strongly varying depending on the constellation of the groups. The question is whether the use of the German language can be reduced in some groups or whether it can be understood as a natural reaction to a situation (following the idea of transcurricular teaching). Interesting in this context is the use of further languages other than German and English. Data show that two groups used Russian and French when creating their stories. While two fifth graders use their family language Russian, two seventh graders seem to deliberately compare English (L2) and French (L3) words. These two cases indicate how a casual use of linguistic competences can be initiated through learning with tablets, and in which way they are integrated in the learning process by the pupils.

I: Ja? Ehm welche Aufgaben hast du übernommen während eurer Partnerarbeit? (Which parts did you speak during your role play?)
S: Den Weihnachtsmann. (Santa Claus.)
I: Den Weihnachtsmann, okay. Ehm ja und ihr habt ja, habt ihr Englisch gesprochen? (Santa Claus. Ok. And did you speak English?)
S: Deutsch. (German.)
I: Deutsch. Habt ihr- (German. Did you-)
S: Am Anfang Englisch, es fiel uns schwer, dann halt auch ab und zu mal russisch geredet. (English at first, but it was hard, and then we spoke Russian occasionally.)
I: Ja. (Ok.)
S: Und dann hab ich mit der nächsten Partnerarbeit gemacht und da haben wir einfach deutsch geredet. (And then I worked with another pupil and we just spoke German.)
I: Okay. (OK.)
S: Das fiel uns leichter. (That was much easier.)
I: Ja. Also Englisch ist dir schwer gefallen, deswegen habt ihr das dann, seid ihr dann in eure andere Sprache gewechselt und warum habt ihr Russisch genommen? (Ok, so, speaking English was hard for you and so you changed languages. And why did you use Russian?)
S: Ist mir ausgerutscht bei Russisch. (It just slipped out.)
I: Ja, ah okay, aber ihr habt das nicht geplant, das auf Russisch zu machen? (Ok, so you did not plan to do it in Russian?)
S: Ähäh. (No.)

The use of the L1 German and the L2 English

The German language is mainly used for the negotiation of meanings and the review of the language products. The interviews show that the pupils almost exclusively use the English language for the recording of their dialogs.

I: Und wann habt ihr denn Englisch gesprochen in der Partnerarbeit? (So, when did you speak English during your group work?)
S: Eigentlich fast die ganze Zeit wo wir das gemacht haben, ham wir fast kein Deutsch gesprochen, nur Englisch, wir ham's versucht Englisch zu sprechen, ham's auch ganz gut gemeistert und ja. (Actually the whole time we were doing it we barely spoke German, only English, we tried speaking English and did it pretty well.)
I: Und als ihr die Geschichte besprochen habt, vor der Aufnahme, habt ihr da Englisch gesprochen? (And when you were speaking about the story, before the recording, did you speak English then?)
S: Ja, ham wir. Wir ham das erst geübt, damit wirn bisl sicherer werden. Und dann haben wir gesagt: so, jetzt geht's los und jetzt machen wir das

Ding einfach. (Yeah, we did. First we practiced it so that we were a bit more confident. And then we said: ok, here we go and now let's just do it.)

I: Und die Aufnahme habt ihr in welcher Sprache gemacht? (And in what language did you do the recording?)

S: In Englisch. (In English.)

I: Komplett? (The whole thing?)

S: Ja. (Yeah.)

For the use of English, insights into the recorded working phases as well as the final products show the use of diverse and spontaneous linguistic structures as well as learned vocabulary and chunks. Video and audio data show that the pupils discuss the meanings of English terms and make text proposals in English. The most complex ones are done by the learners of 3.5 years (Grade 4) and 4.5 years (Grade 7) of English language learning. But even pupils at younger age levels are motivated to talk about language when working with production-oriented apps. In the case of the pupils using French, this scenario is explicitly extended to a third language. However, this fact showed once more that, through the tasks and with the support of the tablet, it is possible to utilise language as a tool. This need to also use the family language is especially reflected in the Russian pupils and their unconscious switching to the family language (see interview above). Hence, the results show that target language learning can also take place using the family languages. However, this study cannot make any statements about the progress made in learning English, but only describe the situation and the processes involved in learning. Nevertheless, it will be interesting to see in the future to what extent the family languages can be extended to metalinguistic discourses in strongly multilingual learning groups and how they affect language use in class. Moreover, the question remains to what extent the motivation for creating stories with peers survives over time.

Conclusion and Outlook

After the first study cycle, it can be stated that production-oriented apps seem to be suitable for the initiation of discourse. Young learners in particular seem to benefit from the graphic scaffolding of the apps. The settings and characters in the app Puppet Pals encourage the imagination and support the use of language through haptic experiences and visualisations. Particularly weak learners can quickly achieve a positive speaking experience as the professional design supports complex communication with even short statements. Linguistically competent learners similarly benefit from the openness of story-making apps because no limits are set to the complexity of their stories. Characters and backgrounds can be used just as the pupils like. Stories can be told in a way that an enormous range of differentiation is made possible by means of the app. By the use of language, it becomes clear that the learners draw on more than just target language competences in order to create their stories. They use not only the school language German but also their L1. The use of the Russian (L1) and French (L3) language indicates that learners are self-motivated to take full advantage of their language competences.

The second study cycle will specifically address a teaching–learning context, which is characterised by a high degree of lived multilingualism. The aim is to find out whether multilingual talk also frequently occurs in classes with very heterogeneous family languages, for what purpose the pupils use which language and how the target language products are designed. Further, the focus on the content aspect will be strengthened. Even though the focus of the first study cycle was on language use, it could be shown that specific content is necessary in order to be able to negotiate meaning. So far, this content has been set as a framework by the task and filled individually by the learners. The aim now is to network content in an interdisciplinary approach such as transcurricular teaching and to find out which learning processes pupils take from other subjects or from their social environment. Currently, it can already be said that the work with story-making apps stimulates individual language productions and the negotiation of meanings using different linguistic systems. As it seems, the learners draw on a variety of themes, knowledge and competences from their life and from school. It will be exciting to see the extent to which tablets can be helpful in the context of transcurricular teaching.

References

Altrichter, H. and Posch, P. (2007) *Lehrerinnen und Lehrer erforschen ihren Unterricht: Unterrichtsentwicklung und Unterrichtsevaluation durch Aktionsforschung.* Bad Heilbrunn: Klinkhardt.

Anstey, M. and Bull, G. (2006) *Teaching and Learning Multiliteracies: Changing Times, Changing Literacies.* Newark, NJ: International Reading Association.

Bach, G. and Breidbach, S. (2009) Fremdsprachenkompetenz in der mehrsprachigen Wissensgesellschaft. In G. Bach and J.-P. Timm (eds) *Englischunterricht* (pp. 280–303). Stuttgart: UTB.

Bär, M. (2013) Standardisierung vs. Individualisierung: Zur Rolle von (komplexen) Lernaufgaben in einem kompetenzorientierten Fremdsprachenunterricht. In A. Grünewald, J. Plikat and K. Wieland (eds) *Bildung – Kompetenz – Literalität: Fremdsprachenunterricht zwischen Standardisierung und Bildungsanspruch* (pp. 98–109). Seelze: Kallmeyer.

Bonnet, A. and Breidbach, S. (2013) Blut ist im Schuh: Wie gut kleidet der Kompetenzbegriff die literarisch-ästhetische Bildung beim Tanz auf dem Hofball der Standardisierung? In A. Grünewald, J. Plikat and K. Wieland (eds) *Bildung – Kompetenz – Literalität: Fremdsprachenunterricht zwischen Standardisierung und Bildungsanspruch* (pp. 20–35). Seelze: Kallmeyer.

Buendgens-Kosten, J. (2015) Multilingual CALL: More than just translation drills? See http://www.openeducationeuropa.eu/sites/default/files/asset/Language-Learning-and-Technology_From_Field_45-7.pdf (accessed 01 August 2017).

Bündgens-Kosten, J. and Elsner, D. (2014) Rezeptives Code-switching ein- und mehrsprachiger Lerner/innen in multilingualen Settings. *Fremdsprachen Lehren und Lernen* 42 (2), 56–73.

Cope, B. and Kalantzis, M. (2000) *Multiliteracies: Literacy Learning and the Design of Social Futures*. New York: Routledge.

Dausend, H. (2014) *Fremdsprachen transcurricular lehren und lernen: Ein methodischer Ansatz für die Grundschule*. Tübingen: Gunther Narr.

Dausend, H. (2015) Kompetenzen als Chance? Wie Sprachhandlungen in der Grundschule erzeugt werden könnten. In S. Méron-Minuth and S. Özkul (eds) *Fremde Sprachen Lehren und Lernen: Aktuelle Fragen und Forschungsaufgaben. Inquiries in Language Learning* (Vol. 15; pp. 63–80). Frankfurt/Main: Peter Lang.

Dausend, H. and Nickel, S. (2017) Tap'n'talk: Förderung differenzierter Sprachproduktionen durch tabletgestützte Lernaufgaben. In S. Chilla and K. Vogt (eds) *Heterogenität und Diversität im Englischunterricht: fachdidaktische Perspektiven* (pp. 179–203). Frankfurt: Peter Lang.

Dezuanni, M., Dooley, K., Gattenhof, S. and Knight, L. (2015) *iPads in the Early Years: Developing Literacy and Creativity*. London: Routledge.

Engel, G., Groot-Wilken, B. and Thürmann, E. (eds) (2009) *Englisch in der Primarstufe: Chancen und Herausforderungen. Evaluation und Erfahrungen aus der Praxis*. Berlin: Cornelsen.

Falloon, G. and Khoo, E. (2014) Exploring young students' talk in iPad-supported collaborative learning environments. *Computers & Education* 77, 13–28.

Flick, U. (2014) *Qualitative Sozialforschung: Eine Einführung*. Hamburg: Rowohlt.

Gattenhof, S. and Dezuanni, M. (2015a) Arts education and iPads in the early years. In M. Dezuanni, K. Dooley, S. Gattenhof and L. Knight (eds) *iPads in the Early Years: Developing Literacy and Creativity* (pp. 30–43). London: Routledge.

Gattenhof, S. and Dezuanni, M. (2015b) Drama, storymaking and iPads in the early years. In M. Dezuanni, K. Dooley, S. Gattenhof and L. Knight (eds) *iPads in the Early Years: Developing Literacy and Creativity* (pp. 86–103). London: Routledge.

Gee, J.P. (1990) *Social Linguistics and Literacies: Ideology in Discourses. Critical Perspectives on Literacy and Education*. London: Falmer Press.

Gomolla, M. (2009) Heterogenität, Unterrichtsqualität und Inklusion. In S. Fürstenau and M. Gomolla (eds) *Migration und schulischer Wandel: Unterricht* (pp. 21–43). Wiesbaden: VS Verlag für Sozialwissenschaften.

Hallet, W. (2011) *Lernen fördern: Englisch. Kompetenzorientierter Unterricht in der Sekundarstufe I*. Seelze: Kallmeyer.

Haß, F. (2006) *Fachdidaktik Englisch: Tradition, Innovation, Praxis*. Stuttgart: Klett.

Hufeisen, B. (2011) Gesamtsprachencurriculum: Weitere Überlegungen zu einem prototypischen Modell. In R. Baur and B. Hufeisen (eds) *„Vieles ist sehr ähnlich": Individuelle und gesellschaftliche Mehrsprachigkeit als bildungspolitische Aufgabe* (pp. 265–282). Baltmannsweiler: Schneider Verlag Hohengehren.

Kirsch, C. (2012) Luxemburgisch lernen durch Geschichtenerzählen: Ein Fallbeispiel einer luxemburgischen Vorschule. *Forum* 324, 46–48.

Kirch, M. (2014) Tablets integrieren: Methodenvielfalt erweitern. Apps als methodisches Werkzeug im Unterricht. *Die Grundschulzeitschrift* 28, 48–51.

Kleemann, F., Krähnke, U. and Matuschek, I. (2013) *Interpretative Sozialforschung: Eine Einführung in die Praxis des Interpretierens* (Vol. 2). Wiesbaden: Springer VS.

Kucirkova, N., Messer, D., Sheehy, K. and Fernández Panadero, C. (2014) Children's engagement with educational iPad apps: Insights from a Spanish classroom. *Computers & Education* 71, 175–184.

Kuckartz, U. (2012) *Qualitative Inhaltsanalyse*. Weinheim: Beltz.

Lütje-Klose, B. (2004) Mehrsprachigkeit als Herausforderung im Anfangsunterricht. In G. Becker (ed.) *Friedrich-Jahresheft 2004: Heterogenität – Unterschiede nutzen, Gemeinsamkeiten stärken* (pp. 50–53). Seelze: Friedrich Verlag.

Mayring, P. (2015) *Qualitative Inhaltsanalyse: Grundlagen und Techniken*. Weinheim/ Basel: Beltz Verlag.

Müller-Hartmann, A. and Schocker-v. Ditfurth, M. (2009) *Introduction to English Language Teaching*. Paderborn: Schöningh/UTB.

Nohl, A.-M. (2010) *Konzepte interkultureller Pädagogik: Eine systematische Einführung* (Vol. 2). Bad Heilbrunn: Klinkhardt.

Roos, J. (2007) *Spracherwerb und Sprachproduktion: Lernziele und Lernergebnisse im Englischunterricht der Grundschule*. Tübingen: Gunter Narr.

Rösler, D. (2013) Sprachstandsnotgebiet A: Herausforderungen an die Fremdsprachenforschung. *Zeitschrift für Fremdsprachenforschung* 24 (2), 151–170.

Siebert-Ott, G. (2010) Mehrsprachigkeit und Bildungserfolg. In G. Auernheimer (ed.) *Schieflagen im Bildungssystem: Die Benachteiligung der Migrantenkinder* (pp. 145–160). Wiesbaden: Verlag für Sozialwissenschaften.

Strauss, A.L. and Corbin, J.M. (1996) *Grounded Theory: Grundlagen qualitativer Sozialforschung*. Weinheim: Beltz.

Sturm, T. (2013) *Lehrbuch Heterogenität in der Schule*. München: UTB Reinhardt.

The New London Group (2000) A pedagogy of multiliteracies designing social futures. In B. Cope and M. Kalantzis (eds) *Multiliteracies: Literacy Learning and the Design of Social Futures* (pp. 9–37). New York: Routledge.

Weinert, F.E. (2001) Vergleichende Leistungsmessungen in Schulen: eine umstrittene Selbstverständlichkeit. In F.E. Weinert (ed.) *Leistungsmessungen in Schulen* (pp. 17–31). Weinheim: Beltz.

Apps

Polished Play (2012): Puppet Pals (1.9)

Red Jumper Limited (2014): Book Creator (4.2.3)

The Open University (2011): Our Story (1.1)

6 Über die Grenzen des einsprachigen Habitus: Application of Computer Assisted Language Learning through Home Language Content in Secondary Level Classrooms

John Michael Alvarez

The Issue

Monolingual ideologies shape educational decisions that result in a marginalised status for the multilingual learner. Rather than viewing the existing language skills of the learner as an asset that can be harnessed to rapidly develop skills in a new language, the majority of secondary schools in the United States compel emergent bilingual learners (EBs) to gain knowledge of English without leveraging home language skills. Instruction is in English, texts are offered in English and, for the majority of secondary level EBs, understanding is limited to what they can glean through the target language. On the one hand, this would seem to be an ineffective instructional decision. Yet, this perspective presumes that the goal of the educational system in America in regard to its population of EBs is to maximise educational opportunity. In reality, the monolingual habitus that governs the American education system promotes stability of the value of English over other languages. Similarly, in the European Union, nations that embrace recognition of the importance of multilingualism yet find shelter in the monolingual habitus marginalise EBs as they assert the primacy of the dominant language within that nation. Gogolin (1997) wrote at length of the assertion of the monolingual habitus in classrooms within Europe, and while the stated goals of the European Union may overtly be to embrace plurilingualism (European Commission, 2008), the monolingual habitus (in which the teacher asserts the eminence of the dominant language of the society within classrooms of learners with different language backgrounds) remains. More recently, Jordens *et al.* (2016: 1) revealed consistent assertions by educators of the monolingual habitus in classrooms in Flemish-speaking Belgian classrooms, underscored by educators who 'exceptionally' applied a multilingual habitus in two mainstream Flanders primary classrooms.

Although in its 'infancy' (Buendgens-Kosten, 2015: 76), multilingual computer assisted language learning (MCALL), or the study of multilingual language teaching and learning, represents an opportunity for societies around the world to align educational practices with the continued recognition by researchers of the value of harnessing existing language assets in facilitating the development of a target language. As an educational researcher in the United States, I have devoted considerable interest to the findings of researchers from the European Union who are exploring the boundaries of the monolingual habitus through the recognition of the enormous existing language assets of learners. In an effort to provide practitioners with insight into the territories of the multilingual habitus that could effectively be leveraged by MCALL application, I provided students in an American secondary school class with the opportunity to capitalise on their existing language assets as they explored two different issues presented to them in their content area classes. My findings indicate that student learning in content area accelerated through use of a native language, as anticipated; however, a potentially more significant finding (from the perspective of additive language development) was that student spoken language production in the target was much more robust as students engaged in discussions using the target language subsequent to their native language exploration of content. Moreover, student writing in the target language after reading content in native languages was considerably more detailed and more cohesive in comparison with exposure to texts in the target language. Although practical challenges in harnessing classroom technologies are present, as I discovered in my work with a diverse collection of EBs, the increased level of student involvement and the enriched application of the target language in productive modalities both underscore the benefits of instruction rooted in the recognition of the vitality of the multilingual habitus.

Making the 'Switch': Multilingual Computer Assisted Language Learning (MCALL)

Taking recent neurological discoveries (Garbin *et al.*, 2010; Green & Abutalebi, 2013; Krizman *et al.*, 2012; Macizo *et al.*, 2010) into account, the utilisation of the native language as a learner makes inroads into a new language should be a valuable consideration for any instructional approach designed to facilitate language development. For adults who seek a new language by readily utilising texts in their native languages as they discover the new language, this consideration is of paramount importance. McDonough (2002) reflected on this very practice; however, in the classrooms in which children and adolescents seek a new language, the 'doggedness of dogma' (Butzkamm, 2003: 31) results in the refusal to entertain the very notion of curriculum or instruction in different languages. Elsner *et al.* (2015) found value in providing students with texts in multiple languages, allowing the learners to negotiate meaning based on their unique needs. MCALL reduces the practical argument of having to 'teach' in a dozen languages in a classroom of immigrants, by providing learners with tailor-made instructional opportunities in which learners can activate the critical development of switching capabilities between their native languages and the target language.

Yet, the realities of the classroom environment (as well as the existing dearth of proven research in support of MCALL curriculum options) considerably diminish application by educators who seek to facilitate target language development among EBs. Nevertheless, researchers are beginning to demonstrate the practicality and validity of MCALL options. Bündgens-Kosten (2015) explored the potential benefits of Erasmus+ project's 'MElang-E' (Multilingual Explorations of Languages in Europe, melang-e.eu) game, which capitalises on the language assets of each learner even as it promotes the critical junction of code-switching, essential to additive language development on the neurological level (Garbin *et al.*, 2010). Featuring simulated code-switching capabilities, MElang-E differs from another promising MCALL application called MuViT (Multiliteracy Virtual Talking Books) that offers receptive code-switching (Elsner, 2013). Similarly, Bündgens-Kosten *et al.* (2015) have explored different groupings of a range of language learners as they engaged with MCALL curricular options. Yet, findings from these important research efforts have yet to be evaluated across a range of environments. In actuality, MCALL has only recently begun to consider multiple language possibilities in content area classrooms. As Buendgens-Kosten (2015) pointed out, the notion of a multilingual form of language instruction, which could then be utilised in a heterogeneous classroom remains practically uncharted territory.

With scant robust software to evaluate for effectiveness, research has not been able to register the benefits or limitations of MCALL applications in classrooms. My research seeks to, at the very least, open the door to further studies in the field that will harness the capabilities of modern technologies in restoring what Butzkamm (2003: 38) referred to as 'the two-thousand-year-old productive alliance between the mother tongue and foreign [sic] languages'.

The Study

This qualitative study sought to gain insight into the process of content learning and target language development by second language (L2) learners through the application of student-selected, academic topic-specific, internet-based home language texts. Instead of the sole use of teacher-provided traditional English language curriculum for content learning, I augmented instruction through the application of MCALL in the form of content area home language texts (CAHLT) that students generated through directed internet inquiry.

My study attempted to obtain insight into the process of content learning by secondary level EBs through MCALL by seeking the answers to the following research questions:

- How does the inclusion of CAHLT influence target language production in speaking?
- How does deliberate code-switching methodology influence students as they engage with the content in productive and receptive modalities?

Description of sample

Using a purposive sample, I assembled a population of students (n = 10) who ranged in age from 14 to 18, and who registered a range of language abilities as measured by the California English Language Development Test (CELDT), an annual assessment administered by the State of California in order to measure the level of a student's fluency in English in four domains: listening, speaking, reading, and writing. Sample student's scores ranged from 338 to 647, with a mean score of 404, and a median score of 544 out of a possible 726, with 653 as an indicator of fluency. Three of the students were in ninth grade (14–15 years of age) at the time of the study, four in tenth grade, one in eleventh grade and two in twelfth grade.

The students in the sample population were fluent speakers in one of the following languages: (a) Swiss-French, (b) Austrian-German, (c) Mexican-Spanish, (d) Vietnamese, (e) Japanese and (f) Mandarin. The student who was fluent in Swiss-French also commanded a fluency in Italian. Each student had demonstrated grade-level proficiency in their respective native languages.

Data collection

All students in the sample attended a support class designed to meet the language development needs of English learners. The class provided remedial reading instruction, as well as individualised support in content area classes. For means of identification of the various levels of language development, I used an initial quantitative analysis that included formal measurement of English language ability as evaluated by a standardised English language development test used in California schools (CELDT).

Students at different levels of L2 were observed in a traditional lesson in the class, as they were engaged in a sequence of reading an article in English, followed by writing in English and discussing in English.

Subsequently, one week later, students used computers to access CAHLT that addressed a topic drawn from a life science class: genetically manufactured organisms (GMOs). Students were provided with a range of home language links, including major newspapers as well as Wikipedia sites focused on the academic topic.

Students had an opportunity to read the CAHLT, and were then asked to write a response to a sequence of questions in their respective home languages. Subsequently, the students were encouraged to engage in a small group discussion in the target language, English. The questions were:

- Do you think GMOs are helpful?
- Do you think GMOs are dangerous?

I used a digital video recorder to capture the students' actions and words as they read, wrote and engaged in discussion.

After completing initial analysis of the observation data, I used individual semi-structured[1] interviews to discover the various perspectives of students during their respective encounters with a learning process that included a text in their home languages. I also collected student-produced written responses that I used to inform my research, even though I did not engage in rigorous evaluation of this aspect of the data.

Data analysis of lesson observation

I had observed the students completing a similar lesson that utilised only English texts instead of CAHLT, and only English writing. The difference in the degree of involvement was striking, especially for higher-level English learners. After collection of the initial data from observation, I engaged in a process of open coding of the initial impressions that emerged from the data. Subsequently, I applied an axial coding process following observation of the video recording to determine potential relationships of the discoveries. Finally, I completed a selective coding to gain insight into the most significant findings of the data collection. Students who previously were very reluctant to engage in the target language during discourse were considerably more detailed and comprehensive in their responses after reading CAHLT. Two distinct axial codes emerged from the subsequent evaluation of the video recording of the observation of the lesson and the discussion: (a) differential initiation of extended discussion and (b) negotiation of accurate vocabulary between native and target language.

Students in the study were at different levels in their English language development, and this stood out as an obstacle as the students were encouraged to engage in discussions using English texts. For lower-level English learners, the use of complicated CAHLT fostered considerably greater degrees of side discussions in the respective home languages; however, this did not always translate to initiating discussion in English. Yet more advanced learners using CAHLT initiated considerably greater degrees of the extension of their respective ideas of the benefits and drawbacks of GMOs in group discourse.

Differential initiation of extended discussion

Students at higher levels of English proficiency demonstrated an increase in their initiation of extended discussion in comparison to their performance on the traditional English-only lesson, depending on the degree of target language proficiency.

Student H, a 14-year-old Japanese student at the 65th percentile in the CELDT, had been very reluctant to participate in discussions after he read texts in English, yet he was extremely verbal in his discussion with a partner in his home language. This increased verbalisation transferred to the target language during the group discussion. After reading about GMOs in his home language, his initiation of spoken language in English was much more expansive than previous discussions. When the group was asked about the drawbacks of GMOs, Student H initiated discussion without prompting. He volunteered to speak first, saying that he saw a danger in GMOs.

Question: Do you think GMOs are dangerous to people?
Student H: Dangerous, because, they can break their nature...natural transfer...if they do that, more...the organism going to breed more than usual...so I think that it is dangerous.

Interestingly, Student H's contribution sparked Student E, also a 14-year-old Japanese student at the 75th percentile, to follow Student H and add precision to the gaps that were present in Student H's answer. Immediately after Student H, Student E explained that GMOs could be dangerous, clarifying Student H's ideas.

Student E: I agree, in his opinion. I think it's dangerous, too, because... it may destroy the...yeah, the natural balance and the natural organisms. Yes.

Student E, who scored at a higher percentile in the standardised test (74%), was able to sharpen the idea that his classmate had presented. The most interesting aspect of this juncture of the discussion was that Student H, who did not have as strong a command of English, felt confident enough to initiate the discourse, and Student E, who typically initiated discussion in other class activities, instead used his contribution to refine the meaning of his classmate.

Student I, a 15-year-old Mandarin speaker who was in the 80th percentile of CELDT, disagreed with Student H and Student E, initiating a detailed discussion of the benefits of GMOs:

Question: Do you think GMOs are helpful to people?
Student I: (Nodding) Because...because, the changes genetics, so it will be like easier to grow and could grow like more than when it when it's not, like when it hasn't changed yet, and like, many people couldn't afford original thing, so if the GMO could make the food cheaper, I think there might be like more people could like get more food.

Student I took a different viewpoint, and initiated discussion of a facet of the issue that was present in her article, but which had not been discussed previously. She extended her line of reasoning using supporting evidence, and even offered a practical example of how her evidence would address the needs of the poor. Student I's response was followed by Student G (a 15-year-old Mexican-Spanish speaker in the 65th percentile of CELDT). Student G did not volunteer until both sides had answered each of the questions, but then reacted strongly, stating:

Student G: I don't really know if it can good thing, because we can say it can help for to something health, but you don't know what effects can have!

Student G did not perceive that her idea had emerged during the discussion, and found it important to initiate it in response to Student I. Student G could have asserted her view following the initial prompt; however, she found greater confidence in providing a counterpoint to Student I than in an initiation of her view following the prompt. She did not initiate her view in response to the teacher's prompt; instead, she initiated her response after a fellow student had provided a viewpoint with exemplification.

Even as students engaged in robust side discussions in both English and their respective home languages, students at lower levels of English proficiency were reluctant to initiate expanded discourse in the larger group discussion. Each student did contribute, with two students (Student D, a 17-year-old Vietnamese speaker at the 56th percentile; and Student C, a 14-year-old Mexican-Spanish speaker, also at the 56th percentile) speaking only when directly prompted:

Question: Do you think GMOs are dangerous to people?
Student D: I don't know. I am sorry. Maybe earth age, maybe long (makes expansive gesture with hand). It is dangerous because they create new organism, and then everything fake, not true, not new, and make environment, they...(looks at text) pollution...
Student C: I don't have words for this question.

Student B, a 16-year-old Austrian-German speaker in the 60th percentile raised her hand, yet when she spoke, she was unable to finish her thought. She followed Student E's response of the harms of GMOs, saying:

Question: Do you think GMOs are dangerous to people?
Student B: Yes, it is because of killing the (long pause) insects? Killing the animals? That's it.

Each student was engaged in reading, wrote extensively and engaged in considerable side conversations in English, and, if they had a language partner, in their respective native languages. Yet, initiating discussion in the larger group proved to be too great a challenge for the students with lower degrees of English proficiency.

Negotiation of accurate vocabulary between native and target language

The negotiation of meaning between the home language and the target language during the discussion was very clear as evidenced by the pauses in the students' verbalisations, and glances downward to the text. The students appeared to be looking for words that they knew in their home languages, and may have been present in the CAHLT, but for which the students did not have an English equivalent. For lower-level English speakers, this discontinuity did not engender the confidence that otherwise would have led them to initiate extended discussion. As Student C had indicated, some students did not have 'the words' for the questions. For the students who had a greater command of English, an attempt was made to find the words; however, for the students who did not have the same degree of proficiency, the search for an appropriate vocabulary term to convey exactly what they wanted to reflect of the complicated content with the CAHLT created frustration.

For Student H, finding words meant using words that were not necessarily perfect, but which did not entirely distort meaning. When extending his discussion on the benefits of GMOs, he drew out the rationale for his support, arriving at a found conclusion:

Question: Do you think GMOs are helpful to people?
Student H: It may be benefit, because there are many people who are poor, and they can't eat their food, so if they make the plants that can produce more than usual, I think this is the... (looks for word on text) *root* of the good.

Another strategy for more proficient English users was to use correct words that did not match the context. Student E, in his discussion of the benefits of GMOs explained:

Question: Do you think GMOs are helpful to people?
Student E: Um, the benefit of GMO is maybe we can make more healthier and more...analogous food. And one more thing, we may make a new medication that can cure some really dangerous um...illness. We may make it.

Student E was searching for the correct word, and while his use of the word *analogous* was not precise, he knew from the text the relationship between natural food and the GMO version; he just could not label it with precision, using instead a word that he felt represented that relationship. Student I's strategy was to use simplified English to create a more comprehensive context from which the more difficult concepts could emerge.

In trying to find complex English words that would allow them to communicate ideas that they understood in their native languages, students demonstrated differential strategies, dependent upon their degree of English proficiency.

Data analysis of interviews

I used a semi-structured interview technique seeking understanding of the unique experiences of EBs in their use of CAHLT in learning (see Appendix for interview guidelines). During my observation of the lesson, students demonstrated different degrees of participation in the group discussion, with the students commanding higher degrees of English fluency initiating discussion with greater confidence. Yet, during the interviews, the students were much more verbal in their responses. Students were asked to describe their experiences as they moved from CAHLT to writing in English, and speaking in English. From the short interviews, two distinct codes emerged: (a) performance strategies of target language usage and (b) cognitive resistance.

Performance strategies of target language usage

Students provided distinctly different experiences with CAHLT and English texts, dependent upon whether the texts were used for a class assignment or test, or for understanding. Dependent upon the purpose, students explained that they were engaged in a clear, strategic use of language. Student A, the Swiss-French speaker, reflected that he engaged in a strategic use of English. He explained that for him, learning English was a tool to get higher grades. For him, achievement in school was not about understanding; it was about scoring well on tests. He explained that he enjoyed reading the French texts, but that in a class setting he would rather read it in English. I asked him if it helped him to understand the subject better by reading the text in French, and he agreed. Yet, he clearly stated that if he was in a class, he would rather have the text in English:

Question: If you had an assignment or test, which article would you choose? Why?

Student A: I would use article in English because you can't use the words in article in French for the answer in question of teacher about GMO. I read in English to do better on test. To do better on test.

This strategic use of the target language for performance and not for understanding was underscored by Student I, who suggested that even if she didn't have an understanding of the text, she would rather use English to perform better in the class assignments and tests:

Question: If you had an assignment or test, which would you choose? Why?

Student I: If I read in English it helps me write in English because the sentence are already there. The words I don't understand, but I read the sentence around it, and I can understand it. Because like if I summarize, I read it in English, I don't have to think of the words, or something else, I can just write in English. Even if I don't know the words I use them anyway.

Both students did not look at learning the target language as requiring understanding of the words; instead, they looked at the words in the target language as templates that they could use to demonstrate understanding of the content.

Even while Student A and Student I described with candour the way they used English text, they also confided that they would appreciate text that was in the native language that they could use alongside the text in English. Student G had a similar perspective, maintaining that if possible she would like to have access to texts in the target language as well as the native language. The question was one of strategy.

Question: Which would you rather have to understand the subject?
Student G: Both, because I can, if I don't understand a word in English, I can read in Spanish and understand, and yeah, I can...it's like, I can read it in English, but the Spanish can help me understand a few words.

When I clarified my questioning to ask students if the use of CAHLT helped them understand the content of the article better, they were universal in their agreement. The question was really one of strategy. If the strategy was used to get a grade in a class, it was different than those used for gaining understanding. For understanding, the students wanted access to both texts. Student H, who demonstrated an affinity for the use of CAHLT in the discussion, also explained that the use of a Japanese CAHLT would help him in understanding the topic, and that he would like access to both articles:

Student H: I can understand the articles, because I read in Japanese, then it is easier to read English, so I can explain it more easier in English.

Similarly, Student E held that use of both texts would help him develop understanding, and that he would prefer to have access to both texts instead of only one in English:

Student E: Because when I read only English article, it will be really hard, but before that, before reading English article if I read Japanese article and understand, and then read English, it would be really easy to understand, so it will be great successful, I think.

Students were universal in their agreement that they would like access to both texts to gain understanding of content. Student C, who did not 'have the words' to participate in the class discussion, explained that if she was trying to understand a subject, she would like to have access to the article in Spanish and in English:

Question: Which article would you rather have to understand the subject?
Student C: Both, it's helpful, because my home language is Spanish, and my second language is below, it is English, so both are helpful to me, because both.

Students in the sample universally welcomed the opportunity to access their existing language assets, which were not fully tapped through exposure to content solely in the target language of English.

Cognitive resistance

As students negotiated meaning from CAHLT to target language production, each of them reported considerable cognitive difficulties that created varying levels of frustration. Some of the students – particularly those at higher proficiency levels in the target language – were able to reconcile the resistance, but even these students reported difficulty. For students at the lower end of the target language proficiency, the difficulties complicated productive language use in discourse. For these students, who were fully capable of interpersonal communication in the form of side-talk with native language partners and with heterogeneous language partners, the resistance did not preclude communication; however, in the more formal discourse setting, students who did not have greater degrees of confidence in target language production were very reluctant to contribute to the discussion.

Student A, a Swiss-French speaker at the 58th percentile, explained his frustration in moving from one language to another:

Student A: I cannot understand the words, but I know because (struggles to find words in English)...this is Swiss words, 'Tâter le terrain.' I go back. I get confused in the order of the words.

The junction for Student A between home and target language created frustration, because while he understood what he was trying to say, he was unable to generate the 'terrain' in English that would render his response viable.

Similarly, Student I, a higher-level target language learner, acknowledged the difficulties of the required transfer from home language to target language owing to her meta-linguistic awareness of the characteristics of the text:

Question: You said that it was hard to write in English after reading in Chinese...why?

Student I: In Chinese, every individual letter is a word. And, but in English, it's like different thing have different names, so like in Chinese, you can just combine letters together to like form a vocabulary, but in English, like each thing its own name, so it's kind of hard to match it with it? I'm better with Chinese. Chinese is putting letters together to form words, I don't know how to explain. It doesn't translate from Chinese to English, because I have to still have to rearrange the order,

> and the vocabulary. There are just characters, and sometimes you don't understand what a single character mean. It's hard to...to like, they don't have definition of these words, because they are made up of bunch of characters...I kind of need to change my brain to the English version.

For Student I, the transfer from one language to another was complicated by the different features of each language. She spoke of a 'change' that was required in thinking, and this change could very well be a junction that will develop with greater frequency of switching, offering greater measures of transfer between languages as she becomes more familiar with this particular function.

Discussion

As Dr Bündgens-Kosten (one of the editors of the present volume) provided me with a translation clarification in one of countless emails, she commented on the 'deliberate code-switching' that I proposed in my study. I believe that what I set out to do with my study is just that: deliberate code-switching, to enhance target language development. I was propelled by the findings of Green and Abutalebi (2013) and I wondered if perhaps we could more rapidly facilitate target language development by working diligently at the junction; by working on the circuit of the code-switching; by developing this circuit. After observing and interviewing a sample of EBs at a suburban Los Angeles secondary school, I discovered the considerable challenges in applying methods of instruction and curriculum that could potentially harness existing language assets in the development of a target language by working at the junction, as it were.

The primary obstacle is institutional. In America, the monolingual habitus is supported by the viewpoint that if students are given access to solely English curriculum, they will not be confused, and will learn English. However, as I discovered at the secondary level, students are quite literally deprived of rigorous content because they cannot read texts that they could understand in their home languages. Using technology to provide students with texts in their home language as well as the target language could provide a valuable bridge for students as they learn content and the target language. In fact, as I learned in my research, the productive language of students who read in their home languages was far more evolved than when they only read English texts. Admittedly, there was a considerable differential dependent upon target language ability in regard to oral production in a class discussion; however, the written production was universally more detailed in comparison to the English-only lesson that the students were typically provided. In fact, lower-level

English students wrote much more in the target language when they were able to access the content in their home language. Although it was not a focus of this study, the written production did not seem to be as stunted for lower-level students as it was for oral production, and this was a consistent finding throughout all levels of English development. Structural features in written responses were much more involved in comparison to those that emerged from an English-only method, as was the use of supporting details. In regard to oral production of language in a formal classroom discussion, for more advanced learners, a willingness to engage in discourse was much more likely when they actually had a store of knowledge that was gained through reading complex texts in their home languages. Interestingly, students did not have computer access during discussion. It remains possible that scaffolding support provided by smartphones or computers during discussion may well have assisted students in greater exploration of discourse.

The research findings are certainly interesting, and the improved generation of target language production would appear to be at the very least correlated to the MCALL intervention described in this report. Yet, the novelty effect of educational technology has long been noted by researchers (Phipps & Merisotis, 1999; Schramm, 1962), as has the general novelty effect of language intervention (Izumi & Bigelow, 2000). Indeed, a new person providing a new intervention can motivate students to engage more fully in learning. In order to gain greater insight into the impact of the MCALL intervention, longitudinal analysis would serve to demonstrate greater discernment of the impact of this intervention; however, policy would have to be in place to make such intervention possible. More than any other factor, the research requires additional time to evaluate the language development gains of the students. Additionally, a greater range of students at different grade levels and socio-economic levels would add precision to findings.

Implications for Teaching

Even as the application of CAHLT presents secondary level teachers with a remarkable opportunity to facilitate more rapid target language development in tandem with content area knowledge among secondary students, this integration requires keen command by teachers of instructional capabilities that may necessitate the cultivation of new practices. Beyond the practical challenges in harnessing technology that makes CAHLT possible, teachers must be able to differentiate instruction and assessment based on the diverse language levels and content understanding of students. Moreover, teachers must be able to tolerate ambiguity in productive language among students as they negotiate content area understanding. Yet, perhaps most critically, in recognition of the necessity of purposeful 'joint intentionality' (Crowley, 2014: 78) that teachers must rely upon to maximise the results of CAHLT, teachers who wish to successfully engage students in this methodology must endorse an asset-based paradigm that recognises the existing language assets of students.

Harnessing technology

As I discovered in my efforts in a suburban Los Angeles secondary school, providing effective CAHLT in a range of languages that shared content alignment was more difficult than simply applying computer-generated translations to existing texts. To maximise student development, teachers will need to have consistent access to a cohesive technology application form that will allow learners with diverse mother tongues to access content area knowledge in their home languages. Many programs that I tried in pilot studies guaranteed multilingual access to content; however, these programs largely provided incomprehensible texts for students, and were not productive in facilitating language development or in providing access to content. I was eventually able to find ways to provide students with academically rigorous texts in their native tongues. Yet, this was an arduous task that may not be surmountable by classroom teachers who are already overwhelmed with existing demands placed upon them. Application of technology is a critical component to the use of CAHLT in secondary classrooms, and in my limited experience, I found that the rewards of spending time discovering aligned, academically rigorous texts from a range of diverse languages added considerable value to the language development and academic achievement trajectories of EBs.

Differentiated evaluation

Beyond the technological challenges that teachers can surmount if they are willing to expend the energy to prepare CAHLT that can reflect accuracy in meaning as well as rigor in academic content, teachers must be able to consistently differentiate in their formative and summative evaluations of the language development and academic understanding of learners. This is not a simple process, as the application of singular forms of assessment administered and evaluated by teachers to the entire class is certainly more convenient. The reliance of teachers on the productive and receptive language capabilities of additive language learners to determine understanding (coupled with the different mother tongue and target language levels of students) offers a considerable challenge to teachers. Yet, through differentiated evaluations, teachers can propel student learning. This requires that teachers first identify with precision the instructional objectives for each student for content as well as language development, and then determine each student's capability in realising those objectives. This is not a simple proposition, and it is conceivable that teachers will need to learn new skills in evaluation. One method that has proven to be effective is the use of self-assessment of language development (Tassinari, 2012). Tassinari's dynamic model encourages learner autonomy in language development, drawing from Dörnyei and Murphey's (2003: 105) underscoring of the vitality of student choice and self-assessment (Ekbatani & Pierson, 2000; Murphey, 1994) in shaping a student's sense of 'genuine authority'. Teachers who are willing to cede control of traditional expectations of instruction and assessment can encourage this 'genuine authority' by having students participate in shaping their own learning trajectories, potentially including student choice of 'activities, teaching materials, topics, assignment, due dates, the format and pace of their learning, the arrangement of the furniture, or the peers they want to work with' (Dörnyei & Murphey, 2003: 105). The use of CAHLT in secondary classrooms invites this critical dimension of student participation in their own learning; however, it is incumbent upon teachers to scaffold opportunities that would provide learners with what might be unprecedented levels of autonomy to maximise productivity of the CAHLT application.

Tolerance of ambiguity in productive language

For teachers to maximise the productivity of CAHLT in secondary classrooms, they must be able to disassociate the quality of productive language from expectations for content achievement. Students who are using CAHLT texts may not be able to produce language that would allow teachers to determine content capabilities. Yet, this does not mean that the content may not be understood by the students, particularly when they are accessing that content in their mother tongues. As students produce target language, it is very likely that considerable ambiguity in meaning may emerge. Yet, working at the critical junction of code-switching (Garbin *et al.*, 2010) significantly enhances target language development, even as it can advantage EBs with greater capabilities in reflecting deepened content knowledge gained through CAHLT. Teachers applying CAHLT in secondary classrooms must provide learners with the freedom to explore new territories in their productive language, and by having teachers embrace ambiguity in productive language rather than seeing this ambiguity as indicative of a lack of content knowledge, teachers will be better able to assist students in navigating their own language discoveries while also gaining deeper understanding of content knowledge.

Teacher endorsement of an asset-based paradigm of learners

Developing the understanding among teachers that students can command a considerable asset in the form of their mother tongues can help those teachers leverage the existing knowledge of learners. Assertion of the value of existing language assets of learners can assist learners by giving them greater degrees of confidence in negotiating the junction of code-switching (Garbin *et al.*, 2010), in turn encouraging their ability to moderate cognitive resistance – especially when teachers are able to provide strategic instructional supports such as meta-cognitive modelling in producing target language. CAHLT leverages existing language assets to propel target language development and content area achievement; however, if teachers are compelled by paradigms that insist on the privileging of the target language over the existing languages of students, the benefits of CAHLT will be diminished. Perhaps the most difficult challenge to overcome by teachers who wish to benefit from the application of CAHLT in secondary classes is in cultivating dispositions that will allow them to recognise the value of a multilingual habitus. In some nations, this process may be easier than others; however, in largely monolingual nations, educators may face considerable challenges in establishing and perpetuating a paradigm that forges practices that may involve the relinquishment of the privileged power of the target language in the classroom in favour of the existing assets of learners.

Conclusion

At one time, existing educational resources may have made it very difficult, if not impossible, to entertain a multilingual approach to education. To be sure, bilingual educational opportunities for students did exist in rare cases; however, the notion that a classroom of students with entirely different native tongues could use their existing linguistic resources as they developed mastery of a target language would have been perceived as an impossibility. Even if Richter's (1807) seminal notion of the 'Muttersprache' were to be entertained by the classroom teacher, the logistical reality of creating the range of curriculum in each of the native languages of the students in a diverse class would make it impossible. Yet, the advent of technology has erased this 'impossibility'. It is now very possible to gain access to a given text in a host of languages with a simple mouse-click or screen tap. The practical excuse for avoiding a multilingual habitus can no longer be justified. Since any secondary teacher with an internet connection can provide students with native language texts on a common subject, at the very least Butzkamm's (1973) enlightened monolingualism – and at the very most a comprehensive multilingual learning environment – is only a mouse-click or screen tap away from becoming a reality.

Note

(1) Bogdan and Biklen (2007) maintained that this particular form of interviewing enables the researcher to gain data that can be used comparatively, as commonalities of responses in more specific areas can facilitate targeted inquiry. At the same time, the semi-structured interview offers room for expansion or contraction of questions that can invite entirely unanticipated avenues of discovery. Structured interviews can 'distort' (Briggs, 1986: 13) the totality of the data collected, in that the researcher confines the parameters of a participant's response. Mishler's (1991: 27) underscoring of the inductive potency of the unstructured interview in providing 'a flexible strategy of discovery', while certainly compelling, may not necessarily align with the more focused nature of this stage of data collection. Given the relatively limited time frame of the study, I utilised the semi-structured interview as it provided me with a degree of focus that facilitated understanding of the influence of CAHLT in target language production by L2 secondary learners.

References

Bogdan, R.C. and Biklen, S.K. (2007) *Qualitative Research for Education: An Introduction to Theories and Methods* (5th edn). Boston, MA: Allyn and Bacon.

Briggs, C.L. (1986) *Learning How to Ask: A Sociolinguistic Appraisal of the Role of the Interview in Social Science Research.* Cambridge: Cambridge University Press.

Buendgens-Kosten, J. (2015) Multilingual CALL: More than just translation drills? *eL Papers* 45, 74–77.

Bündgens-Kosten, J., Elsner, D. and Hardy, I. (2015) Videoanalyse ein- und mehrsprachiger Lerner/innen bei der computerbasierten Textarbeit: die Rolle von Code-Switching und Negotiation im frühen Englischunterricht. In U. Rauin, M. Herrle and T. Engartner (eds) *Videoanalysen in der Unterrichtsforschung: Methodische Vorgehensweisen und Anwendungsbeispiele* (pp. 225–241). Weinheim: Beltz Juventa.

Butzkamm, W. (1973) *Aufgeklarte Einsprachigkeit: Zur Entdogmatisierung der Methode im Fremdsprachenunterricht.* Heidelberg: Quelle & Meyer.

Butzkamm, W. (2003) We only learn language once. The role of the mother tongue in FL classrooms: Death of a dogma. *Language Learning Journal* 28 (1), 29–39.

Crowley, K.A. (2014) Second language learning strategies using first language acquisition methods. *Studies About Languages* 25, 77–87.

Dörnyei, Z. and Murphey, T. (2003) *Group Dynamics in the Language Classroom.* Cambridge: Cambridge University Press.

Ekbatani, G. and Pierson, H. (2000) *Moving toward learner-directed assessment. Learner-directed assessment in ESL.* Mahwah, NJ: Erlbaum.

Elsner, D. (2013) Fostering multilingualism with computer-based multilingual storybooks: The European Comenius project MuViT. Presentation at the World CALL Conference on Global Perspectives on Computer-Assisted Language Learning. Glasgow, 10–13 July.

Elsner, D., Bündgens-Kosten, J. and Hardy, L. (2015) Affordanzen und Nutzung mehrsprachiger Lernumgebungen: erste Ergebnisse aus der Pilotierung zum Forschungsprojekt LIKE. In M. Kötter and J. Rymarczyk (eds) *Englischunterricht in der Primarstufe: Neue Forschungen – weitere Entwicklungen* (pp. 35–57). Frankfurt: Peter Lang.

European Commission (2008) *Multilingualism: An Asset for Europe and a Shared Commitment.* Brussels: European Commission.

Garbin, G., Sanjuan, A., Forn, C., Bustamante, J.C., Rodriguez-Pujadas, A., Belloch, V., Hernández, M., Costa, A. and Ávila, C. (2010) Bridging language and attention: Brain basis of the impact of bilingualism on cognitive control. *Neuroimage* 53 (4), 1272–1278.
Gogolin, I. (1997) The 'monolingual habitus' as the common feature in teaching in the language of the majority in different countries. *Per Linguam* 13 (2), 38–49.
Green, D.W. and Abutalebi, J. (2013) Language control in bilinguals: The adaptive control hypothesis. *Journal of Cognitive Psychology* 25 (5), 515–530.
Izumi, S. and Bigelow, M. (2000) Does output promote noticing and second language acquisition? *TESOL Quarterly* 34 (2), 239–278.
Jordens, K., Van den Branden, K. and Van Gorp, K. (2016) Multilingual islands in a monolingual sea: Language choice patterns during group work. *International Journal of Bilingual Education and Bilingualism* 19 (7), 1–13.
Krizman, J., Marian, V., Shook, A., Skoe, E. and Kraus, N. (2012) Subcortical encoding of sound is enhanced in bilinguals and relates to executive function advantages. *Proceedings of the National Academy of Sciences* 109 (20), 7877–7881.
Macizo, P., Bajo, T. and Martín, M.C. (2010) Inhibitory processes in bilingual language comprehension: Evidence from Spanish–English interlexical homographs. *Journal of Memory and Language* 63 (2), 232–244.
McDonough, J. (2002) The teacher as language learner: Worlds of difference? *ELT Journal* 56 (4), 404–411.
Mishler, E.G. (1991) *Research Interviewing: Context and Narrative*. Cambridge, MA: Harvard University Press.
Murphey, T. (1994) Tests: Learning through negotiated interaction. *TESOL Journal*, 4(2), 12–16.
Phipps, R. and Merisotis, J. (1999) *What's the Difference? A Review of Contemporary Research on the Effectiveness of Distance Learning in Higher Education*. Washington, DC: The Institute for Higher Education Policy.
Richter, J.P.F. (1817) *Levana oder Erziehlehre*. Stuttgart: Cotta'sche Buchhandlung.
Schramm, W. (1962) What we know about learning from instructional television. In W. Schramm (ed.) *Educational Television: The Next Ten Years* (pp. 52–76). Stanford, CA: The Institute for Communication Research, Stanford University.
Tassinari, M.G. (2012) Evaluating learner autonomy: A dynamic model with descriptors. *Studies in Self-Access Learning Journal* 3 (1), 24–40.

Appendix: Interview Guidelines

Students in a secondary English language support class were observed reading CAHLT and English texts in a specific subject: genetically modified organisms. They were then observed as they wrote in English and in their home languages, to the prompt: Do GMOs help or harm people? How do they help or harm people?

Finally, students were observed as they engaged in classroom discourse, following two specific questions:

- Question one: Do you think GMOs are helpful to people? How?
- Question two: Do you think GMOs are harmful to people? How?

Following the observation, students were interviewed, using a semi-structured interview with two specific questions, followed by probing questions based on responses:

- Question one: If you had an assignment or test, which article (CAHLT or English) would you choose? Why?
- Question two: Which text (CAHLT or English) would you rather have to understand the subject? Why?
- Probing/follow-up questions:
    - How did the text in your home language help you understand GMOs?
    - How did the English text help you?
    - Why was it harder to write in English (after reading your CAHLT)?
    - Why was it harder to write in your home language? (after reading your English text)?

7 Playful Plurilingualism? Exploring Language(s) with the Multilingual Serious Game MElang-E

Judith Buendgens-Kosten and Daniela Elsner

Introduction

This volume as a whole introduces multiple ways in which languages beyond the target language can be given a place within the language classroom, be it through multilingual stories, intercomprehension exercises or multilingual practices online. One type of media, though, generally receives very little attention, even though its potential is especially pronounced: multilingual digital games.

Digital games in the language classroom

Talking about 'digital games' is somewhat like talking about 'film'. Just as there are documentaries and dramas, comedies and news programmes, there is a plethora of genres of digital games (cf. e.g. Adams & Rollings, 2007: 433ff.).

In language learning contexts, 'drill-and-kill' type games get the most attention. These are short and simple casual games that focus on units of language such as vocabulary or grammatical forms.

At the same time, many researchers and practitioners also realise that any game that contains language can be a means of language learning, regardless of whether or not it has been designed specifically for this purpose. The use of commercial-off-the-shelf (COTS) games like World of Warcraft (Rama *et al.*, 2012) falls into this area.

However, while fitting World of Warcraft into an average English as a foreign language (EFL) curriculum might pose challenges, integrating serious games might be easier. In its broadest sense, any game that has been designed to cover extra-game educational content can be considered a serious game, including simple drill-and-kill games (e.g. vocabulary games on Quizlet). In this context, we are using the term *serious game* in its narrower definition, not encompassing *all* games that have educational goals, but rather limited to two types of games:

- Games that focus on serious topics such as health and body, peace and conflict, family and relationships from an educational perspective (e.g. excluding many war-themed COTS games, which have a serious topic at their core, but do not deal with it from an educational perspective).
- Games that focus on specific curriculum content in a mode that goes beyond drill and kill.

For example, the literacy/numeracy game Winterfest, which integrates reading and math challenges into an overarching story plot is a serious game by this definition, a spelling-trainer is not.

These serious games provide opportunities to use language, but often also tie in well with the themes and topics of the language classroom. A serious game can be used in the classroom just like an essay or a short story, as a form of linguistic input to be enjoyed, understood, interpreted and creatively reacted to. Whereas DepressionQuest (http://www.depressionquest.com/), for example, could be used with an older age group as part of a unit on mental health, MElang-E would fit well into a unit about friendship, music/casting shows or travel.

Serious games are often created for a native speaker audience, and can linguistically be fairly complex. Of course, many serious games created for younger learners can be of interest here. At the same time, just as a complex text can be supported by illustrations and diagrams that make its comprehension easier, a serious game may feature both written and spoken texts, images that provide context (e.g. objects to choose from, facial expressions of interlocutors) and, by the nature of a game as a game, allow learners to test their interpretations by acting within the game and experiencing the consequences of their choices. The actual design features of the game can therefore function as scaffolding for understanding the game language.

Serious games developed specifically for language learning contexts also exist, and they benefit from the same advantages. Excellent examples are the current serious games offered by the Goethe Institut. In *Lernabenteuer Deutsch: Ein Rätselhafter Auftrag* (https://www.goethe.de/de/spr/ueb/mis.html) for instance, each utterance is provided in written and spoken text and supported by visual context. The game play allows for trial and error, and more complex linguistic tasks receive extra support (e.g. choice between reading a letter or receiving only a summary of the text) (see Figure 7.1).

Figure 7.1 Lernabenteuer Deutsch, context (open fridge door) and accompanying text ('The fridge door is open')

(Source: Goethe-Institut)

Multilingual digital games

Multilingual digital games exist. In the COTS game GTA, for example, you can observe (often merely decorative) use of a second language. Some COTS games, such as the Myst series, use (often fictional) languages (in the case of Myst: D'ni) as content for puzzles. Drill-and-kill type games often include elements of translation (see e.g. Quizlet).

Language learning games that go beyond drill-and-kill types of tasks, though, do not usually feature more than one language. Even *Lernabenteuer Deutsch*, which features a non-native speaker of German as a main character, only lets this character speak in native-like German.

Projekt MElang-E

MElang-E[1] (the acronym stands for 'Multilingual Exploration of Languages in Europe') is a serious game based on the adventure game genre, which is defined by Adams and Rollings as

> (...) an interactive story about a protagonist character who is played by the player. Storytelling and exploration are essential elements of the game. Puzzle-solving and conceptual challenges make up the majority of the gameplay. Combat, economic management, and action challenges are reduced or non-existent. (Adams & Rollings, 2007: 619, italics in the original)

MElang-E (Figures 7.2 and 7.3) has been designed explicitly as a multilingual game. This was motivated by hopes for both linguistic and affective outcomes. On the linguistic level, practicing languages (especially English on the A2/B1 level) in a realistic setting (including native and non-native speakers of languages) and practicing plurilingual communication skills using all existing language skills, was the target. On the affective level, creating a language-friendly environment that seamlessly integrates heritage languages and modern foreign languages, that creates appreciation for and interest in a wide range of languages and that helps learners see the importance of developing plurilingual and intercultural skills, was the main target.

In the game, learners take up the role of Mali, a young Brit from Oxford, who travels across Europe to persuade his former band mates to

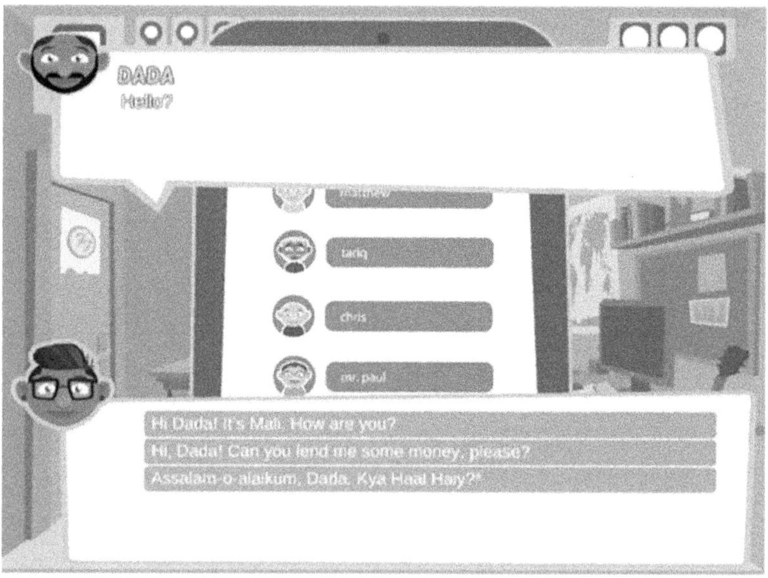

Figure 7.2 Screenshot MElang-E (prototype2): Mali having a phone conversation with his grandfather

Figure 7.3 Screenshot MElang-E (prototype): Mali at the airport check-in desk, talking to Ashley

join him for a youth band contest in Tallinn. During five separate chapters – Oxford, Frankfurt, Luxembourg, Barcelona and Tallinn – the player navigates through places and through dialogue trees, selecting shops to enter, people to talk to and utterances to make, in order to solve in-game problems (e.g. 'find Nicki', 'get your parents to agree with your plans for the trip'). In doing so, learners will often have the option to act multilingually through Mali (see below for details). Also, other (non-player) characters in the game model a range of multilingual practices. The game provides all dialogues (English and all other languages) in both written and spoken form, making them more accessible to players, especially when non-Latin scripts are used (Figures 7.2 and 7.3).

As the focus of this game is on (plurilingual) language learning, the language content of the game adds an additional level of (linguistic rather than primarily conceptual) challenge to the game. In addition to conversing with non-player characters, the player can explore the environment and manipulate some items in it (Adams & Rollings, 2007: 622), but these elements are much less pronounced in MElang-E than in COTS adventure games.

MElang-E simulates effective communication in the plurilingual tradition, allowing players to choose from different dialogue options (scripted conversations/dialogue trees), and to see the reactions of the interlocutor to the choices made. This is quite similar to how other serious games may, for example, provide a simulation of an electric circuit, and allow the player to manipulate it by, for example, switching the position of the lamp and battery to observe the effects this has. By taking up a plurilingual role in the game, players not only acquire occasional words and grammatical structures in different languages, but also develop a better understanding of language ecology and multilingual communication strategies. In ideal circumstances, this may even function as transformational play (see below).

Code choice and code diversity in MElang-E

One challenge in designing a multilingual game such as MElang-E lies in the design of language options. MElang-E features a wide range of places and in each place, a plethora of individuals with different backgrounds, including linguistic backgrounds. Relevant questions during the early design phase were, for example: Can the player choose at all times what language to use? If yes, how many languages can be offered at all times? How does code choice happen? With the click of a button, the selection of a flag? Are all dialogues translated into all languages?

As stated above, in MElang-E, players act through a player character, Mali. This player character shapes what language options are available overall. Mali is defined as bilingual in Urdu and English, with basic, school-acquired skills in French and German (~A1). When travelling to a country where he does not speak the majority language, he takes a few minutes on his flight/train trip to learn some basic phrases (greeting, thanking, etc.). This *language background*, in combination with *considerations of appropriateness* depending on the interlocutor and overall communicative setting, determines what choices are available to the player. Estonian greetings, for example, are only available as choices in the Tallinn chapter, while a scholarly discussion in Japanese is never an option, as this would neither fit the linguistic profile of Mali, nor the settings in which Mali finds himself. This also means that for some languages there are more opportunities for use within the game than for others, and these may be concentrated in one of the five chapters. As an example, Table 7.1 provides an overview of some of the communicative situations learners can navigate in German and in English, respectively, within the Frankfurt chapter.

Please note that, generally, when more than one language option is available, these different language options are not just translations of each other. For example, while Mali speaks both English and German, his English is at a native speaker level, while his German is around A1. The German utterances, therefore, tend to be shorter, simpler in structure and feature less breadth of vocabulary.

For example, at a small souvenir shop near Frankfurt's main station, after having established whether he wants to communicate in German or English, Mali, in effect, responds to the same questions, either to 'OK. Was suchst du?' ['*OK. What are you looking for?*'][3] or to 'Are you looking for

Table 7.1 Communicative situations in English and German within the Frankfurt chapter of MElang-E

Communicative situation	In English	In German
Check-in at a hostel	Yes	Receptive only
Buy something at a bakery	Yes	Receptive only
Buy souvenirs	Yes	Yes
Interview people about age, nationality, shopping habits	Yes	Yes
Describe a person	Yes	No[a]
Talk about emotions	Yes	No
Talk about hobbies	Yes	No
Make an order at a café	Yes	Receptive only
Change a flight booking	Yes	Yes

[a] This dialogue integrates French.

anything special?'. If the player has chosen the English track, he/she can choose between the responses 'I'm looking for a souvenir. Maybe something typical for Frankfurt?' and 'I don't know what I am looking for exactly, but you seem to have lots of knick-knacks. What would you recommend?'. In the German track, there is only one option: 'Ein Souvenir für Mum and Dad'. While both English response options heavily depend on common chunks of language (*I'm looking for…*, *I don't know…*), they are longer and more complex than the German option. In the second English option, there is even specialised vocabulary – *knick-knacks* – the meaning of which can be deduced from the context. In contrast, the (partially) German response helps players with a simple structure and internationalisms. Other utterances depend heavily on the basic phrases learned during early language studies, such as 'Wie alt bist du?' (used pragmatically inappropriate in this setting, where the formal 'Wie alt sind Sie?' would have been appropriate) or 'vielen Dank!'

This, of course, is not a bug, but a feature. It not only models how we can communicate efficiently even with limited linguistic skills. It is also written in a way to make it as accessible as possible (while remaining sociolinguistically realistic) for learners of German or speakers of other Germanic languages. While German is taught as a foreign language in many European countries (Eurydice, 2012), its status as usually second or third foreign language (after English) means that for the target group (seventh-grade learners), only relatively low German skills (if any) can be presumed (unless the players are situated in a German-speaking country or area).

Mechanics of code choice

In a conversation, the player is offered a range of utterances at each step of the dialogue. The player then chooses which one will be used by Mali. Instead of abstractly switching languages ('clicking on a language button'), the player chooses which utterance to make. Often, utterances in several languages are possible, and by choosing the utterance in German, for example, the player increases the probability that the response will be in German too:

Shopkeeper, at a Frankfurt souvenir shop:	Hallo! Suchst du nach etwas bestimmtem? Kann ich dir helfen?
Mali's response, Option 1:	Hallo! Ehm, I'm sorry, what did you say? I don't speak much German.
Mali's response, Option 2:	Helfen? Ja? Ehm, Ich spreche nur wenig Deutsch.

While, certainly, some languages dominate in some places, this does not mean that, for example, Frankfurt is displayed as a place where only German and English as a foreign language are spoken. Other languages are integrated in the same chapter, though not all can be actively used by the player. For example, Mali can talk in French and English to a small child that got lost in the city centre, and he has the opportunity to interview a businessman who talks in English with Mali, and Turkish with his child. This way, a more realistic image of the true diversity of languages in a German metropolis is created, without requiring the player character, Mali, to be unusually skilled in languages.

As the language skill of players does not necessarily match those of the player characters, players are given a lot of freedom in choosing what language they want to use in a certain situation. For example, in the souvenir shop scene quoted above, the shop vendor is introduced as a native speaker of German with strong English language skills, who originally addresses Mali in German, but offers to switch to English if this is more convenient for him. The player can actively *choose* to navigate this conversation in German, or to continue in English.

Other conversations, though, may require some use of German to be completed successfully. To assist players without previous language skills in German, these may then heavily rely on scripted language, previously taught by another (non-player) character.

Mali:	Sounds easy enough. Can you teach me some German key words that might be helpful?
Marie:	Yes. 'Excuse me please, do you have a minute' is 'Entschuldigung, hätten Sie einen Moment Zeit?' ['*Excuse me please, do you have a moment?*'] 'Would you mind if I asked you a few questions for a university project?' is 'Dürfte ich Ihnen ein paar Fragen für ein Uniprojekt stellen?' [*Excuse me please, do you have a moment?*].

'Es geht ums Shoppen' ['*It is about shopping*'] which means 'It is about shopping'.
(Dialogue structure has been simplified for print.)

Diversity of linguistic codes

Of course, code choice is not limited to language choice. Mali's dialogue options cover different registers and levels of politeness, which may or may not be pragmatically suitable for a specific encounter.

Within the game as a whole, additional dimensions of linguistic diversity can be found. Characters in the game have a range of regional backgrounds, and may speak local varieties of the language. In those cases, the spelling is in standard orthography (dialect respellings are only used in select instances when these spellings are well conventionalised, eye dialect is avoided in all cases, cf. Preston [1985]), but the voice acting reflects the regional background of the character.

A similar approach is used with non-native speakers of a language: Standard orthography is used, but voice acting reflects a non-native accent. Whenever possible, the linguistic profile of voice actors is matched with the linguistic profile of the game characters to make the accent more realistic.

Non-native language is, of course, marked not only by phonetic, phonological and prosodic features, but also by lexical and grammatical features. Taking into consideration the concern of many teachers regarding 'bad linguistic models', the absolute majority of characters in this game use impeccable, though often very simple, grammar (see example).

Example of simple grammatical structures:

Julia (woman shopping): Hauptwache sind nur zwei Stops. [*Hauptwache are only two stops*] I mean two stops. I also have to go to Hauptwache. You can come with me. But you need to buy a ticket first!

Example of more advanced grammatical structures:

Robin Baumgartner (works at a coffee shop): She used to play in a band? No way! I would have never thought she was a band girl! Her shift just ended and I think she wanted to do some homework for uni. I am not sure though. Maybe Laura knows more. They study together.

Non-standard lexical items are included when these are typical of the local English (such as the German English *Handy* for cell phone), but may receive some form of correction (explicit correction or simple recasts) by other game characters (see example).

Mike Noak:	Yes, I am German. I am from Berlin. You know, the main city.
Mali, Option 1 (explicit correction):	The main city? You mean the capital city? Like London in the UK or Paris in France? Or Tallinn in Estonia?
Mali, Option 2 (focus on communicative intent):	Berlin! I bet shopping in Berlin is great, too.
Mike Noak:	Yo!

Non-standard grammar is only used by characters who are strongly marked as having extremely low skills in this language. For example, when Mali tries to communicate in Catalan, the final forms are not correct, but the probability of mistakes is signalled by hesitation, self-correction, etc. The same applies to a small number of non-player characters of very low linguistic level in a language. In other words, whenever a character in the game speaks fluently, the grammatical forms are correct, the lexical forms are mostly standard forms, but may include a small number of fossilised local variants, and the pronunciation covers the whole range of native-likeness and native-unlikeness found in that region. If a character is notably struggling with communicating in the target language (A1 and below), more deviations from the linguistic norms taught at school might be observable.

Code-switching in MElang-E

In this context, we understand code-switching as 'the receptive and productive use of and alternation between two or more linguistic varieties in discourse situations, including interaction with others and texts' (Elsner & Lohe, 2013).

MElang-E can be viewed as text. From this perspective, the mechanism of choosing languages outlined above, i.e. selecting from dialogue options, constitutes an example of receptive code-switching, as the player decides the language of the input he/she receives (Buendgens-Kosten & Elsner, 2014: 62; also see Elsner & Buendgens-Kosten, this volume).

Unlike most other settings in which receptive code-switching is used, MElang-E does not just provide the same text in different versions, between which the player can then switch, but rather *simulates* productive code-switching. Therefore, it may be more helpful to view this game as a form of simulated plurilingual communication, or even, at times, *simulated* translanguaging (García *et al.*, 2015: 200), than as a classic receptive code-switching product.

Code-switching can also happen without the player's active choice, i.e. not only when the player actively changes languages between utterances.

Many utterances, both by the player character Mali and by non-player characters, are composed of more than one code.

The wealth of examples of code-switching within the game is reminiscent of the wealth of purposes of code-switching in the real world. When Mali code-switches with his grandfather, the use of both Urdu and English is closely connected to his identity. When using a few phrases of Estonian, it is a marker of his linguistic courage and his attempt to signal politeness. When Jürgen, a polyglot youth hostel manager, code-switches, it is both a way to help his customer understand, and a way to play with words and languages, as the following two examples demonstrate (translations in brackets have been added for the readers' convenience).

Code-switching to help comprehension

Jürgen: Na, das war ja ein kurzes Intermezzo. Ich drucke dir schnell die Rechnung aus. [*Well, this was a short intermezzo. I'll quickly print the invoice for you.*] I'll print the invoice.
Mali Option 1: Invoice? But i didn't stay overnight?
Mali Option 2: Rechnung? Warum? [*Invoice? Why?*]
Jürgen: Naja, du hast ja immerhin den ganzen Tag das Zimmer blockiert. [*Well, after all you blocked the room for the whole day.*] You blocked the room the whole day. Ich muss dir zumindest den halben Preis berechnen [*I have to bill at least half the price*] half price. Umsonst ist nur der Tod... und der kostet das Leben. [*Only death is for free – and it costs you your life.*] HAHAHA.

Code-switching as language play

Mali: Excuse me, what do you need? A Personal...?
Jürgen: Ausweis! Card with your picture. Or Passport, Pasaport, Pasaporte, Pass, Pasupouto.

Insofar as MElang-E is a simulation of communication, code-switching in MElang-E is 'locally functional' (Auer, 1984: 7) within the fictional interactional episode. This does not exclude the possibility of occasional code-switching due to lacunae or gaps in vocabulary knowledge, though these do not dominate within the game.

Marking language choice

To reflect real-world multilingual practices, in which individuals do not normally explicitly mark or even announce what language they use at which time, the game does not provide meta-information about language choice and does not typographically highlight code-switching between utterances. In the case of intrasentential code-switching, one language is marked in italics. The language highlighted is not necessarily the non-English language.

This highlighting of one language in intrasentential code-switching is problematic in so far as it may contribute to a certain exotisation of code-switching: Why, after all, should this specific (socio-)linguistic phenomenon be highlighted, when no other linguistic phenomena are? The decision to highlight intrasentential code-switching derived from an awareness of the didactic context in which the game is to be used. It was added to help learners distinguish between the range of languages that appear in the game. For a person first confronted with e.g. Spanish and Catalan, or Luxembourgish and German, identifying which language is which, when both are spoken in the same environment, can be challenging. When intrasentential code-switches are unmarked, this may become impossible. While in the real world accepting uncertainty when navigating linguistic landscapes might be unavoidable, for the didactic linguistic environment created by the game, highlighting one language in within-utterance code-switches to aid the development of budding language identification skills has been chosen.

Another way in which learners are supported in identifying languages that appear in the game is through the badge system (see below), which informs learners of the name of a language the first time it appears in the game through awarding the 'language explorer badge' for that language.

Intercomprehension

Intercomprehension, that is the ability to understand one language or language variety based on another language or language variety (Klein, 2014: 405), is a valuable source of receptive language skills. A range of materials to help learners discover intercomprehension strategies (e.g. the EuroCom project – Klein, 2014), or to apply intercomprehension strategies to linguistic material in their environment (e.g. for Sorbian in Germany, see Pohl, this volume) already exists. MElang-E aids learners in the development of intercomprehension skills in two ways. First, learners will be confronted with languages that may not be part of their linguistic repertoire, forcing them to accept non-comprehension or to use context and intercomprehension to deduce meaning. Learners who enjoy this kind of challenge have plenty of options of creating extra practice situations through strategic code choice. Second, non-player characters within the game model intercomprehension as a viable strategy: In the Frankfurt chapter of the game, Senora Cortés has panicked in a stuck elevator. She speaks Spanish only, which nobody else in the elevator speaks. Sofia, though, speaks Italian, German and English. She uses Italian to talk to

Senora Cortés, who then responds in Spanish (dialogue structure has been simplified for print, all emphasis mine):

Mali: Tell her to stay **calm**. They are fixing it.
Sofia: Signora, stia **calma**. Stanno **riparando l'ascensore**. [*Signora, stay calm! They are repairing the elevator*!]
Senora Cortés: ¡Ah, entiendo! Están **reparando el ascensor**. Gracias a Dios vamos a salir pronto. [*Ah, I understand! They are repairing the elevator! Thank God! We'll soon get out of here.*]
Mali: We should be fine in less than **thirty minutes**.
Sofia: **Tranquilla** Signora! In meno di **trenta minuti** saremo salvati. [*Stay calm, Signora. We will be saved in less than thirty minutes.*]
Senora Cortés: ¡Menos de **treinta minutos** no es mucho! Ahora estoy más **traquila**. [*Less than thirty minutes isn't much! Now I am much calmer*!]

In this sequence, learners can discover how intercomprehension can be used for communicative purposes. As an added benefit, they also have the opportunity to directly compare Spanish, Italian and English utterances, and to discover, for example, cognates.

Gamifying multilingual practices: The badge system

Badges are a type of reward structure (Kapp, 2012: 33ff.). Simply speaking, a badge is a symbolic representation of an achievement, similar to boy scout/girl scout badges. They represent past behaviour, often interpreted as evidence of competence. On the Kahn Academy video learning platform (https://khanacademy.org), for example, badges are awarded for watching a certain number of videos or solving a number of math problems.

Badges can serve two basic functions. They can increase enjoyment in the game, for example by demonstrating game success for achiever-type players, or to give explorer-type players (Bartle, 2003) surprises to seek out. At the same time, they can impact behaviour in a way desired by the designers of badges. Just as the badge system of the Kahn Academy makes it clear to users that watching many videos or solving math problems is valued, a multilingual game can use badges to signal that a specific type of (linguistic) behaviour is considered valuable.

In any product, be it a game or a learning platform, reward structures only make sense if the behaviour that is to be rewarded is possible. Also, many players consider it frustrating if badges are contradictory, i.e. if you cannot earn one badge once you have earned another badge. While this is acceptable in games with a high replay value, contradictory badges might be less than optimal in a serious game.

These two observations have a direct impact on the possible game design. On the one hand, many types of badges are very interesting from a didactic point of view, but integrating opportunities to earn these badges into the game play would be difficult. On the other hand, while MElang-E certainly wants to encourage learners to use a broad range of languages in different situations, rewarding both language choices (e.g. allowing for English or German, and providing two different badges depending on which one is used) could lead to contradictory badges. For example, in an early design, players could have earned a badge for navigating a certain number of service encounters in English. At the same time, some of these could be navigated in other languages, and players could earn badges for using these other languages. In the final badge design, this was modified to eliminate the possibility of contradictory badges.

The current badge design focuses on four types of achievements:

(1) Language achievements, i.e. having encountered or used a language in the game.
(2) Communicative achievements, i.e. successfully navigating a range of communicative situations of special interest for the target group.
(3) Pragmatic achievements, i.e. the ability to use situationally appropriate politeness.
(4) Action achievements, i.e. having achieved some desirable game outcome, such as receiving a job offer after a job interview.

Some of these rewards encourage players to do things within the game that are not strictly necessary to complete the game, such as talking to additional non-player characters or making an extra effort in those conversations that are mandatory. In other words, these rewards encourage deep engagement with the dialogues, rather than just random clicking, and extend the amount of input by encouraging engaging in extra dialogues. The other rewards focus specifically on language choice, and encourage exploration and use of a wide range of languages. As an example, a 'Language explorer' badge is earned whenever a new language is encountered. The badge (e.g. 'Language explorer: French') is earned automatically as soon as the first utterance in this language appears in the scripted dialogue. At this point, the player is not only told the name of the language, which might, in itself, already be useful, but also finds out whether by using this language, another advanced badge, the 'Language user: French' badge, can be earned. If he/she is motivated by earning badges, this might encourage him/her to use some French within the game to earn this 'Language user' badge.

Putting it into practice: Teacher handbook and teaching material

Any digital learning object that aims to be implemented in the classroom has to fit the logic of the classroom. Digital games, especially COTS games that have lengthy play durations, are chronically difficult to integrate into the classroom. The same issue applies to the serious game MElang-E, with a total estimated play duration of several lessons. Even the structure of MElang-E – chapter-like 'cities', which can be played as meaningful units – does not fully solve the problem of integration into the classroom.

In the teacher handbook, the pedagogic background of MElang-E and strategies for incorporating it into the classroom are outlined. As MElang-E is browser based, free and does not require registration, it is possible to play it as a group using a projector or interactive whiteboard; as small groups clustered around computers or laptops; or individually, using, for example, tablet PCs. Learners are able to play parts of the game in school, and some as homework, and switch contexts and locations seamlessly, if they register as users.

To further support use in the classroom, and to increase acceptance by teachers, a range of worksheets and activity suggestions focusing on communicative competence, intercultural competence and language awareness are available to teachers free of charge, ordered according to the different city chapters in the game and labelled with information on learning goals. As the communicative situations in MElang-E closely follow the Common European Framework of Reference for Languages (CEFR) requirements for levels A2 and B1, the game and the accompanying teaching material are ideally situated to practice, for example talking about oneself and one's interest, or engaging in common service encounters in English. Some of the worksheets and activity suggestions are fairly conventional, while others involve multiple languages, non-native English, etc. This is a strategic choice, to allow teachers to experiment with multilingual resources like MElang-E without having to commit to a full-blown plurilingual approach to language teaching.

Conclusion

The aim of this chapter was to demonstrate the value that multilingual serious games have for the language classroom, focusing on engaging with the MElang-E language learning game on the descriptive and conceptual level. While aspects of the game and the accompanying teaching material (e.g. difficulty level of text, acceptance of multilingual game texts by learners, acceptance of multilingual games by teacher training students, test teaching with teaching material) have already been tested with the target group, it is difficult to fully assess the quality of a game before it is playable *as a game*. The game will be published in 2018 (see melang-e.eu for details), and subsequently, research on the actual game and how it is used by learners can commence in full.

Once the game has been completed, research will explore how the game and the extensive supporting material are actually being used in the classroom by learners and teachers. The plurilingual outlook of the game – even though it reflects the demands of the CEFR (Council of Europe, 2001: 4f) – may be challenging for many teachers and learners alike. To assist teachers, a range of teacher materials explaining the key notions behind the design are currently in preparation. For students, it is hoped that the experience of playing MElang-E will not just result in the acquisition of a few 'travelling' words, but in a new understanding of the role of language(s), acquired through what – in the context of science learning – Barab *et al.* (2010) call 'Transformational play'. In other words, MElang-E could help in taking yet another chip out of the no-longer unshakable wall of the 'monolingual habitus' (Gogolin, 1994) and contribute to a 'language-friendly environment' as proposed by the Council of Europe in 2008.

Notes

(1) Development of MElang-E has been funded by the European Union through Erasmus+. For a complete list of project partners, see http://melang-e.eu/.

(2) As this is a prototype version, not all details are final yet. The asterisk after Mali's final text option indicates that this text (Arabic and Urdu) still needs to be set in the correct script.

(3) Throughout the text, translations that do not appear in the actual game dialogues have been added. They are set in brackets and marked in italics: [*translated text*].

References

Adams, E. and Rollings, A. (2007) *Game Design and Development: Fundamentals of Game Design*. Upper Saddle River, NJ: Pearson.

Auer, P. (1984) *Bilingual Conversation*. Amsterdam: Benjamins.

Barab, S.A., Gresalfi, M. and Ingram-Goble, A. (2010) Transformational play: Using games to position person, content, and context. *Educational Researcher* 39 (7), 525–536.

Bartle, R.R. (2003) *Designing Virtual Worlds*. Berkeley, CA: New Riders.

Buendgens-Kosten, J. and Elsner, D. (2014) Rezeptives Code-Switching ein- und mehrsprachiger Lerner/innen in multilingualen Settings. *Fremdsprachen Lehren und Lernen* 42 (2), 56–73.

Council of Europe (2001) *Common European Framework of Reference for Languages: Learning, Teaching, Assessment*. Cambridge: Cambridge University Press.

Elsner, D. and Lohe, V. (2013) Fostering Multilingualism with Computer-Based Multilingual Storybooks: The European Comenius Project MuViT. Presentation at WorldCALL Conference 2013. See https://prezi.com/pbjnxpu-ybnj/fostering-multilingualism-with-computer-based-multilingual-storybooks-the-european-comenius-project-muvit/ (accessed 8 April 2018).

Eurydice (2012) *Key Data on Teaching Languages at School in Europe. 2012 Edition. Eurydice Report*. Luxembourg: Publications Office of the European Union.

García, O., Flores, N. and Homonoff-Woodley, H. (2015) Constructing in-between spaces to 'do' bilingualism: A tale of two high schools in one city. In J. Cenoz and D. Gorter (eds) *Multilingual Education: Between Language Learning and Translanguaging* (pp. 199–224). Cambridge: Cambridge University Press.

Gogolin, I. (1994) *Der monolinguale Habitus der multilingualen Schule*. Münster: Waxmann.

Kapp, K.M. (2012) *The Gamification of Learning and Instruction: Game-Based Methods and Strategies for Training and Education*. San Francisco, CA: Pfeiffer.

Klein, H.G. (2014) L'eurocompréhension (eurocom), une méthode de compréhension des langues voisines. *Ela: Études de linguistique appliquée* 4, 403–418.

Preston, D.R. (1985) The Li'l Abner syndrome: Written representations of speech. *American Speech* 60 (4), 328–336.

Rama, P.S., Black, R.W. and van Es, E. (2012) Affordances for second language learning in World of Warcraft. *ReCALL* 24 (3), 322–338.

Part 3
Intercomprehension and CALL

8 (A) CALL for Slavic Intercomprehension: The Promotion of Minority Languages in the Modern Foreign Language Classroom

Manuela Pohl

Introduction

Members of multilingual societies are not automatically aware of the cultural wealth with which they are surrounded. Making them aware of it is a political responsibility. Citizens should have the opportunity to learn different foreign languages at school; public administration should offer its services in different languages; and diversity within the linguistic landscape should be supported. This is how raising multilingual awareness should work according to agreements like the European Charter for Regional or Minority Languages, which deals with the protection and promotion of these languages in all European countries that have ratified the charter – including Germany (Council of Europe, 1992: Preamble). Education bears a special responsibility for promoting diversity among European citizens as it allows less commonly spoken languages to be promoted within the member states. This chapter aims to make the case for raising language awareness by utilising the linguistic landscape surrounding schools in a specific multilingual area. In particular, the chapter presents a suggestion for the integration of a minority language in a small region of Germany. In Lower Lusatia, the region in question, the minority language Lower Sorbian is used alongside the official language, German. According to established guidelines and federal laws, schools in the federal state of Brandenburg, particularly in Lower Lusatia, are obliged to integrate the issue of minority languages into their curricula (Land Brandenburg, 2016: §4 (5)). However, this does not result in an appropriate representation of the topic in learning material, course books and so on (Ratajczak, 2011: 21).

That is why the idea of using the linguistic landscape in a bilingual settlement area arose. Foreign language classes are well suited for topics like crosslinguistic comparisons, which is why language teachers could attempt to integrate Lower Sorbian into a foreign language classroom, as well. As it is based on a classroom experiment, this chapter first presents the sociolinguistic background of the idea, followed by methodological explanations concerning the intercomprehension approach, and Sorbian-Russian crosslinguistic comparisons. For reasons of mobility, for better access to authentic language material and to enable real-time collaboration, mobile technology is suggested as a way of improving the original classroom experiment. This chapter presents a computer assisted language learning (CALL) task in which technological devices could be used as tools to accomplish given tasks and as a result, would improve the media literacy skills of the learners involved. In this way, pupils can learn *through* new media *about* a new language while applying skills they are familiar with as well as gaining new competencies in both fields.

The Sorbs, A National Minority in Germany

The Slavic language, Sorbian, is spoken by the Sorbs – one of Germany's four national minorities. They live in an area called Lusatia and form part of the linguistic landscape of this distinctive region of Germany. While there are two Sorbian languages (Lower and Upper Sorbian spoken in Lower and Upper Lusatia), this chapter will concentrate on the smaller of them, Lower Sorbian. This 'endangered minority language' (Moseley, 2010: 37) is spoken in Lower Lusatia, an area in the federal state of Brandenburg.

Because Germany ratified the Framework Convention for the Protection of National Minorities (Council of Europe, 1995), a multilateral treaty of the Council of Europe, as well as the European Charter for Regional or Minority Languages (Council of Europe, 1992), the federal government of Brandenburg in particular, is responsible for preserving the Lower Sorbian cultural identity and language (Bundesministerium des Innern, 2015: 10; Land Brandenburg, 2014: Preamble).

Since 1992, the European Charter for Regional or Minority Languages has been ratified by almost all EU member states. It supports the protection and promotion of regional or minority languages in the different countries and regions of Europe as a 'contribution to the building of a Europe based on the principles of democracy and cultural diversity' (Council of Europe, 1992: Preamble). Celebrating diversity and appreciating plurality are important values shared between the nations of the European Union. Thus, Germany has to protect the cultural heritage of its four recognised national minorities: the German Sinti and Roma, the Sorbian, the Frisian and the Danish people (Bundesministerium des Innern, 2015: 10).

Within this group, Sorbian has a special status, as the Slavic minority of the Sorbs does not have – as Glaser (2007: 219) puts it – 'a kin-country or "mother-state" of their own'. There are only two small settlement areas in north-eastern Germany: Lower Lusatia in the federal state of Brandenburg and Upper Lusatia in the federal state of Saxony. There are many different numbers circulating regarding the amount of Sorbian mother tongue speakers: According to Spieß (2002: 323), there are 20,000 Lower Sorbs living in the South of Brandenburg, while according to the German Ministry of the Interior there are about 30,000 (Lower and Upper) Sorbs in Germany (Bundesministerium des Innern, 2015: 47). However, the ministry admits that no statistics based on ethnicity have been gathered since the end of World War II (Bundesministerium des Innern, 2015: 11; Schön & Scholze, 2014: 37). As a result, the exact number of people belonging to a minority, or speaking the minority's language, is difficult to estimate.

In order to protect the language from dying, the Sorbian culture as well as the language has attained a special status in Brandenburg's legislation (Land Brandenburg, 2014: Preamble; Land Brandenburg, 2016: §4) and knowledge of the minority is a requirement of Brandenburg's schools, as well (Senatsverwaltung Berlin and MBJS Brandenburg, 2015a: 7). Accordingly, the school curriculum contains the obligation to discuss the issue of the Sorbian culture in non-linguistic subjects too. Unfortunately, apart from some rare attempts initialised by the University of Potsdam (cf. Neumann, 2008), there is a rather small amount of materials designed in accordance with these demands (Ratajczak, 2011: 21). That is why this chapter is proposing making the linguistic landscape itself a proper provider of learning material, in order to integrate Sorbian meaningfully as a worthwhile subject.

Sorbian in the Russian Language Classroom

When looking for a subject that offers strong ties to Sorbian, Russian as a foreign language seems to be a good match. Being one of the regularly offered foreign languages in German secondary schools (EACEA/Eurydice, 2012: 75), Russian is taught in schools of the Sorbian settlement area, too. There is an obvious connection between these languages as both derive from the same language family. Belonging to the Slavic branch of the Indo-European language family, both show various similarities that are worth exploring. Exposing pupils to other languages in their regular foreign language class is in line with the Council of Europe's demands for 'linguistic diversity' and 'plurilingual education' (cf. Trim, 2001). Therefore, these languages can be compared in order to raise language learners' meta-linguistic awareness, which is an important factor of multilingual learning. Making pupils aware of the procedures of language comparisons might improve their ability to interact in multilingual situations too. In the words of The New London

Group (1996: 67–68): 'When learners juxtapose different languages, discourses, styles, and approaches, they gain substantively in meta-cognitive and meta-linguistic abilities and in their ability to reflect critically on complex systems and their interactions'.

For pupils in the Sorbian settlement area, the minority language in question is highly visible in their everyday life: Looking at street signs or public facilities, such as municipal buildings or railway stations, which are (at least) bilingually signposted, reveals a vivid multilingual linguistic landscape in the Sorbian settlement area (Land Brandenburg, 2014: §11). This is why this promising real-life case study should be transferred into the foreign language classroom as well. On the one hand, monolinguals might benefit from addressing this issue by extending their meta-linguistic awareness. On the other, members of minorities suffering from negative self-concepts (Neumann, 2014: 112) may be encouraged to feel more valued by majority members. Thus, the 'symbolic function [...] the visibility of a language has in the public space can have a special meaning in the case of minority learners' (Cenoz & Gorter, 2008: 281), which is why addressing this topic might lead to an increase in some pupils' self-esteem.

Another reason for integrating Sorbian as a further Slavic language into the Russian language classroom is the connection to the learners' everyday life. There is quite a distance – geographically as well as linguistically – between Germany and Russia. For most pupils, the sole opportunity to experience this foreign language in an authentic way will be to get in contact with Russian bilinguals, migrants or tourists outside of Russia. Experiencing the language in Russia happens very rarely. However, other Slavic countries are close: Germany's eastern neighbours, Poland and the Czech Republic, are more likely to be visited by German pupils. As both their official languages, Polish and Czech, are West Slavic languages, they can be compared with and understood via Russian too. Thus, intercomprehensive skills as presented in the Framework of Reference for Plurilingual Approaches (Council of Europe, 2012: 56) can be trained for this purpose. Trying to understand some Sorbian words taken from street signs next to the school, for example, could be the first step towards working with other Slavic languages in the Russian language classroom (Behr, 2011; Paul, 2002; Seidel & Wächter-Springer, 1997). This way, learners' language awareness could be raised and the benefit of learning Russian in order to understand other Slavic languages becomes clear.

Reasons for Using the Linguistic Landscape of the Sorbian Settlement Area

The conditions that might evoke learners' attention in that matter are quite convenient. According to Landry and Bourhis (1997), who coined the term 'linguistic landscapes', many multilingual traces are to be found in the Sorbian settlement area. The linguistic landscape in question offers rich multilingual input, which is – according to Landry and Bourhis (1997) – a characteristic trait of the concept. There are many multilingual traces to be found in the Sorbian settlement area: Public road signs, street names, place names, and public signs on government buildings which form the linguistic landscape of the region (Landry & Bourhis, 1997: 25) can be found in Sorbian and German. They influence the perception of a special area as being multilingual and multicultural. According to Article 10 of the European Charter for Regional or Minority Languages 'the use or adoption, if necessary in conjunction with the name in the official language(s), of traditional and correct forms of place names in regional or minority languages' (Council of Europe, 1992: 9) is an obvious characteristic of the linguistic landscape in minority language regions. That is why the bilingual street signage in the Sorbian settlement area represents a model linguistic landscape that puts both minority and majority languages on an equal footing.

All these different multilingual elements can be used to fulfil the function of learning material (Chern & Dooley, 2014: 2). In the context of foreign language learning, the urban signage provides a range of opportunities to analyse authentic linguistic material, which is useful for the development of language awareness and the promotion of linguistic diversity (Cenoz & Gorter, 2008: 283). As mentioned above, dealing with minority languages in school not only gives native speakers of German an opportunity to learn about other languages and widen their horizons, but it can also have positive effects on the status of minority identities. Therefore, policy makers should recognise the importance of bilingual signage for the identity of minority speakers – especially in the case of endangered languages like Lower Sorbian (Austin & Sallabank, 2011: 19). Bilingual signage is also closely linked to the discussion around a minority's reputation or status in a given society. Considering sociolinguistic ideas with greater political and ethical relevance, and at the same time promoting cultural diversity in the language classroom, is also a required part of the curriculum (Senatsverwaltung Berlin and MBJS Brandenburg, 2015b: 25). Learners can become aware of their own perception of a multilingual region; minority rights can be discussed and measures for ensuring equal treatment of all members of a community can be analysed cautiously and critically.

Other important arguments for using bilingual street signage as a starting point for the analysis of Sorbian words in the Russian foreign language classroom are the manageable length of text pieces, as well as the repetitive linguistic forms occurring on street signs. As Chern and Dooley (2014: 7) convincingly conclude from these reasons, 'reading their way through the linguistic landscape can be motivating' for learners, which is why it seems to be a good starting point for crosslinguistic comparison.

Reasons for Applying the Intercomprehension Approach

The conditions outlined above allow for the use of authentic Sorbian material in the Russian foreign language classroom. Crosslinguistic comparison and reflection about languages promote language awareness, which is why, in a Russian classroom scenario, learners of Russian were requested to work with an unknown Slavic language applying intercomprehensive strategies. These strategies enabled the learners to understand a language they were unfamiliar with by exploiting their existing linguistic and general knowledge (Braunmüller, 2002; Doyé, 2004; Klein & Stegmann, 2000). As intensive research led to the development of the Framework of Reference for Pluralistic Approaches to Languages and Cultures (Council of Europe, 2012), national as well as federal curricula cover this topic, such as Berlin-Brandenburg's curriculum for modern foreign languages. The latter encourages the application of the crosslinguistic approach to enable pupils to reflect on language itself (Senatsverwaltung Berlin and MBJS Brandenburg, 2015b: 10). It also encourages the comparison of words and chunks of different languages – like pupils' languages of origin, foreign languages or regional languages – with each other in order to convey language awareness (Senatsverwaltung Berlin and MBJS Brandenburg, 2015b: 10).

By making learners think about words, their structure and their meaning, such crosslinguistic comparisons provide ample opportunities to increase the learners' meta-linguistic awareness and spread the concept of linguistic diversity. This means so much more than the current practice of *multiple monolingualism* that replaced the *monolingual habitus* in German mainstream schools (Marx, 2014: 9). It is rather a question of exposing pupils to different languages, enlarging their receptive lexicon in different related languages, improving their individual comprehensive strategies and also enabling them to apply these intercomprehensive strategies in other areas of intercultural interaction. And because the system 'one nation – one language' is an artificial construct, and as such monolingual communication is a rarity (Cenoz & Gorter, 2013: 593), boundaries between different languages have to be reduced too. In order to establish a strong feeling of community among the members of all European countries, we should focus on similarities rather than differences. This could be the key to the development of a real multicultural society.

Before learners are able to notice the similarities between Sorbian and Russian however, they need to acquire some code-breaking strategies. In the present proposal, this knowledge is provided by intercomprehensive strategies.

The efficacy of intercomprehension – in a German Russian language classroom in particular – has been described in detail by Mehlhorn (2014). She investigated the positive effects deriving from intercomprehensive tasks. Having investigated the influence of the first language (L1) and the second language (L2) on the acquisition of Russian as a third language (L3), she concluded that the method is beneficial for language learners even at a very early stage – as soon as they are motivated to explore transferable chunks of international words (Mehlhorn, 2014: 158). Furthermore, other researchers outlined the benefits of using intercomprehensive strategies to compare languages belonging to the Romance branch (Bär, 2009; Klein & Stegmann, 2000; Meißner, 1993). According to them, no L2 or L3 – especially from within the same language family – can really be considered unknown or foreign, because in some ways it belongs to a system already well understood. In order to apply this system adequately, learners have to be made aware of the underlying principles of crosslinguistic comparisons. Therefore, the so-called 'EuroCom' system was developed for intercomprehension between different European language families (Klein & Stegmann, 2000). This concept is based on the assumption that when learning a third or fourth foreign language, the learner uses knowledge from familiar languages and earlier acquired language learning strategies and from that, stimulates the constructivist language learning process (Mazza, 2004: 37). The 'EuroComRom' idea was originally developed for intercomprehension between Romance languages and provides seven analytical steps that make the interpretation of unknown words and texts easier (Klein & Stegmann, 2000). For the Slavic languages, Zybatow and Zybatow (2004: 70) have proposed discrete steps to follow when applying this specific strategy.

After having analysed a piece of text according to the following seven steps, the information hidden in a foreign language text can be easily deduced (Zybatow & Zybatow, 2004: 70):

- similarities on the basis of international vocabulary;
- similarities on the basis of Pan-Slavic vocabulary;
- sound correspondence;
- similarities in spelling or pronunciation;
- similarities in Pan-Slavic syntactic structures;
- similar morphosyntactic structures;
- similar pre- or suffixes.

These steps can therefore serve as an analytical framework for the understanding of unknown Sorbian words and texts too. The pupils' role is thus transformed from 'language learners' to 'language researchers' (Sayer, 2010: 153). In this way, their methodological skills are enhanced and their ability to discover and understand related languages is strengthened.

Reasons to Apply Technology-Enhanced Learning

In a first project scenario, (analogue) materials based on intercomprehension strategies were developed for pupils in their fourth year of learning Russian. Learners living in Cottbus, which is the biggest town in Lower Lusatia, were supposed to compare Lower Sorbian words to Russian, their second foreign language. By using Sorbian street signs as a starting point, the pupils were given many opportunities to find language examples that are easily deducible – mostly because of lexical similarities. The application of different intercomprehensive strategies then enabled them to decode a Lower Sorbian location plan without any explicit knowledge of this language.

Next to the positive results (learners being able to recognise similar word patterns, transfer their knowledge and make use of inference), disadvantages were noticeable too. For example, the preparation of material was comparatively complex. Additionally, providing different language material according to the learners' interests or offering suitable scaffolding material (e.g. Lower Sorbian dictionaries, sound files) proved to be difficult. Moreover, it would have helped to have had a platform for regular interactive exchange of results or the technological tools to design attractive post-analysis activities. As a result, taking this project to the next level by transferring it into a digital setting seemed to promise several advantages.

Advantages of Mobile Technology

One of the main advantages of applying mobile technology in this setting is the free access to the internet – anytime, anywhere. Not only does the internet enlarge the linguistic landscape of minority regions virtually, it also allows for minority groups to benefit from the opportunity of presenting themselves to a broader audience (Cenoz & Gorter, 2008: 283). For example, Nitzsche's (2015) web research reveals a growing repertoire of Sorbian online texts and material on Facebook, Wikipedia and so on. This leads to the assumption that there might be a growing body of multimodal material accessible with suitable technological equipment. Making use of web material, and including it meaningfully into language lessons, might further develop learners' multiliteracies (Busch, 2013: 133) in terms of critical text research and multimodal source selection. Supporting the learners' multiliteracy development helps them to understand that '[...] language and other modes of meaning are dynamic representational resources, constantly being remade [...] as they work to achieve their various cultural purposes' (The New London Group, 1996: 63). To teach learners to understand these multimodal representations, their meanings and functions is as well in line with Brandenburg's media curriculum (Senatsverwaltung Berlin and MBJS Brandenburg, 2015b).

For the task proposed later in this chapter, it is necessary that each pupil (or small group of pupils) is provided with mobile devices (ideally tablet computers) as they allow for the convenient storage and retrieval of learning outcomes. They also provide opportunities for sharing and recycling materials, synchronous communication and a lot more. Tablet computers suggest themselves for multimodal tasks, because they provide several useful features in one device – which not long ago would have been different units: recorder, camera and data storage. Moreover, touchscreens provide another beneficial feature for non-natives, or Russian language learners: the use of a touchscreen with Cyrillic letters makes writing in Russian much easier than with traditional keyboards. Furthermore, pupils would have all kinds of online resources available – be these online dictionaries, sound files, pictures or anything else that might help them complete their task. Moreover, they can upload their material onto learning platforms and get constructive feedback from their fellow pupils in real time, or link it to other material. In doing so, they get a sense of control and ownership of their learning outcomes, which might make an important contribution to their degree of motivation and personal involvement in the task.

Nevertheless, it has to be taken into account that learners – although belonging to the generation of 'digital natives' (Prensky, 2001) – are not always confident using the technological tools provided, which is why training them to use technology to their benefit is one of the prerequisites for complex digital tasks (Blake, 2016: 130). These benefits include the possibility to take and edit photos, to listen to audio files or record oral explanations, to do research online, to write texts and design graphics. As further importance for the learning process, the social aspect has to be emphasised: learners have the opportunity to work collaboratively, share their ideas online, use hyperlinks to refer to each other or show their learning results to their peers who then could give feedback, all the while improving their media literacy.

Certainly, one of the most obvious benefits of using technological devices is the massive pool of authentic online resources that provides many opportunities to generate language learning material. As a result, individual and autonomous work could be created much more easily. The suggestion is to use tablet computers as one tool among others as tasks should still force learners to go out, talk to people and find and share information, because this is supposed to have a positive effect on their motivation. Moreover, Warschauer's study on motivation in computer-assisted learning 'found that the impact of Web-based work rested in large part on the social and cultural relevance of [...] assignments. When students felt they were contributing something of value to the public arena, they put in a great deal of effort in the process and attention to the product ...' (Warschauer & Healey, 1998: 64). It therefore becomes evident that the types of resources young learners use in their everyday life might be considered motivating. Producing their own digital products is in accordance with today's learners routinely using digital tools to produce new web content (Blake, 2016: 131) and with tasks that make use of digital features, teachers could certainly engage learners' interest in the topic.

The Intercomprehensive CALL Scenario

A task that introduces the Sorbian language into the Russian language classroom making use of digital devices could read as shown in Figure 8.1. This means that learners have to pass through the three basic phases of analysis, documentation and creation:

(1) Analysis of language patterns:
- Examples for crosslinguistic comparisons are presented and rules are recognised.
- Scaffolding techniques are offered (audio files, online dictionaries).
- Recognising similarities among Russian and Sorbian is practiced through matching activities.

(2) Documentation of the town's linguistic landscape:
- Examples of Sorbian street names have to be discovered on the real street signs in the town.
- Photos of these bilingual signs have to be uploaded as evidence and support for other groups.
- Findings and results have to be shared and recorded in a collaborative learning database.

(3) Creation of new material:
- Sorbian-Russian games (crosswords, word squares, etc.) have to be created with the aid of online authoring tools.
- Street sign memories could be designed using the (edited) photos taken by different groups.
- QR codes could be produced explaining the meaning of different street signs in Russian.

To complete this task scenario, the language detectives first have to be enabled to recognise Slavic traces in their surroundings. In a second step – based on their understanding of this matter – they can apply their knowledge when finding traces and documenting them. Thirdly, they are supposed to complete the task by creating new learning material with the help of different online resources.

The tourist information office needs your help:

A group of Russian tourists will visit your home town Cottbus. They are interested in the traces of Slavic languages to be found in and around Cottbus.
During the next few weeks

- you will work as language detectives and look for Slavic traces in Lower Sorbian street signs.
- you will translate the traces found into Russian and transliterate the information online.
- you will work cooperatively and inform each other about the traces found on the school's learning platform.
- you will prepare material for the tourists' children, too. They want to learn about this unfamiliar language in an enjoyable way and like games and riddles.

Figure 8.1 Example of classroom task

Here, it becomes clear that, for the completion of the task, they have to combine a deep understanding of the linguistic procedures with an appropriate degree of media competence.

The first linguistic patterns they have to analyse should be provided by the teacher. Learners have to be introduced to the seven steps of analysing unfamiliar languages and from this, learn about similarities between related languages (Paul, 2002; Seidel & Wächter-Springer, 1997). For practising the analytical steps, students should try to figure out the meaning of basic Sorbian words that have Russian equivalents that are already part of their active learner vocabulary. In order to explain what they are supposed to do as language detectives, photos of bilingual street signs could be used.

The Lower Sorbian street name 'Stara postowa droga' (Figure 8.2) serves as an ideal example. According to the previously mentioned analytical steps (Zybatow & Zybatow, 2004: 70), this street name could be easily analysed by applying only three of the seven steps:

- check for similarities on the basis of international vocabulary:
  - Sorbian: postowa => Russian: почтовая [počtovaja] = English: *post*
- check for similarities on the basis of Pan-Slavic vocabulary (including sound correspondence, spelling, pronunciation):
  - Sorbian: stara => Russian: старая [staraja] = English: *old*
  - Sorbian: droga => Russian: дорога [doroga] = English: *way/ street*
- similarities in Pan-Slavic morpho-syntactic structures:
  - inflection of adjectives: the feminine adjectives agree both in gender and number with the noun they are referring to: all feminine endings => [-a]

Afterwards, learners would have to analyse different randomly chosen Sorbian street names – first and foremost – with the help of Russian, and find them in the town. In a second step, they would document the correct German translation by uploading a photo of the street sign found onto their school's learning management system (e.g. Moodle platform).

This way, pupils would be motivated to share their knowledge, comment on each other's findings and ask for support or help wherever they are. This kind of treasure hunt might also motivate them to discover their hometown and surrounding villages more attentively in the future. This, in turn, will have a positive effect on the recognition of Sorbian as part of their everyday life and might even lead to the recognition of further multilingual traces in other (European) bilingual areas as well.

Finally, they have to create new material in their second language, Russian. For the Russian transliteration of Sorbian street signs and for the creation of riddles or games, they are supposed to use basic vocabulary,

Figure 8.2 Bilingual street sign in Cottbus (English: *Old post way/street*)

which prevents them from feeling overwhelmed by the linguistic complexity of the underlying comparative processes. Although in the proposed scenario, learners do not have to negotiate in the target foreign language – in this case Russian – they have to use their language awareness skills and existing foreign language skills to find solutions for a challenging problem. The role of the teacher in the whole process is to provide learners with meta-linguistic strategies and advise them on how to proceed. He or she would have to monitor the learner output online and provide feedback whenever it is needed. This way, learners can work autonomously but can get back to the teacher whenever they feel the need to do so.

Conclusion and Prospects

Referring to Sayer (2010: 144), who developed a linguistic landscape project with EFL learners in Mexico, ideas like the one presented above aim at engaging students 'in investigating and talking about how language is used [...]'. Sayer's (2010: 152) pupils collected photographs and analysed them according to sociolinguistic categories. In his view, projects like this not only help learners to make 'connections between the content of [...] classroom lessons and the world beyond the classroom walls', they also enhance learners' ability to 'think creatively and analytically about how language is used in society and become more aware of their own socio-linguistic context' (Sayer, 2010: 153). The latter aspect is especially important for monolingual pupils in the Sorbian settlement areas. They should be confronted with the special linguistic features of their surroundings more often in order to increase the acceptance of the regions' biculturalism (Ratajczak, 2011: 69). That is why sending learners out to explore their surroundings linguistically is highly recommended. As well as this, combining the linguistic analysis with a proper amount of socio-linguistic discussions is strongly encouraged – especially when learners are already able to reflect on their own perceptions and expectations regarding cultural diversity and the role of minorities.

In a multicultural Europe, members of majority cultures have to take particular responsibility for the protection of common goods – such as diversity and the protection of minorities. All learners – no matter what cultural or linguistic background they come from – should internalise that at an early stage of their education process. This objective could be well achieved by scenarios like the one proposed. By highlighting similarities rather than differences, the proposed task presents a way to include a minority language meaningfully into a foreign language classroom. Also, applying the intercomprehension approach is one way in which students could get the opportunity to make use of their linguistic capital in a multicultural situation.

To design this task to be as activating and authentic as possible, the use of mobile technology has been suggested. Thereby, learners would be given ample opportunities to create material on their own and as a result, not only learn about crosslinguistic comparisons but also about design thinking and digital collaboration. For the proposed task, among the advantages of mobile technology would be the constant internet access that enables learners to do all kinds of research, real-time photography in order to present findings, and ensure constant communication for feedback from others (teacher, learners). Moreover, through constant presenting, commenting and re-writing in a virtual space, regulation of the learning process is possible: pupils reflect on their work, monitor each other and evaluate their results based on the uploaded material. This fosters responsible planning and serious work. By being involved in meaning-making processes, learners solve problems, make decisions, find reasons, create new materials and evaluate their own and other's work (Pellerin, 2014: 11).

It could also be interesting to send pupils working as language detectives into a virtual space and connect with learners in other bilingual areas of Europe to exchange perceptions and experiences online. One or another of these groups could prepare intercomprehensive learning materials for learners of Russian not living in a Slavic area, like learners in Lusatia or the border regions of Germany do. This could work as an exchange project as well as an e-learning cooperation. It would be beneficial for all participating pupils, because any interaction with people not sharing the same background provides new positive impressions and might give inspiration for thought-provoking discussions. That is how computer- and mobile-assisted language learning can help to overcome geographical borders, enhance language learning experiences and support the promotion of lesser used languages.

References

Austin, P.K. and Sallabank, J. (eds) (2011) *The Cambridge Handbook of Endangered Languages*. Cambridge: Cambridge University Press.

Bär, M. (2009) *Förderung von Mehrsprachigkeit und Lernkompetenz*. Tübingen: Gunther Narr Verlag.

Behr, U. (2011) Sprachenübergreifendes Lehren und Lernen: ein Plädoyer aus der Sicht des Russischunterrichts. *Die Neueren Sprachen* 2, 33–44.

Blake, R. (2016) Technology and the four skills. *Language Learning & Technology* 20 (2), 129–142.

Braunmüller, K. (2002) Semicommunication and accomodation: Observations from the linguistic situation in Scandinavia. *International Journal of Applied Linguistics* 12 (1), 1–23.

Bundesministerium des Innern (2015) *Nationale Minderheiten- und Regionalsprachen in Deutschland* (3rd edn). See https://www.bmi.bund.de/SharedDocs/Downloads/DE/Broschueren/2015/Minderheiten_Minderheitensprachen.pdf?__blob=publicationFile (accessed 06 April 2018).

Busch, B. (2013) *Mehrsprachigkeit*. Stuttgart: UTB.

Cenoz, J. and Gorter, D. (2008) The linguistic landscape as an additional source of input in second language acquisition. *IRAL* 46, 267–287.

Cenoz, J. and Gorter, D. (2013) Towards a plurilingual approach in English language teaching: Softening the boundaries between languages. *TESOL Quarterly* 47 (3), 591–599.

Chern, C.-I. and Dooley, K. (2014) Learning English by walking down the street. *ELT Journal* 68 (2), 113–123.

Council of Europe (1992) *European Charter for Regional or Minority Languages*. Strasbourg. See http://www.coe.int/t/dg4/education/minlang/textcharter/default_en.asp (accessed 06 April 2018).

Council of Europe (1995) *Framework Convention for the Protection of National Minorities*. Strasbourg. See https://rm.coe.int/16800c10cf (accessed 06 April 2018).

Council of Europe (2012) *A Framework of Reference for Pluralistic Approaches to Languages and Cultures*. Strasbourg. See http://www.ecml.at/tabid/277/PublicationID/82/Default.aspx (accessed 06 April 2018).

Doyé, P. (2004) A methodological framework for the teaching of intercomprehension. *Language Learning Journal* 30 (1), 59–68.

EACEA/Eurydice (2012) *Key Data on Teaching Languages at School in Europe 2012*. Brussels: Education, Audiovisual and Culture Executive Agency (EACEA). See http://eacea.ec.europa.eu/education/eurydice/documents/key_data_series/143EN.pdf (accessed 06 April 2018).

Glaser, K. (2007) *Minority Languages and Cultural Diversity in Europe: Gaelic and Sorbian Perspectives*. Clevedon: Multilingual Matters.

Klein, H. and Stegmann, T. (eds) (2000) *EuroComRom – die sieben Siebe: romanische Sprachen sofort lesen können*. Aachen: Shaker.

Land Brandenburg (2014) Gesetz über die Ausgestaltung der Rechte der Sorben/Wenden im Land Brandenburg. See https://bravors.brandenburg.de/gesetze/swg#6 (accessed 06 April 2018).

Land Brandenburg (2016) Gesetz über die Schulen im Land Brandenburg. http://bravors.brandenburg.de/gesetze/bbgschulg_2016 (accessed 06 April 2018).

Landry, R. and Bourhis, R. (1997) Linguistic landscape and ethnolinguistic vitality: An empirical study. *Journal of language and Social Psychology* 16 (1), 23–49.

Marx, N. (2014) Häppchen oder Hauptgericht? Zeichen der Stagnation in der deutschen Mehrsprachigkeitsdidaktik. *Zeitschrift für Interkulturellen Fremdsprachenunterricht Didaktik und Methodik im Bereich Deutsch als Fremdsprache* 19 (1), 8–24.

Mazza, E. (2004) Konstruktivistische Lerntheorien und fremdsprachliche Unterrichtspraxis am Beispiel Italienisch als Tertiärsprache. In B. Hufeisen and N. Marx (eds) *Beim Schwedischlernen sind Englisch und Deutsch ganz hilfsvoll: Untersuchungen zum multiplen Sprachenlernen* (pp. 33–46). Frankfurt am Main: Lang.

Mehlhorn, G. (2014) Interkomprehension im schulischen Russischunterricht? Ein Experiment mit sächsischen Schülerinnen und Schülern der Klassenstufe 8. *Zeitschrift für Interkulturellen Fremdsprachenunterricht* 19 (1), 148–168.

Meißner, F.-J. (1993) Interlexis: ein europäisches Register und die Mehrsprachigkeitsdidaktik (Französisch/Spanisch). *Die neueren Sprachen: Zeitschrift für Forschung und Unterricht auf dem Fachgebiet der modernen Fremdsprachen* 92 (6), 532–554.

Moseley, C. (ed.) (2010) *Atlas of the World's Languages in Danger* (3rd edn). Paris: UNESCO Publishing.

Neumann, I. (2014) *'Weil es eine sprechenswerte Sprache ist': Einstellungen von Schülern des Niedersorbischen Gymnasiums Cottbus zur sorbischen Sprache und Kultur.* Bautzen: Sorbisches Institut.

Neumann, M. (2008) *Sorben (Wenden): eine Brandenburger Minderheit und ihre Thematisierung im Unterricht; Sorben (Wenden) in Brandenburger Rahmenlehrplänen.* Potsdam: Universitätsverlag.

Nitzsche, J. (2015) Das virtuelle sorbische Siedlungsgebiet wird urbar gemacht: einige Aspekte der Digitalisierung im sorbischen Kontext. In E. Tschernokoshewa, I. Keller and F. Jacobs (eds) *Einheit in Verschiedenheit. Kulturelle Diversität und gesellschaftliche Teilhabe von Minderheiten auf dem Prüfstand* (pp. 53–70). Münster/New York: Waxmann.

Paul, E. (2002) Zur Herausbildung des Leseverstehens an polnischen, tschechischen, und obersorbischen Texten als einer rezeptiven Kompetenz vor dem Hintergrund von Spracherfahrungen des Russischen. *Praktika: Forum für den Russisch-Unterricht* 1 (2002), 6–12.

Pellerin, M. (2014) Language tasks using touch screen and mobile technologies: Reconceptualizing task-based CALL for young language learners. *Canadian Journal of Learning and Technology* 40 (1), 1–23.

Prensky, M. (2001) Digital natives, digital immigrants. *On The Horizon* 9 (5), 1–6.

Ratajczak, C. (2011) *Vom Image einer Minderheitensprache.* Bautzen: Domowina-Verlag.

Sayer, P. (2010) Using the linguistic landscape as a pedagogical resource. *ELT Journal* 64 (2), 143–154.

Schön, F. and Scholze, D. (eds) (2014) *Sorbisches Kulturlexikon.* Bautzen: Domowina-Verlag.

Seidel, A. and Wächter-Springer, L. (1997) Wenn Anfänger keine Anfänger sind – Sprachgeschichte und originale Texte: Empfehlenswertes für den Russischunterricht in Klasse 11. Teil I. *Fremdsprachenunterricht* 5 (1997), 364–372.

Senatsverwaltung für Bildung, Jugend und Wissenschaft Berlin, Ministerium für Bildung, Jugend und Sport des Landes Brandenburg (2015a) *Rahmenlehrplan Berlin-Brandenburg. Teil A: Bildung und Erziehung in den Jahrgangsstufen 1–10.* See bildungsserver.berlin-brandenburg.de/fileadmin/bbb/unterricht/rahmenlehrplaene/Rahmenlehrplanprojekt/amtliche_Fassung/Teil_A_2015_11_16web.pdf (accessed 06 April 2018).

Senatsverwaltung für Bildung, Jugend und Wissenschaft Berlin, Ministerium für Bildung, Jugend und Sport des Landes Brandenburg (2015b) *Rahmenlehrplan Berlin-Brandenburg. Teil B: Fachübergreifende Kompetenzentwicklung.* See bildungsserver.berlin-brandenburg.de/fileadmin/bbb/unterricht/rahmenlehrplaene/Rahmenlehrplanprojekt/amtliche_Fassung/Teil_B_2015_11_10_WEB.pdf (accessed 06 April 2018).

Spieß, G. (2002) Niedersorbisch. In M. Okuka (ed.) *Lexikon der Sprachen des europäischen Ostens* (pp. 323–325). Klagenfurt: Wieser.

The New London Group (*Cazden, C., Cope, B., Fairclough, N., Gee, J., Kalantzis, M., Kress, G., Luke, A., Luke, C., Michaels, S. and Nakata, N.M.*) (1996) A pedagogy of multiliteracies: Designing social futures. *Harvard Educational Review* 66 (1), 60–92.
Trim, J.L.M. (ed.) (2001) *Common European Framework of Reference for Languages: Learning, Teaching, Assessment* (12th edn). New York: Cambridge University Press.
Warschauer, M. and Healey, D. (1998) Computers and language learning: An overview. *Language Teaching* 31, 57–71.
Zybatow, L.N. and Zybatow, G. (2004) Die EuroCom-Strategie als Weg zur europäischen Mehrsprachigkeit: EuroComSlav. In D. Rutke (ed.) *Europäische Mehrsprachigkeit: Analysen – Konzepte – Dokumente* (pp. 65–96). Aachen: Shaker.

9 When Non-Romance Languages Break the Linguistic Contract in Romance Languages Chat Rooms: Theoretical Consequences for Studies on Intercomprehension

Sílvia Melo-Pfeifer

Introduction

In this contribution, different concepts and contexts of multilingual interaction will be mapped to explain a preference for 'intercomprehension' in the field of foreign language (FL) education. Subsequently, interactional instances of linguistic contract (see Bono & Melo-Pfeifer, 2011; Degache, 2006) violation within the scope of communication between Romance languages (RL) in chat rooms will be analyzed, as a particular lens for the study of intercomprehension. The interactions that will be part of the empirical study occurred on the Galanet platform, which was conceived to understand the functioning of online interaction between speakers of different RL. The communicative contract for the project stated that all (and only) RL (e.g. Catalan, French, Italian, Portuguese, Spanish and Romanian) could be used to communicate in the chat room, following the principle that each participant should use their RL and try to understand the other speakers'. However, as noted in previous studies (Bono & Melo-Pfeifer, 2011; Melo-Pfeifer, 2014), English, Flemish, German or Fulani were also brought into the communicative scenario, challenging the rather monoglossic, Romance-only communicative contract. The specific reasons why those non-RL were used in this communicative scenario remain unexplored. In this contribution, the following research questions will be answered:

- Which non-RL are mobilized in multilingual RL chats, during a Galanet session? What are the relationships to students' multilingual biographies?
- What roles do these instances of linguistic and communicative contract violation play in the interaction?
- How do interactional partners react to the introduction of non-RL? What interactional dynamics follow a violation of the communicative contract?

Our hypothesis is that students' use of their entire communicative and linguistic repertoires is an act of multilingual identity performance (Norton, 2013; Pavlenko & Blackledge, 2004) and a sign of multiple affective belongings.

What are We Talking About? Mapping Multilingual Interaction through Coexisting Concepts

Multilingual interaction designates the fact that interlocutors taking part in a communicative event make use of several linguistic resources (combined with other semiotic resources). This does not automatically mean that speakers do not share a common mother tongue or that they do not share some part of their linguistic repertoires. Indeed, interlocutors may have many different motivations when using several languages. Play, humor and 'identity work', parallel to pragmatic needs, may prompt the utilization of more than one language and this combined use of semiotic resources may not be a direct consequence of linguistic deficit or lack of communicative skills.

Whether speakers resort to two or more languages in a communicative event in order to solve communicative problems, achieve shared meaning or play with words and repertoires, the truth is that multilingual interaction challenges a common (mis)conception: that communication, in order to be efficient or to promote equality between speakers, should be monolingual. As Canagarajah (2012: 1) recalls, interactional multilingual practices challenge a 'monolingual orientation to communication' and, indeed, to the analysis of communication, we would add.

Several concepts used in Applied Linguistics and Language Education challenge this monolingual orientation and defend *ad hoc* multilingual norms. Table 9.1 offers a glimpse of those concepts, organized alphabetically, and tries to provide a standard mainstream definition for them.

Some of these concepts are, we are tempted to say, quite similar, and trying to distinguish them is a hard task, condemned to be Sisyphean, as new terms to talk about multilingual communication are constantly being proposed. Furthermore, it may be somewhat unimportant to frame these concepts, as, from our perspective, they are more the result of individual

Table 9.1 Concepts referring to multilingual interaction

Concept	Definition	Author(s)
Codemeshing	Mixed use of vernaculars with standard majority language of communicative modes and symbol systems in texts[a] and text production.	Canagarajah (2011)
Code-switching	Interlocutors switch between languages intra- or inter-sententially to achieve communicative purposes or solve a situated linguistic problem.	Auer (1998)
Crossing	Merged or alternate use of linguistic resources as a sign of identity affiliation and identity indexicality.	Rampton (1995)
Intercomprehension	Each interlocutor speaks one language and understands the one(s) of the other(s), adjusting productive strategies in the mother tongue to interlocutors, mainly within the scope of a linguistic family.	Degache (2006); Doyé (2005)
Interproduction	Each interlocutor makes (additional) efforts to adapt the production in the mother tongue, facilitating the comprehension of their interlocutors.	Capucho (2011, 2012)
Lingua receptiva	Combination of receptive multilingualism and intercomprehension, but not restricting either to closely related languages or to speakers using their mother tongue.	Ten Thije (2013, 2014)
(Linguistic) Mediation	Situation, usually bilingual, where speakers do not share a language of communication and a third party functions as 'bridge builder'.	Council of Europe (2001); Reimann and Rössler (2013)
Metrolingualism	Collaborative and creative management of linguistic resources in everyday life, in urban hyper-complex and hyper-diverse visual and sound linguistic landscapes.	Pennycook and Otsuki (2015)
Polyglot dialog	Symmetric communication form, each interlocutor uses their own language and has enough passive linguistic skills in the language of the other.	Posner (1991)
Polylanguaging	Speakers use a collection of linguistic entities, which are bound up and articulated, for achieving communicative aims.	Jørgensen (2008)
Receptive multilingualism	Interlocutors understand each other's languages, because of the receptive competence they possess, due to linguistic familiarity.	Braunmüller and Zeevaert (2001)
Semi-communication	Situation where speakers, because they do not share a mother tongue, use their first languages and partially those of their interlocutors simultaneously.	Braunmüller and Zeevaert (2001)
Translanguaging	Speakers use the full length of their plurisemiotic repertoires, without any consideration of linguistic borders,[b] which are strategically combined to achieve communicative goals.	Canagarajah (2012); García and Wei (2014); Lewis *et al.* (2012)
Translingual practices	All communicative practices that go beyond monolingual orientations to communication and that consider other meaning containers.	Canagarajah (2011, 2013)

[a] Blommaert (2008) calls it 'heterography'.

[b] The concept of translanguaging posits that multilingual speakers have just one linguistic system, in which several semiotic resources (among them linguistic resources) combine or even merge together to constitute the full communicative potential of individuals. It also sees that 'named languages are social, not linguistic, objects' (Otheguy *et al.*, 2015: 281).

positioning, ideological standing points, disciplinary backgrounds or research and linguistic traditions than a clear-cut distinction of communicative situations (see García & Wei [2014] for an attempt previous to ours). As stated by Lewis *et al.* (2012: 656) 'the terminology list [above] reveals the recent profusion of a multiplicity of overlapping terminology. Do they all refer to the same concept, or are there subtle variations and differences, or even different concepts? The danger, in breaking new ground, is that we are setting up a maze of terminology'.[1]

Table 9.1 provides some answers to Lewis *et al.*'s questions: there are indeed more or less subtle differences and some are actually different concepts, thus referring to relatively different situations and 'mechanics of communication'.

With this conceptual profusion in mind, Suresh Canagarajah proposes the umbrella term 'translingual practice' to designate all communicative practices dealing with more than one language and encompassing several semiotic resources. More recently, a new challenging concept has emerged: translanguaging. This concept posits the inseparability – or even the merging – of different linguistic codes and other semiotic tools. From this perspective, translanguaging is quite close to 'polylanguaging', but quite different from code-switching, which emphasizes separate codes playing together within a clear linguistic and pragmatic 'grammar of use'.

Some of these concepts (e.g. polyglot dialog, receptive multilingualism, intercomprehension, interproduction and lingua receptiva) bring forward the role of linguistic similarities across languages, often *within* but not *limited to* the same linguistic family, and previous knowledge (even if not consciously retrieved) in the co-construction of meaning. The theoretical framework that has been privileged by researchers is one that analyzes communication between speakers of languages of the same linguistic family (e.g. Romance, Germanic or Slavic) and thus languages partially transparent, even if recent attempts open up this narrow perspective (see 'interproduction'). Among these concepts, receptive multilingualism, intercomprehension and lingua receptiva value the ability to understand the utterances of other interlocutors (as we can guess from the names 'receptive' and 'comprehension'). Interproduction, in turn, values the ability to co-construct meaning (even if, from the very beginning, this co-construction was put forward in studies dealing with intercomprehension from an interactional perspective, as Araújo e Sá & Melo [2007] illustrate) and goes beyond linguistic families.

Other concepts, such as crossing, polylanguaging and metrolingualism, are better suited to refer to communicative acts embedded within a strong identity affirmation in hyper-complex linguistic scenarios. Here then, identity and group affiliation is performed through the use of different linguistic resources, belonging or not belonging to the same linguistic family. Codemeshing, in turn, has been applied to describe processes of crosslinguistic practices in writing.

All these concepts can potentially cover a range of situations when two or more languages (or linguistic resources, depending on the paradigm) are present. The only exception could be the concept of 'linguistic mediation', as it is usually described in terms of someone facilitating the contact in bilingual situations, where the mediator (a third person) has the command of the two languages being separately used by the two interlocutors or the two groups.

Even if the conceptual borders are difficult to draw, it is undeniable that the proliferation of terms and expressions in the field of multilingual interaction is a sign of two realities: (i) a paradigm shift that considers multilingual interaction worth researching, beyond monolingual orientations to communication; and (ii) the increasing visibility and frequency of multilingual communication phenomena. Additionally, our empirical analysis of instances of violation of the communicative contract will show that a clear-cut separation of these concepts is even more difficult when analyzing the *hic et nunc* of multilingual interaction, even when it is produced within a specific framework (intercomprehension between RLs).

Intercomprehension between RLs

From all the concepts available, we will refer in this work to the concept of intercomprehension. The obvious question is: Why?

If we look at the complex conceptual landscape used to analyze multilingual interaction, we see that some of the concepts privilege multilingual interaction among speakers of a certain linguistic family – this is precisely the context of our study. Furthermore, the concept of intercomprehension was the first to be included in studies in FL education (even if mainly in the field of written comprehension of neighboring languages), across linguistic and educative scenarios and in initial and continuous teacher education. Another important argument, directly related to the theme of this volume, is the fact that it was intercomprehension that first paid attention to multilingual electronic communication (email, discussion forums and chats) among speakers of closely related languages. Summing up, the combination of these three criteria – communication between speakers of one language family, usage in academic fields of education/pedagogy and its connection to online multilingual interaction in several European projects – has led us to adopt this concept.

Intercomprehension refers to a mode of communication where each speaker uses his/her language(s) and understands the language(s) of the other(s). Not needing a common lingua franca, it stresses the role of interlinguistic transparency in order to access and co-construct meaning. For intercomprehension to occur, it is necessary to combine those transparencies with the mutual effort of comprehension between speakers, who thus have to make a double effort. Firstly, the effort to understand and capture the meaning of the combination of several sense containers (posture, gaze, languages, etc.). Secondly, the effort to produce accessible output, namely by reducing the linguistic distance between utterances and interlocutors (selection of transparent vocabulary), combining several meaning-makers (transsemiotic compound) that can eventually improve understanding and providing sense-redundancy through the conscious use of communicative strategies (use of synonyms and paraphrases, for example). These efforts of understanding and production, which are dialectic and interdependent, are indispensable in overcoming linguistic and communicative barriers and therefore in negotiating and constructing meaning in the multilingual interaction.

Accordingly, intercomprehension promotes more authentic communication (since production occurs in the mother tongue or in an RL of each speaker's choice), while understanding, which is always present in any interaction, is mediated by the presence of cognates and context ingredients, among others. This means that each interlocutor is simultaneously an expert of his/her language(s) and a potential learner of other languages. Such symmetry of the linguistic status potentially reduces hierarchy among participants and promotes a more balanced sharing of voice, floor and communicative roles. As a result, intercomprehension in RLs from an interactional perspective could be said to assume the following principles (Melo-Pfeifer, 2015: 102):

- RLs establish a linguistic *continuum* that allows interlocutors to effectively engage in conversations, as languages have many lexical cognates and are also syntactically partially transparent;
- interlocutors develop creative and additional strategies to co-construct meaning, which go beyond linguistic resources;
- intercomprehension involves interlocutors in the ongoing co-construction of context, forms and meaning, community solidarity and linguistic well-being;
- productive and receptive skills in RLs are interdependent and reliant on multiple linguistic and non-linguistic resources at the same time;
- intercomprehension between RLs is multisemiotic and multimodal.

Empirical Study: Instances of Linguistic Contract Breakdown

The Galanet project

Galanet[2] was a European project that gave birth to a homonym online platform aimed at creating multilingual interaction conditions among students mastering at least one RL, either as a so-called mother tongue or as a 'reference language' (that could act as a 'bridge' between RL speakers). The Galanet platform includes synchronic (chat) and asynchronic communicational tools (discussion forum and email) conceived to provide situations for intercomprehension. Creating multilingual conditions to communicate was thus the main goal of Galanet, i.e. not to teach/learn FLs (which may however happen in parallel to communication), but rather the actual communicative practice of intercomprehension.

The platform (Figure 9.1) follows a project-oriented approach, as the participants are meant to develop a collaborative project: the production of a multilingual 'press dossier' on an intercultural theme previously negotiated between participants.

The platform can be said to be visually organized around two representations: a temporal and a physical representation. In terms of the temporal representation, a Galanet session develops in four interdependent and sequential phases (see Araújo e Sá *et al.* [2010] for details on tasks), as shown in Figure 9.1 (left side): (1) breaking the ice and choice of a theme; (2) brainstorming; (3) collecting documents and debate; and (4) elaborating and publishing the press dossier.

In terms of physical representation, the platform visually reproduces different work locations: a welcome desk (center), a private bureau, the library (bottom left, where participants can deepen their knowledge about a particular RL or about the functioning of online and multilingual communication) and a resource center (next to the library, where participants can develop particular competences, usually written or oral receptive skills in several RLs), a forum (top left) and a meeting room (top right, a space to complete collaborative tasks and produce the 'press dossier').

During the Canosession (the second intercomprehension session in the Galanet platform, between February and May 2004, presented here; see also Araújo e Sá *et al.* [2010] and Melo-Pfeifer [2014, 2016]), 13 teams from six countries (Argentina, Belgium, France, Italy, Portugal and Spain) participated in the session (with 236 participants, students and tutors counted together), discussing the theme '*Ridiamo per le stesse cose?... Y*

Figure 9.1 The home page of the Galanet platform (http://deste.umons.ac.be/galanet/)

a-t-il un humour romanophone?' ('*Do we laugh at the same things?... Is there a RL humour?*'). Even if almost all participant teams share at least a bilingual experience and all of them have a multilingual goal (several target languages), French was an RL known in all teams and also the language that was most often signaled as the 'target language'. We can thus characterize the communicative situations happening within this project (and even being stimulated by it) as multi-plurilingual (Ehrhart, 2010), as plurilingual individual repertoires and a multilingual social space co-exist (Melo-Pfeifer, 2015, 2016).

Corpus and methodological path

The sequences analyzed here were collected through the Galanet project. They were chosen as analytical objects because they show the violation of the RL-only linguistic contract, making us wonder whether or not it is possible to define intercomprehension within multilingual but monoglossic Romance-only norms, without taking into account subject agency and complete linguistic repertoires.

We identified 25 chat sequences (from a much larger corpora, Melo [2006]), ranging from 4 to 84 turns, where non-RLs were used. The sequences are delimited in such a way that the context in which a non-RL was used would be clear and what kind of meta-linguistic or meta-communicative comments (if any) they triggered.

Table 9.2 shows how many times each non-RL emerged during the session and if they were elicited by interlocutors or spontaneously used or both, answering our first research question.

It is interesting to observe that only mother tongues not belonging to the RL family were elicited (Flemish) or announced (Fulani) by speakers. All the other languages that integrate students' repertoires as an FL were spontaneously used (as the students themselves clarify in the chat interventions).

After identifying all the sequences where non-RLs were used, we developed a detailed analysis of the roles played by those languages (expanding the results from Melo-Pfeifer [2014]) and of the communicative

Table 9.2 Violations of the linguistic contract

Languages	Elicited/announced by interlocutors	Spontaneously used	Number of sequences
English	–	14	14
Flemish	1	–	1
German	–	5	5
Fulani	1	–	1
Chinese	–	2	2
Arabic	–	2	2

work that followed those contract violations. The results are presented in the next section.

Results: Identity, Humor and Linguistic Policing

A preliminary observation can be made: sequences, generally occurring in the beginning of a chat session, introducing languages less known and less shared (Arabic, Chinese, Fulani and Flemish), are shorter and limited to salutations. So, they are clearly used to define the communicative situation as multilingual.

Regarding the roles played by those languages – our second research question – they can be seen as remediation tools helping to solve communicative problems, signs of identity, markers of play and humor, and socialization tools in a multilingual environment (Table 9.3). As a remediation tool, languages can be used to overcome linguistic opacities and restore intercomprehension, being accompanied by non-verbal cues specific to chat conversation (symbols, smileys, capital letters, expressive punctuation, etc.) (Melo-Pfeifer, 2014). Identity marks refer to languages that, not being shared by other speakers, are used to accentuate or value an affective affiliation or a personal trait. This may be a special relationship to a heritage language or to the learning of an FL, considered special or worthwhile mentioning (Norton, 2013) because of the linguistic mark or the cognitive consideration it may stimulate in other interlocutors. Forbidden languages may also be used to foster play and humor in multilingual communication, namely when combined with other sense containers as smileys or capital letters, which help uncover pragmatic intentionality. As for socialization tools, unpredicted languages are used to greet, to salute or to end a conversation. They perform precise speech acts and they are attached to the communicative goals of language learning.

Again, from the categories described above, we can see that English has a particular role in the interaction. Besides the frequency of use (we must acknowledge it is the most common FL included in students' linguistic repertoires), English is the only language that is used in three different

Table 9.3 Roles played by non-RLs

Languages	Remediation tool	Identity mark	Markers of play and humor	Socialization tool	Total occurrences
English	8	–	6	4	18
Flemish	–	2	–	–	2
German	–	–	–	5	5
Fulani	–	1	–	–	1
Chinese	–	–	–	2	2
Arabic	–	–	–	2	2
Total	8	3	6	14	30

Table 9.4 'My name is Bond'

Sequence 1: Play and humor	**English translation**
[JavierT] alexander?	[JavierT] alexander?
[xander] nao	[xander] no
[xander] pedro	[xander] pedro
[xander] pedro	[xander] pedro
[xander] my name is bond	[xander] my name is bond
[xander] pedro bond	[xander] pedro bond
[JavierT] ;)	[JavierT] ;)

Table 9.5 'Menda es una palabra típica del español'

Sequence 2: Remediation tool	**English translation**
[SaulL] Menda es una palabra típica del español	[SaulL] Menda is a typical Spanish word [palabra]
[bogdana] palabra = ?	[bogdana] palabra = ?
[colombia] mot = palabra	[colombia] word [mot] = palabra
[SaulL] word	[SaulL] word
[AnnaïkG] = parole	[AnnaïkG] = word [parole]

roles, the only language that is used for purposes of humor (Sequence 1, Table 9.4) and the only forbidden language used as a remediation tool (Sequence 2, Table 9.5).

Sequence 1 (Table 9.4) illustrates the making of or the interactional merging of fiction (reference to British James Bond) and reality (as the student's name really is Pedro) in identity construction and/or performance online, in a scenario marked by the physical invisibility of participants and their anonymity.

In Sequence 2 (Table 9.5), resorting to English fulfills a different goal: solving Bogdana's linguistic trouble related to the opacity of the Spanish noun 'palabra'. English, however, does not occur in isolation as a strategy of repair, but is used aside legitimate RL: French ('mot') and Italian ('parole').

It is interesting to observe that only non-RLs with mother tongue status are used as identity marks. Sequence 3 (Table 9.6) illustrates how one participant explicitly related his/her origin through the use of a heritage language.

It is also interesting to note the fact that (Portuguese) students who have been learning Arabic and Chinese for only a couple of months already feel free to use those languages for communicative purposes, relating them to their linguistic learning biographies (Sequence 4, Table 9.7).

This means that less shared languages are used less frequently and with only some specific purposes: to increase the communicativeness of the platform, increase the possibilities of multilingual contact and perform learner or personal identities. Chinese and Arabic are indeed used solely to greet other participants, in very stereotyped contexts and situations.

Regarding the third research question, we can say there are two major communicative events that take place with the violation of the communicative contract: discussion of linguistic biography and linguistic

Table 9.6 'Ça ne dérange pas si je parle en poular'

Sequence 3: Identity mark	English translation
[Ana] ça ne dérange pas si je parle en poular	[Ana] will you be bothered if I speak Fulani
[Jean-PierreC] C'est quoi le poular?	[Jean-PierreC] What is Fulani?
[Ana] jc'est ma langue natale	[Ana] It's my mother language
[Ana] no la conoces??	[Ana] don't you know it??
[Jean-PierreC] Tu peux toujours essayer.	[Jean-PierreC] You can always try
[Ana] tana alla ton?	[Ana] tana alla ton?
[Jean-PierreC] Tana alla ton doit vouloir dire comment ça va?	[Jean-PierreC] Tana alla ton could mean « how are you »?
[Ana] très bien!!!	[Ana] very good!!!
[Ana] que fuerte !!	[Ana] whowww !!

Table 9.7 'ni hao !!! = Ola, salut hola em chines'

Sequence 4: Socialization tool	English translation
[lusitana] ni hao !!! = Ola, salut hola em chines	[lusitana] ni hao !!! = Ola, salut hola em chines [Hello in Chinese]
[AnnaïkG] Salut	[AnnaïkG] Hello
[tita] ni hao	[tita] ni hao
[carla] nihao	[carla] nihao
[tita] ni men hao	[tita] ni men hao
[xander] ola	[xander] Hello
[guidiguidi] nimen hao	[guidiguidi] nimen hao

policing (Blommaert *et al.*, 2009). Indeed, when students break the linguistic contract, one positive consequence may be a discussion of the reasons why the students acted that way and articulation with their multilingual biography (origin or learning trajectories for example). So, this first consequence is related to biographic and identity aspects of students' profiles and may lead to the acknowledgment or even praise of individuality. The other consequence – linguistic policing – is potentially face threatening, because linguistic policing reminds others of the linguistic contract and often expresses a clear prohibition of language use. Table 9.8 illustrates which languages prompt which reactions.

Once again, it is noticeable that English plays a particular role. It is the language that most prompts linguistic policing and generates least curiosity, being taken for granted in the linguistic biographies. Indeed, only less shared languages originate discussions about linguistic biographies and learning paths (Sequence 5, Table 9.9). It is also quite remarkable that when English is used to solve intercomprehension problems (see category 'remediation tools'), it rarely leads to linguistic policing, being considered as 'the better of two evils' or 'the lesser evil': between misunderstanding and use of a forbidden lingua franca.

Sequence 6 (Table 9.10) illustrates how linguistic policing is performed in multilingual RL chat rooms, in this case related to the emergence of German and English in the Galanet platform. We can, however, observe that both languages are object of policing for different reasons (which

Table 9.8 Communicative paths opened up by non-RLs

Languages	Discussion of linguistic biographies	Linguistic policing	None/unspecific	Total sequences
English	–	5	9	13
Flemish	1	–	–	1
German	2	2	1	5
Fulani	1	–	–	1
Chinese	–	–	2	2
Arabic	1	–	1	2
Total	5	7	12	25

Table 9.9 'Pourquoi qalbu dis-tu toujours salame-alekum?'

Sequence 5: Discussion on linguistic biography	English translation
[qalbu] salame-alekum	[qalbu] salame-alekum
[AvataraA] hola qalbu	[AvataraA] hello qalbu
[AvataraA] de donde eres?	[AvataraA] where are you from?
[lusitana] alekum salam ,9	[lusitana] alekum salam ,9
[lusitana] ;)	[lusitana] ;)
[guidiguidi] portugal	[guidiguidi] portugal
[ChristianD] Pourquoi qalbu dis-tu toujours salame-alekum?	[ChristianD] qalbu why do you always say salame-alekum?
[carla] hola,salut ,olá a todos!	[carla] Hello everybody [in 3 languages]!
[guidiguidi] nao sabe dizer outra coisa	[guidiguidi] he cannot say anything else
[tita] salut	[tita] hello
[AvataraA] hola carla	[AvataraA] hello carla
[carla] qalbu dit ça parce qui'il etude arabe	[carla] qalbu says that because he studies Arabic

means that translanguaging outside the RL family is not always censored for the same motives).

Indeed, English is banned from the discussion and clearly proscribed from the conversation, this act of linguistic policing being frequently followed by the recalling of the project's philosophy: RLs only. This explains communicative acts of discouragement or prohibition like the ones shown in Table 9.11, from different excerpts.

Linguistic policing can get close to 'multilingual moral panic' (Heller & Duchêne, 2007) since English tends to be perceived as a 'language killer' and such speech acts are usually performed with the help of play and humor, to diminish their impact on speakers' faces. In turn, the prohibition of German is based on the common assumption that it is a difficult language that should therefore be kept aside (see Sequence 6 in Table 9.10). Its ban is not related to the communicative contract, but to the fact that students, even those who partially know this language (sometimes far more than Chinese or Arabic), have consciously banned it, supporting their decision primarily by resorting to a shared image of the language anchored on ideas of difficulty or incomprehensibility. This may even include linguistic policing in the forbidden language: „*[colombia] hier wird nicht deutsch gesprochen*" [Here German is not spoken] and „*[AnnaïkG] Es ist richtig das Deutsch*

Table 9.10 'hier wird nicht deutsch gesprochen'

Sequence 6: Language policing	English translation
[AlejandroG] Hallo, Wie geht's?	[AlejandroG] Hello, how are you?
[AnnaïkG] Gut gut!	[AnnaïkG] good good!
[romautos] :((	[romautos] :((
[romautos] nao percebo nada de alemao	[romautos] I don't get anything from Germam
[romautos] é uma nova língua romana???	[romautos] is it a new RL???
[romautos] ;)	[romautos] ;)
[AntonioR] ¿Qué te pasa Alejandro?	[AntonioR] what's wrong with you Alejandro?
[bogdana] je 'ai pas très bien compris...	[bogdana] I didn't really understand
[CristinaV] el alemán es muy complicado para mí	[CristinaV] German is too complicated for me
[AlejandroG] :)	[AlejandroG] :)
[colombia] hier wird nicht deutsch gesprochen	[colombia] Here German is not spoken
[AlejandroG] la hacemos romana pues	[AlejandroG] we should make it a RL
[CristinaV] oye oye, no más alemán , please¡¡¡¡¡	[CristinaV] oh oh, no more German, please!!!!!
[AlejandroG] :-)	[AlejandroG] :-)
[colombia] y tampoco inglés ;)	[colombia] and no English too ;)
[CristinaV] jajajjaja	[CristinaV] jajajjaja
[romautos] Please? Isso também é romano???	[romautos] Please? Is that also a RL???
[CristinaV] vale, de acuerdo	[CristinaV] OK, I agree
[AlejandroG] Bueno, vale, entoncers sólo románicas...	[AlejandroG] Well, ok, just RLs than...
[AntonioR] Amigos un poco de orden en este caos	[AntonioR] Friends, some order in this chaos
[romautos] acho que vou ter de re estudar as minhas bases de língua!!! estou a ficar perdina	[romautos] I think I have to restudy the basis of the language!!! I am getting lost
[AnnaïkG] Es ist richtig das Deutsch ist nicht eine Roman gesprochen (sic)	[AnnaïkG] It's true that German is not a Romance speaking[a] (sic)

[a] AnnaïkG is recalling the fact that German is not a Romance but a Germanic language

Table 9.11 Recalling the linguistic contract

Original	English translation
[floquet] aie quelqu'un qui parle anglais dans ce projet, il vas se faire éjecter :-)	[floquet] aie anybody speaking English here, will be ejected :-)
[djose] silvia no ingles	[djose] silvia no English
[djose] Benedetto qui nos si parla ingles	[djose] Benedetto here is no English spoken
[romautos] Please? Isso também é romano???	[romautos] Please? Is that also a RL???
[Sabrina] pas d'anglais!!!	[Sabrina] no English!!!
[qalbu] esto es un chat romanófico	[qalbu] this is a romanophonic chat

ist nicht eine Roman gesprochen" [It's true that German is not a Romance speaking]. Here, another difference may be observed: linguistic policing of English is never performed in English, a fact that symbolically also performs and accentuates its segregation.

Synthesis and Implications

We have seen that different languages erupt in the communicative scenario with different roles, leading to very different communicative dynamics. Among the languages that illegally erupt in these chat rooms is English, the only language used to solve linguistic problems, such as opacity, and perform a multilingual identity, play and humor. These facts, attached to the frequent instances of linguistic policing they raise, lead us to stress the very different status of English in these chat rooms (see also Melo-Pfeifer, 2014). Indeed, English is perceived as part of a shared plurilingual repertoire, and this entails two other consequences: it is always used without external elicitation and it is never subjected to linguistic policing when used to solve problems.

The other languages have a rather different status as they more frequently serve to socialize, to increase the linguistic diversity of the platform and to foster discussions on individual linguistic biographies. From this perspective, the use of 'non-RLs other than English' fosters reflection about learning and biographical paths: these other languages come to be perceived as exotic linguistic resources, contrary to English, which is 'taken for granted'.

Although the project described in this chapter did not have a focus on teaching or learning a specific FL, these conclusions may be significant from the perspective of third language acquisition and multilingual education both in the classroom and in online environments. Indeed, since English is the most widely taught language in the different European school systems, it may be called upon to be a function of cognitive mediation in FL learning, being an important strategic and linguistic anchor and preparing further learning paths. Furthermore, those results may help us to understand that insisting on shaping the FL learning as a monolingual and monoglossic space does not fit in with students' interests and the way they perceive, use and value their repertoires.

From a conceptual point of view, the instances of linguistic contract violation show that it is difficult to keep a multilingual and yet monoglossic linguistic contract. In fact, even if intercomprehension takes a clear multilingual orientation to communication, it still introduces borders that can be perceived as illegitimate: explored in this contribution is the fact that the full length of plurilingual repertoires is not authorized to communicate (see Melo-Pfeifer [2016] for other 'monoglossic stances'). Or, perhaps worse, that it is only partially considered, namely when it fulfills instrumental needs (solving problems and keeping the interaction going).

A second theoretical consequence, recalling the terminology in Table 9.1 and stemming from the fact that students do not abide by the communicative instruction 'RLs only' (even when the project explicitly stresses that rule), is that intercomprehension from an interactional perspective mainly in the context studied in this contribution, touches closely on other concepts such as 'crossing', 'polylanguaging', 'translanguaging' and 'lingua receptiva'.[3] Indeed, intercomprehension, as we saw in this contribution, generates semiotic behaviors and stances that strategically combine linguistic and non-linguistic resources as signs of identity and tools to achieve communicative aims and co-construct meaning, disregarding linguistic borders, typologically related languages or the use of a mother tongue. This does not mean that intercomprehension subsumes or is subsumed by the other concepts, but instead that it would be fruitful to engage in discussion where the different viewpoints on multilingual communicative practices come close. This dialogue would cross-fertilize research paths and views on different contexts, and legitimate multilingual interaction as a trustworthy research field, namely in language education and teacher training. Bringing all these perspectives together would highlight the 'normality' of interactions that resort to several languages and that activate the full plurilingual and strategic repertoires of social actors, as well as their consciousness about the interplay of linguistic and non-linguistic resources, ingredients of the context and situational constraints.

Notes

(1) Parallel to this one, we can also mention the danger of conceptual stretching inside each of those concepts, depending on research groups and research interests.

(2) Galanet (*Plateforme pour le développement de l'intercompréhension en Langues Romanes*) was a Socrates/Lingua Project, coordinated by Christian Degache of the Université Stendhal, Grenoble 3 (France). The same research group worked on two more recent projects: GALAPRO (www.galapro.eu) and Miriadi (https://www.miriadi.net/).

(3) And even with 'English as lingua franca'. It was not included in Table 9.1 because it does not explicitly refer to the use of more than one language in interaction.

References

Araújo e Sá, M.H. and Melo, S. (2007) On-line plurilingual interaction in the development of language awareness. *Language Awareness* 16 (1), 7–20.

Araújo e Sá, M.H., De Carlo, M. and Melo-Pfeifer, S. (2010) „O que diriam sobre os portugueses": Intercultural curiosity in multilingual chat-rooms. *Journal of Language and Intercultural Communication* 10 (4), 277–298.

Auer, P. (ed.) (1998) *Code-Switching in Conversation*. London: Routledge.

Blommaert, J. (2008) *Grassroots Literacy: Writing, Identity and Voice in Central Africa*. London: Routledge.

Blommaert, J., Kelly-Holmes, H., Lane, P., Peppänen, S., Moriarty, M., Pietikäinen, S. and Piirainen-Marsh, A. (2009) Media, multilingualism and language policing: An introduction. *Language Policy* 8, 203–207.

Bono, M. and Melo-Pfeifer, S. (2011) Language negotiation in multilingual learning environments. *International Journal of Bilingualism* 15 (3), 291–309.

Braunmüller, K. and Zeevaert, L. (2001) *Semikommunikation, rezeptive Mehrsprachigkeit und verwandte Phänomene: Eine bibliographische Bestandsaufnahme*. Hamburg: SFB 538.

Canagarajah, S. (2011) Codemeshing in academic writing: Identifying teachable strategies of translanguaging. *The Modern Language Journal* 95 (iii), 401–417.

Canagarajah, S. (2012) Translanguaging in the classroom: Emerging issues for research and pedagogy. *Applied Linguistics Review* 2, 1–28.

Canagarajah, S. (2013) *Translingual Practice: Global Englishes and Cosmopolitan Relations*. Abingdon: Routledge.

Capucho, M.F. (2011) Cooperating and innovating: Redinter, working together for the implementation of intercomprehension methodologies. In Pixel (ed.) *International*

Conference 'The Future of Education'. Conference Proceedings. See https://www.researchgate.net/publication/228417504_Cooperating_And_Innovating-Redinter_Working_Together_For_The_Implementation_Of_Intercomprehension_Methodologies (accessed 18 July 2016).

Capucho, M.F. (2012) L'Intercompréhension: un nouvel atout dans le monde professionnel [Intercomprehension: A new strength in the professional world]. In Ch. Degache and S. Garbarino (eds) *Actes du colloque IC2012. Intercompréhension: compétences plurielles, corpus, intégration*. See http://ic2012.u-grenoble3.fr/OpenConf/papers/67.pdf (accessed 18 July 2016).

Council of Europe (2001) *Common European Framework of Reference for Languages*. Cambridge: Cambridge University Press.

Degache, Ch. (2006) *Didactique du plurilinguisme: Travaux sur l'intercompréhension et l'utilisation des technologies pour l'apprentissage des langues* [*Didactics of Plurilingualism: On Intercomprehension and the Use of Technologies in Language Learning*]. Habilatation, Université Stendhal: Grenoble 3.

Doyé, P. (2005) *Intercomprehension: Guide for the Development of Language Education Policies in Europe: From Linguistic Diversity to Plurilingual Education. Reference Study*. Strasbourg: Council of Europe.

Ehrhart, S. (2010) Pourquoi intégrer la diversité linguistique et culturelle dans la formation des enseignants au Luxemburg. In S. Ehrhart, Ch. Hélot and A. Nevez (eds) *Plurilinguisme et Formation des Enseignants: une approche critique* (pp. 221–238). Bern: Peter Lang.

García, O. and Wei, L. (2014) *Translanguaging. Language, Bilingualism and Education*. Basingstoke: Palgrave Macmillan.

Heller, M. and Duchêne, A. (2007) Discourses of endangerment: Sociolinguistics, globalization and social order. In A. Duchêne and M. Heller (eds) *Discourses of Endangerment* (pp. 1–13). London: Continuum.

Jørgensen, J.N. (2008) Polylingual languaging around and among children and adolescents. *International Journal of Multilingualism* 5 (3), 161–176.

Lewis, G., Jones, B. and Baker, C. (2012) Translanguaging: Developing its conceptualization and contextualization. *Educational Research and Evaluation* 18 (7), 655–670.

Melo, S. (2006) Emergência e Negociação de Imagens das línguas em Encontros Interculturais Plurilingues em Chat. PhD thesis, Universidade de Aveiro.

Melo-Pfeifer, S. (2014) Intercomprehension between RLs and the role of English: A study of multilingual chat-rooms. *International Journal of Multilingualism* 11 (1), 120–137.

Melo-Pfeifer, S. (2015) An interactional perspective on intercomprehension between RLs: Translanguaging in multilingual chatrooms. *Fremdsprachen Lehren und Lernen. Zur Theorie und Praxis des Sprachunterrichts an Hochschulen* 44 (2), 100–113.

Melo-Pfeifer, S. (2016) Translanguaging in multilingual chat interaction: Opportunities for Intercomprehension between RLs. In W. Congcong and L. Winstead (eds) *Handbook of Foreign Language Research in the Digital Age* (pp. 188–207). Hershey, PA: IGI Global.

Norton, B. (2013) *Identity and Language Learning. Extending the Conversation* (2nd edn). Bristol: Multilingual Matters.

Otheguy, R., García, O. and Reid, W. (2015) Clarifying translanguaging and deconstructing named languages: A perspective from linguistics. *Applied Linguistics Review* 6 (3), 281–307.

Pavlenko, A. and Blackledge, A. (2004) *Negotiation of Identities in Multilingual Contexts*. Clevedon: Multilingual Matters.

Pennycook, A. and Otsuji, E. (2015) *Metrolingualism: Language in the City*. Abingdon: Routledge.

Posner, R. (1991) Der polyglotte Dialog: Ein Humanistengespräch über Kommunikation im mehrsprachigen Europa. In H. Hafner and A. Schwarz (eds) *Semiotik und Didaktik: Festschrift für Otto Keller zu seinem 65. Geburtstag* (pp. 6–10). Frankfurt: Lang.

Rampton, B. (1995) *Crossing: Language and Ethnicity among Adolescents.* Manchester: St Jerome Publishing.
Reimann, D. and Rössler, A. (eds) (2013) *Sprachmittlung im Fremdsprachenunterricht.* Tübingen: Narr Verlag.
Ten Thije, J. (2013) Editorial: Lingua receptiva (LaRa). *International Journal of Multilingualism* 10 (2), 137–139.
Ten Thije, J. (2014) The effectiveness of lingua receptiva (LaRa) in multilingual communication. *Applied Linguistics Review* 5 (1), 125–129.

Part 4
Multilingual Online Exchange and Telecollaboration

10 Developing Plurilingual Competence in the EFL Primary Classroom through Telecollaboration

Euline Cutrim Schmid

Introduction

In many parts of the world including Europe, foreign language classrooms are becoming increasingly multilingual and multicultural. In English as a foreign language (EFL) classes in Germany, for instance, third language (L3) acquisition has become a norm rather than an exception as a result of the migration processes of the last decades. This context creates new opportunities for EFL teachers. Research has shown that under certain circumstances, multilingualism favors the acquisition of additional languages and several authors have discussed advantageous cognitive and meta-linguistic abilities that bilinguals/multilinguals bring to the task of learning an additional language (e.g. Cenoz, 2009; Elsner, 2015; Jessner, 2006). In spite of these potential advantages, the literature has pointed out that the German educational system typically ignores the prior cultural and linguistic knowledge of multilingual learners (e.g. Engel *et al.*, 2009; Gogolin, 1994; Hesse & Göbel, 2009).

Research indicates that L3 learners have language-specific knowledge and competencies at their disposal that second language (L2) learners do not have. The literature has pointed to several aspects, such as enhanced levels of meta-linguistic awareness (e.g. Bialystok, 2009; Bos & Pietsch, 2006; Engel *et al.*, 2009; Jessner, 2006), more extensive and flexible use of language learning strategies (e.g. Schroeder & Stölting, 2005) and enhanced communicative sensitivity (e.g. Thomas, 1992). Nevertheless, research has shown that L3 learners do not always reach appropriate levels of proficiency in their first language (L1; or their L2) in order to be able to experience these cognitive advantages (Cummins, 1991; Wilden & Porsch, 2015), and they are not always aware of the benefits that their multilingual competence can bring to the process of learning an additional language (e.g. Oliveira & Anca, 2009; Volgger, 2010). Furthermore, several studies also indicate (e.g. De Angelis, 2011; Haukås, 2016; Ziegler, 2013) that foreign language teachers are typically not aware of these advantages, and even when they are, they demonstrate insufficient knowledge on approaches and strategies for exploiting language learners' multilingual resources. As a result, current demographic and sociolinguistic changes do not seem to have had a strong impact on foreign language teaching practice in Europe. Empirical school-based research (e.g. Horst *et al.*, 2010; Jessner, 2006) has shown, for instance, that EFL instruction is often perceived as separate from the instruction in the official language of the school, other foreign languages and the minority language of the students.

Over the past decade, a growing body of literature has pointed to the need to invest in the teaching and maintenance of immigrant children's heritage languages (e.g. Mehlhorn, 2010) so that multilingual learners can use their L1 knowledge as a strong foundation for additional language learning. The language teaching literature has also underscored the need to challenge the existing monolingual ideology present in many foreign language classrooms (e.g. Candelier, 2008). In the EFL context, for instance, several authors (e.g. Corcoll, 2013; Jessner, 2006; Piccardo, 2013) have suggested that teachers should encourage learners (especially multilinguals) to reflect and draw on their rich store of language information and skills in order to make them aware of their own meta-linguistic knowledge. Jessner (2006: 135) for instance, suggests that the teaching of EFL should serve to 'activate and support cognitive processes for further language learning, to provide a cognitive foundation for contrastive learning and reflection on language learning and also to create openness to linguistic and cultural diversity'. Along the same lines, Beacco and Byram (2003: 28) point out that the 'teaching of English should be conceived so as to stimulate speakers' plurilingualism and not block its later development in the name of a monolingual ideology'. These recommendations have created a call for the development and evaluation of innovative pedagogical resources and effective teaching practices that can assist teachers in exploiting the cognitive and meta-cognitive skills that multilinguals bring to the task of learning an additional language.

This chapter aims at contributing to this call by discussing the potential of an English as lingua franca (ELF) telecollaboration exchange for supporting the development of primary school learners' cross-linguistic and cross-cultural awareness in the multilingual/multicultural EFL classroom. The chapter reports on a two-year research project that investigated live communication between distant classes of young learners. The project exploited the technical affordances of synchronous computer-mediated communication (CMC) between primary school learners in France and Germany using live audio/video and screen sharing in a task-based framework. It was developed in a funded three-year Erasmus Plus European project to support interactive teaching with technologies

(ITILT2, http://www.itilt2.eu) and research data include class video recordings, participant observation and interviews.

The remainder of the chapter is structured as follows: The second section presents the literature review on pluralistic approaches. Then, the third section describes the research project and provides three examples of the developed computer assisted language learning (CALL) tasks, and the fourth section discusses the main research findings. The final section draws some general conclusions and makes suggestions for future work in this area.

Pluralistic Approaches to Foreign Language Education

In response to the recommendations discussed above, a few innovative pedagogical approaches have been proposed in the literature in the last two decades. Some of these approaches have been grouped together under the general umbrella of 'pluralistic approaches' (Candelier, 2008). Pluralistic approaches have been defined as approaches using teaching and learning activities involving several (i.e. more than one) languages and cultures and whose main goal is to help learners to establish links with what they already know and can already do with languages. In other words, they support the development of learners' plurilingual and intercultural competencies. The literature has discussed four main pluralistic approaches, which vary in terms of goals, objectives and expected outcomes.

The *cross-language approach*, for instance, is directed toward helping learners establish links between all languages studied within the school curriculum. It thus pushes for the comparison of languages rather than the teaching of languages in isolation of one another and is based on interdepartmental cooperation and integrated language pedagogy. Corcoll (2013) for instance, used a 'pedagogically based code switching' approach, in which Catalan and Spanish were integrated into EFL lessons in order to give primary school children in Barcelona the chance to translanguage and discover similarities and differences among the three languages. Horst *et al.* (2010) used the cross-language approach in a slightly different way. They investigated how language instruction can be designed to help learners build on their L1 knowledge. The authors designed and piloted a series of crosslinguistic awareness activities with Francophone learners of English (ages 9–10) at a school in Montreal. Both studies produced findings showing that the pluralistic approaches supported the development of learners' crosslinguistic awareness.

Another pluralistic approach that has become very influential, especially in the primary school context, is the *awakening to languages* approach. In this approach, pupils get into contact with different languages not because they should learn them, but to benefit from a process of 'decentralisation' (Candelier, 2008; Fidler, 2006). It is linked to the *language awareness* movement initiated by Hawkins (1984), and its main aim is to help young learners realize how languages work and how they structure culturally bound experiences. Several implementations of this approach have been discussed in the literature. Elsner (2014) and Lohe (2015) for instance, have reported on the MuViT project, which developed a concept for digitalized, multilingual talking books integrating different activities for the development of language and cross-linguistic awareness, and an authoring tool enabling children to produce and share their own multilingual storybooks within a web community. In Stille and Cummins's (2013) study, English learners experimented with ways to draw upon the multiple languages that they knew during literacy and curriculum learning activities. Both studies have shown that supporting students to express themselves using the full range of their language resources creates a teaching and learning context that validates students' linguistic repertoires and plurilingual identities. In the context of the MuViT project, for instance, Bündgens-Kosten and Elsner (2014) showed that trilingual students made use of their L1 and their L2 during collaborative reading in the L3.

The other two pluralistic approaches are the *intercomprehension* between related languages and the *intercultural* approaches. In the former approach, the learner works on two or more languages from the same linguistic family (Romance, Germanic, Slavic languages, etc.) in parallel. One of these languages is already known, and the main aim is to develop receptive skills in the target language. According to Candelier (2008), there has been little development of intercomprehension in schools (see chapters by Melo-Pfeifer and Pohl, this volume). The *intercultural approach*, on the other hand, has already had a clear influence on the methodology of language teaching and is therefore relatively well known. Most of the work in this area has focused on the use of telecollaboration to connect learners from different cultures, and help them to develop positive attitudes toward cultural diversity (e.g. Kramsch, 1998; Mueller-Hartmann, 2006; O'Dowd, 2006). Recently, there has been an increasing focus on telecollaboration exchanges whereby learners use a common foreign language, a lingua franca, instead of communicating with native speakers (e.g. Clavel-Arroitia & Pennock-Speck, 2015; Dooly, 2011; Guarda, 2013).

While early theories on the integration of culture into language teaching (Byram, 1997) suggested that learners should strive to reach native-like linguistic and sociocultural proficiency, more recent proposals have replaced the native speaker model with the notion of the intercultural speaker (e.g. Dooly, 2011). Lewis *et al.* (2011: 3) discuss the increase of multilateral online exchanges for learning language and culture and point out that 'multilateral exchanges reflect the changing reality of language learning in a globalized world where prolonged and intensive contact with one additional culture has given way to more fleeting encounters with multiple cultures, mediated by Web-based communication tools'. In the EFL context, more specifically, online exchanges increasingly use English as a lingua franca (ELF) for intercultural communication. This may reflect an acknowledgment by English language teachers that EFL learners are more likely to communicate with non-native than with native speakers.

The literature (e.g. Dooly, 2011; Guarda, 2013) has produced some research findings showing the potential advantages of this form of telecollaboration. Guarda (2013), for instance, points out that in these contexts learners are encouraged to move away from the rigid combination 'national language/culture' to explore several cultures at the same time by means of a single foreign language. This was the approach to telecollaboration used in the study described in this chapter. Our project investigated the potential of synchronous videoconferencing (VC) to support the development of learners' plurilingual competencies. VC is a form of computer-mediated communication that permits live, face-to-face interaction without recourse to the written language. During VC exchanges, learners can see and hear their interlocutors, and are involved in understanding and producing oral messages in real time.

Description of the Project

Setting the context

The main aim of the VC project was to exploit the potential of interactive technologies to create more learner-centered environments in which authentic target language communication could take place. Two primary schools in Germany and France were involved in the project from February 2013 to June 2015. Charts provide detailed information about the teachers (see Table 10.1) and learners (see Table 10.2) involved in the project.

Table 10.1 Information about participating teachers

French Teacher	German Teacher
Generalist primary school teacher	Generalist primary school teacher
Twenty years of classroom experience	Five years of classroom experience
Technologically fluent	Low level of technological expertise
Previous experience with VC	First experience with VC
Bilingual (French/Spanish) with special motivation for EFL teaching	Recent pre-service training on teaching EFL (CLT and TBLT approaches)

Table 10.2 Information about participating learners

French Pupils	German Pupils
Year 1: 25 pupils (aged 8-9) in 3rd grade Year 2: 25 pupils (aged 8-9) in 3rd grade	Year 1: 25 pupils (aged 7-8) in 2nd grade Year 2: 25 pupils (aged 8-9) in 3rd grade
One 90-minute session of EFL per week	Two 45-minute sessions of EFL per week
General pattern of EFL activities: • Teacher-led presentation • Carousel activities, Individual listening, exercises, worksheets • Short closing plenary session	Varied EFL activities: • Storytelling • Singing • Role plays • Games, arts and crafts
Used IWB regularly in all classes	Beginner users of IWB
Previous experience with VC exchanges	No previous experience with VC

The main research questions guiding the project were:

(1) How can an interactive whiteboard (IWB) support VC exchange between remote partners involving young learners?
(2) How well do task-oriented materials, activities and teaching techniques seem to promote effective learner–learner exchanges?

Since the German class had a high proportion of children with a migration background (80% of the pupils – 20), and many of them were learning English as a third or fourth language, the German team decided to pursue a third research question in order to investigate the potential impact of the project on the development of the German learners' plurilingual and intercultural competencies:

(3) Can such telecollaborative projects support the development of learners' crosslinguistic and cross-cultural awareness? If so, how?

Findings pertaining to Research Questions 1 and 2 have been discussed elsewhere (Cutrim Schmid & Whyte, 2015; Whyte & Cutrim Schmid, 2014). This chapter focuses specifically on the third research question, and thus only discusses research findings obtained on the German side of the telecollaboration.

The project placed special emphasis on the design of authentic language learning tasks implemented with the use of an IWB-based video communication software (Bridgit Conferencing Software) that supports whole-class online collaboration. The use of this software increases the functionality of the IWB by enabling live screen sharing, with a video and audio channel carried by a dedicated server. Webcam, microphones and speakers were connected to the classroom computers allowing learners in the French and German classes to communicate and interact with learning materials (through screen sharing) during live telecollaborative sessions.

Materials were developed involving information-gap tasks to exploit the affordances of both the VC format and the IWB tools and features. In the following, we describe three activities that were developed in the framework of the project.

Pedagogical activities

Session 1: Identity card

The first VC session was a familiarization session designed as described in Figure 10.1 with interactions in groups of four to five learners.

Session 2: Let's go shopping

In this session, the learners practiced food vocabulary as shown in Figure 10.2 with one pupil playing the shop assistant and two learners playing customers to select and pay for different foodstuffs.

Session 3: Breakfast time

In this VC session, learners prepared a breakfast table for a learner in the remote class, as detailed in Figure 10.3.

Topic	Getting to Know Each Other

Task	Create an identity card for each class member
Materials	IWB file containing a page for each group of 4 learners, including photos, texts (names, numbers), and icons (likes & dislikes).
Language	*Student 1:* What is your name? How old are you? When is your birthday? What do you like? *Student 2:* My name is...., I'm.... years old, my birthday is in..., I like dogs, football, dancing, etc...

Figure 10.1 Session 1: Identity card

Topic	Going Shopping

Task	Choose items from shelves to buy in supermarket
Materials	IWB file containing a page for a German supermarket (REWE) and another one for a French supermarket (E.Leclerc)
Language	*Shopkeeper:* Can I help you? Is that all? It's ... Euros *Customers:* I'd like..... That's all, How much is it?

Figure 10.2 Session 2: Let's go shopping

Data Collection and Data Analysis

Data were collected via a variety of qualitative research instruments, including classroom observations and field notes, video recordings of eight VC sessions, questionnaires, an in-depth interview with the teacher and focus group interviews with learners. The field notes were mainly descriptive of the lesson events as they unfolded, but also contained some of the researcher's thoughts regarding the impact of VC tasks on the pupils' language learning processes. The learner focus group interviews lasted approximately 30 minutes on average. The questions focused on the learners' general perceptions of the VC experience, possible challenges they faced and their suggestions for the design and implementation of future VC tasks. The teacher questionnaires contained nine open-ended questions focusing on the teacher's perceptions regarding the impact of the VC tasks on learners' motivation and language learning achievement. Task-based language learning was the pedagogical framework used for the design and analysis of VC tasks. Figure 10.4 provides an overview of the research procedure in the German context.

Grounded theory (Glaser & Strauss, 1967) was used for the qualitative analysis. Therefore, the research data were approached with relatively little preconceptions, as we endeavored to identify categories of meaning

Topic	Breakfast Time

Task	Make up a plate for a visitor's breakfast
Materials	IWB containing a page with a selection of food items (fridge, food shelf, kitchen table, plate, cutlery)
Language	*Host/hostess:* What would you like for breakfast"? Would you like some...on your....? How many...? *Visitor:* I'd like... please. Thank you.

Figure 10.3 Session 3: Breakfast time

from the data. The process of data collection and data analysis was facilitated by four university students (one per semester), who worked in the framework of the project as teaching assistants. The data were coded and categorized according to prominent themes that emerged from the data in response to the main research questions. Firstly, the transcripts of the teacher questionnaires and teacher in-depth interview, learner interviews, video-recorded VC interactions and field notes were coded for categories on an individual basis and analyzed across transcripts to identify common themes. This process facilitated the identification of the themes or topics that were recurrent in all sets of data. The quotes presented in this chapter are excerpts of general patterns found in the data.

Research Findings

The research findings show that the VC tasks were perceived as relevant and interactive. Both teachers remarked that the VC activities helped their learners to understand the purpose of learning a foreign language, and learners' perceptions revealed enhanced motivation and self-confidence in using the target language. Cutrim Schmid and Whyte (2015) and Whyte and Cutrim Schmid (2014) discuss research findings showing the potential

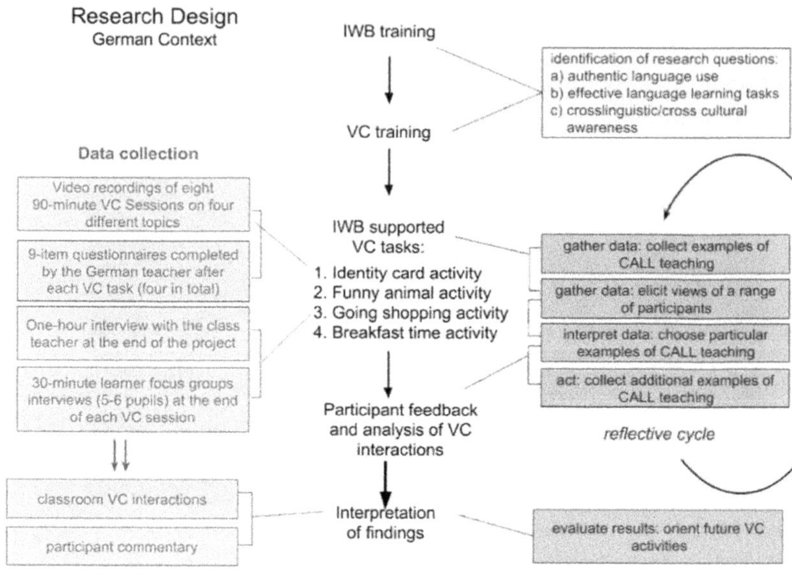

Figure 10.4 Research design and data collection: German context

of VC activities for providing extensive opportunities for language practice in authentic scenarios.

As already pointed out, the student population in the German school was characterized by sociocultural and linguistic diversity. Interview data from Germany indicate that the project created enhanced opportunities for the development of pupils' plurilingual competencies. Our findings have shown that the VC tasks promoted pupils' reflection on their own linguistic repertoires and on the role of ELF, and prompted them to compare and contrast different languages and cultural traditions. In the following, I discuss interview data on the teacher's and learners' perceptions on these issues.

Reflecting upon their own linguistic repertoires

As pointed out in the previous section, 80% (20) of the pupils in the German class had a migration background, and most children spoke German as a second language. Data obtained through interviews and classroom observations showed, however, that this linguistic and cultural diversity was often ignored in the EFL lessons. In fact, prior to the project, the class teacher knew relatively little about the pupils' plurilingual resources, and even the pupils themselves ignored several aspects of their classmates' cultural and linguistic backgrounds. These findings are in line with previous research showing that the German educational system typically ignores the prior cultural and linguistic knowledge of multilingual learners (e.g. Hesse & Göbel, 2009).

Research data have shown that the VC activities triggered spontaneous conversations about language and culture among learners. For instance, prior to the VC activities, the German pupils often heard the French teacher and her pupils speaking French to each other, and video-recorded data revealed that they frequently wondered what they were saying, made guesses and expressed their own opinions about that language. Furthermore, the pupils were invited to reflect systematically on the impact of the VC activities on their language learning processes during focus group interviews. The data have shown that these interviews also generated interesting discussions about the pupils' linguistic and cultural repertoires, as can be seen in the following sequence:

S4: I know a little bit of French. My Dad is Portuguese and he knows a little bit of French and he taught me some French.
T: Do you speak Portuguese at home with your Dad?
S4: Only with my Grandma and my Grandpa.
S5: But you can't really speak, can you?
T: So you can understand a little bit of Portuguese?
S4: Only some words from my Grandpa. For example 'Eis' means 'sorvete'.
T: What have you just said, Stefan?
S5: That I know three words in French.
T: OK
S2: I only know one French word: 'Oui'.
S5: This is not a French word!
S2: Yes, it is.
T: So tell us what it means.
S2: I don't know, but I heard it on TV.
T: 'Oui' means 'yes' in French. (Focus Group Interview – Second Grade, First Year)

This is a short extract of a long interview sequence, in which the pupils shared information about their familiarity with different languages and cultures. Prior to this sequence, the pupils had been asked to evaluate their language performance during the VC tasks and to reflect on possible challenges they faced. These questions generated a lively discussion not only about their English language competencies, but also about their intercultural experiences and skills in other languages. In this sequence, for instance, we learn that S4 has a Portuguese heritage and has limited knowledge of Portuguese, and S2 and S5 have already been in contact with the French language. In fact, the data have shown that the focus group interviews were used by the teacher as useful opportunities to learn more about the pupils' plurilingual repertoires. In the following sequence, for instance, the teacher took advantage of the VC interview to learn more about S2's cultural and linguistic background:

> T: Was it difficult for you to understand the French children?
> S2: Yes/No!
> T: Why was it not difficult for you?
> S2: I can speak good English because I was born in the US.
> T: Do you talk to your parents at home in English?
> S2: No, in Romanian.
> T: Did you go to Kindergarten in the US or in Germany?
> S2: In Germany and in Romania. (Focus Group Interview – Second Grade – First Year)

At the beginning of this sequence, the pupils were asked to evaluate their English comprehension skills in the framework of the VC project. In Line 2, S2 expressed confidence in his/her ability, and the teacher then asked a few follow-up questions in order to better understand his/her reply. The pupil's answers revealed that he/she had been exposed to at least three languages before primary school: English (birth in the United States), Romanian (his home language) and German (in kindergarten). Accounts such as this one were frequent in the interview data, which shows that the reflective discussions about the VC tasks were effectively used by the teacher as opportunities to (a) gain a better overview of the cultural and linguistic diversity present in her classroom, and (b) encourage the pupils to reflect on their own linguistic repertoires.

Reflecting on foreign language learning and the role of English as lingua franca

The research data have shown that the VC tasks enabled the pupils to grasp an understanding of the notion of English as the lingua franca of the contemporary world, since they could experience this abstract concept in a tangible way. In the following interview sequences, the class teacher referred to this aspect as one of the main added values of the project:

> That they can speak with French kids they wouldn't be able to speak otherwise. Because it was the same as last time they said 'Hey they're speaking French how can we talk to them? And it was the same thing as last time, they said.... do they understand German? Ah no! So we have to speak English! (Class teacher – Final Interview)
> They realize it's ... yeah...very important to learn a language you can communicate with everybody in the world. And that they learn this in

the second grade I think it's really great, not in the tenth or twelfth grade. (Class teacher – Final Interview)

In both sequences, the class teacher reflected on what she considered one of the main benefits of the project, i.e. raising pupils' awareness of the special role played by English as a language of international communication. As she explained in the first sequence, some pupils expressed anxiety when they first heard the remote class speaking French with their teacher in the few minutes preceding the first VC task. However, they quickly understood that they could still communicate with the French children because both classes were learning EFL. In the second interview sequence, the teacher added that it is especially valuable that they can develop this awareness very early in their language learning process.

During focus group interviews, the pupils also often reflected on the role of ELF and the potential challenges involved in interacting with non-native speakers of English. For instance, they often compared their language performances with those from the remote class and speculated on possible reasons for pupils' failures and difficulties, as can be seen in the following sequence:

T: So you didn't have any problems talking to the French children?
S4: I found it strange that when they said words like 'My birthday is in basketball'.
T: Did you find it weird that they made mistakes?
S3: Maybe they cannot speak so good English.
S4: We learn a lot of English.
S3: They are French and maybe they don't learn English every day. We learn English since the first grade. And they are in the third grade, I think.
S4: In the second. (Focus Group Interview – Second Grade – First Year)

In this sequence, the pupils were invited to reflect on their computer-mediated interaction with the French children. In the first line, S4 pointed out that the French children sometimes built sentences that made no sense, which he found 'weird'. In Line 3, S3 took the turn and speculated on possible reasons for the French pupils' difficulties. Her statements show that she empathized with the French pupils, and understood that, like them, the remote class spoke EFL, and thus depended on intensity and quality of foreign language instruction to perform well. As she pointed out in Lines 4 and 6, maybe 'they don't speak so good English' because 'they don't learn English every day' (as we do). In subsequent parts of the interview, the pupils continued to reflect on their own language performance and their language learning processes.

The VC tasks also triggered enriching discussions about the topic of 'language accent'. During the focus group interviews, several pupils mentioned that they noticed that the French pupils spoke English differently from them, which sometimes hindered their understanding, as can be seen in the following sequence:

S1: I always noticed that the French spoke English a bit differently from us.
T: And was it sometimes difficult for you to understand?
S1: Yes, they always said 'What do you like' (tried to imitate the French accent) and that I found difficult to understand.
[....]
S2: They also spoke a bit differently from the way we speak English. (Focus Group Interview – Second Grade – First Year)

Pupils' remarks, like those shown in this sequence, were often used by the teacher as opportunities to raise pupils' awareness to the topic of language transfer and the fact that all speakers of a foreign language, no matter what L1 they have, will often speak that foreign language with an accent. It was interesting for the pupils, for instance, to find out that they also spoke English with an accent.

These two sequences illustrate the type of reflection that took place in most of the learner focus group interviews. As the pupils evaluated the effectiveness of the VC project and analyzed their participation in the various VC tasks, they were also actively involved in reflecting on language and language learning, and thus possibly increasing their levels of meta-linguistic awareness. This section has presented research data indicating that the VC tasks created new opportunities for meta-linguistic reflections on key aspects of language awareness, such as: what it means to 'know' a language; how foreign languages are learned; and the role of ELF. The following section focuses more specifically on the development of cross-linguistic awareness, as the pupils compared the different languages involved in the project.

Comparing and contrasting different languages

As already pointed out, during VC tasks the learners used ELF and there was no German or French input in VC interactions. However, there was still some level of exposure to pupils' school languages throughout the project. For instance, the pupils could hear French/German being spoken in the remote classes prior to the beginning of the VC tasks, and the teachers sometimes supported their learners during VC interactions by translating words or sentences for them into their school languages. Furthermore, most French children had typical French names, and during the shopping activity, the names of the supermarkets and the product labels were kept in the original languages in order to enhance the authenticity of the task (e.g. 'Thon entier au naturel Cuit à Coeur').

The research data have shown that, even though the pupils used ELF during VC interactions, they also showed interest in each other's school languages. The German interview data, for instance, have shown that during focus group interviews the pupils talked about features of the French language (e.g. beautiful, easy), evaluated their level of French proficiency and discussed French speakers among their families. This shows that, even though the school languages were not given much prominence during the project, the pupils were still actively involved in comparing these languages with the languages they know. As the pupils engaged in reflection on their linguistic resources for instance, we have seen that a discussion about the French language led some pupils to talk about their proficiencies in other Romance languages (e.g. Romanian and Portuguese).

In the framework of this project, the exposure to at least three different languages could have been better exploited by the teacher for capitalizing on multilinguals' prior language knowledge. For instance, the pupils could have been encouraged to use their linguistic resources to make sense of the food product labels, since this is authentic behavior when shopping in a foreign country. The learners with a Romanian or Portuguese heritage, for instance, could have had an advantage, since these are also Romance languages that share similarities with French. The pupils could have done these analyses prior to their VC interactions with the French pupils to learn more about each product before their VC shopping interactions.

Developing sensitivity and openness toward different cultures

As discussed in the second section, one of the main objectives of pluralistic approaches to language education is to help learners to develop positive representations and attitudes toward other languages and cultures. Therefore, throughout the VC project the learners were engaged in reflecting on similarities and differences between their own and other cultures. For instance, during the preparation phase for the shopping activity (see Figure 10.2), the learners familiarized themselves with traditional products available in different countries, including the ones typically found at a French supermarket (e.g. baguette, croissant and quiche), and with the eating habits of different culture groups. The class teacher reflected on this project objective in the final interview:

> I think the shopping activity is a good thing because the kids see the French products and they really see, ah okay, I am in a French shop now and there are different products, because we talked a lot about different products from different countries, what do you get in different countries, what can you eat, what is special in different countries so it was like an intercultural exchange.

> And I think that they really liked to go shopping in a L. Leclerc and they saw that the French went shopping in Rewe, so they really realized the different shops. (Class teacher, Final Interview)

In this quote, the teacher pointed out that one of the advantages she saw in the project was the fact that the French exchange stimulated her pupils' interest in other ways of living, and it created new opportunities for learning not only about British or French culture, but also about other cultures, including the ones represented in her class (e.g. German, Turkish, Polish, Italian). She also noted that her pupils' motivation was enhanced because they were able to put their new cultural knowledge into practice in 'authentic' interactions with the French remote class.

The data also indicated that this culture-general approach to cultural learning fostered the learners' curiosity for other countries and cultures. In the following sequence of a focus group interview, the learners were asked to make topic suggestions for future VC tasks:

> **S1:** I really liked the Videoconference. I would like to do the next one with Spanish children or children from other countries.
>
> **S2:** Yeah, I would be glad, if we could do a videoconference also with other children. For example, with Brazilian or Spanish or Italian children, or I don't know...But I would be glad if other children came to the videoconference. (Focus Group Interview – Third Grade – Second Year)

In general, learners' interview data have shown that the telecollaboration experience produced a strong emotional involvement of the children, who especially valued the opportunity to use English to make friends in a different country. This sequence showed that this positive experience seemed to have paved the path for future intercultural exchanges, since the pupils expressed their continued interest to use ELF to interact with foreign children in different parts of the world. Another interesting aspect of this sequence is the fact that the children did not specify a target culture, but expressed an attitude of openness toward new cultures in general. These findings confirm the advantages of the ELF approach to telecollaboration discussed in the second section, and reveal the usefulness of the intercultural approach in helping learners develop positive attitudes toward cultural diversity.

Conclusion

This chapter has presented and discussed research findings of a two-year telecollaboration project that investigated the potential of live videoconferencing to support the development of primary EFL learners' plurilingual competencies. Our findings indicate that the project was able to exploit the potential of CALL to respond to some of the literature recommendations discussed in the first part of this chapter, i.e. to create EFL tasks that can 'activate and support cognitive processes for further language learning, to provide a cognitive foundation for contrastive learning and reflection on language learning and also to create openness to linguistic and cultural diversity' (Jessner, 2006: 135). The research findings have shown that the VC tasks promoted pupils' reflection on their own linguistic repertoires and on the role of ELF, and prompted them to compare and contrast different languages and cultural traditions.

The analyses of learner interview data have shown that the VC tasks created enhanced opportunities for meta-linguistic reflections on key aspects of language awareness. In the context of the VC project, these reflections took place mainly during the learner focus group interviews. However, in my view, they could also be incorporated into the EFL syllabus as classroom activities and used in connection with other pedagogical resources, such as the 'European Language Portfolio' (Council of Europe, 2016). It is reasonable to conclude that such meta-linguistic discussions can foster the development of pupils' crosslinguistic and cross-cultural awareness. The data have shown that the teacher capitalized on the pupils' strong cognitive and emotional involvement during the VC project to create space for reflection on the concepts of language and language learning and to help the learners grasp a better understanding of the relevance of cultural knowledge for successful communication and collaboration.

As discussed earlier, even though pluralistic approaches to foreign language teaching have been considered an innovative and efficient response to the new educational demands of the multilingual and multicultural world, research has shown that teachers demonstrate little familiarity with such methods. Therefore, there seems to be a strong need for the development of educational proposals that can support teachers in the process of translating theoretical recommendations into practice. This chapter has attempted to make a practical contribution to this field, by discussing the potential of CALL to foster the development of learners' plurilingual competencies. In the context of this project, the development of crosslinguistic and cross-cultural awareness was seen as a welcome by-product of the VC tasks, since the main aim of the study was to promote the authentic use of the target language English. Therefore, a fruitful topic for further research is to examine how pluralistic activities and meta-linguistic reflections could be more fully integrated into EFL classroom practice in order to better capitalize on the learners' multilingual resources.

References

Beacco, J.C. and Byram, M. (2003) *Guide for the Development of Language Education Policies in Europe: From Linguistic Diversity to Plurilingual Education*. Strasbourg: Council of Europe Language Policy Division. See http://www.coe.int/t/dg4/linguistic/Source/FullGuide_EN.pdf (accessed 6 January 2017).

Bialystok, E. (2009) Effects of bilingualism on cognitive and linguistic performance across the lifespan. In I. Gogolin and U. Neumann (eds) *Streitfall Zweisprachigkeit: The Bilingualism Controversy* (pp. 53–67). Wiesbaden: VS-Verlag.

Bündgens-Kosten, J. and Elsner, D. (2014) Rezeptives code-switching ein- und mehrsprachiger Lerner/innen in multilingualen Settings. *Fremdsprachen Lehren und Lernen* 43 (2), 56–73.

Byram, M. (1997) *Teaching and Assessing Intercultural Communicative Competence*. Clevedon: Multilingual Matters.

Candelier, M. (2008) Awakening to languages and language policy. In J. Cenoz and N. Hornberger (eds) *Encyclopedia of Language and Education: Knowledge about Language* (pp. 219–232). Berlin: Springer.

Cenoz, J. (2009) *Towards Multilingual Education: Basque Educational Research from an International Perspective*. Bristol: Multilingual Matters.

Clavel-Arroitia, B. and Pennock-Speck, B. (2015) Telecollaboration in a secondary school context: Negotiation of meaning in English as lingua franca/Spanish tandem interactions. *Revista D'innovació Educativa* 15, 74–82.

Corcoll, C. (2013) Developing children's language awareness: Switching codes in the language classroom. *International Journal of Multilingualism* 10 (1), 27–46.

Council of Europe (2016) European Language Portfolio. See https://www.coe.int/en/web/portfolio (accessed 2 December 2016).

Cummins, J. (1991) Interdependence of first- and second-language proficiency in bilingual children. In E. Bialystok (ed.) *Language Processing in Bilingual Children* (pp. 70–89). Cambridge: Cambridge University Press.

Cutrim Schmid, E. and Whyte, S. (2015) Teaching young learners with technology. In J. Bland (ed.) *Teaching English to Young Learners: Critical Issues in Language Teaching with 3–12 Year Olds* (pp. 239–259). London: Bloomsbury.

De Angelis, G. (2011) Teachers' beliefs about the role of prior language knowledge in learning and how this influences teaching practices. *International Journal of Multilingualism* 8 (3), 216–234.

Dooly, M. (2011) Crossing the intercultural borders into 3rd space culture(s): Implications for teacher education in the twenty-first century. *Language and Intercultural Communication* 11 (4), 319–337.

Elsner, D. (2014) Multilingual virtual talking Books (MuViT): A project to foster multilingualism, language awareness, and media competency. In D. Abendroth-Timmer and E.-V. Hennig (eds) *Plurilingualism and Multiliteracies: International Research on Identity Construction in Language Education* (pp. 175–190). Frankfurt am Main: Peter Lang.

Elsner, D. (2015) Inklusion und Herkunftssprachen: Mehrsprachigkeit als Herausforderung und Chance. In C.M. Bongartz and A. Rohde (eds) *Inklusion im Englischunterricht* (pp. 71–94). Frankfurt am Main: Peter Lang.

Engel, G., Groot-Wilken, B. and Thürmann, E. (eds) (2009) *Englisch in der Primarstufe – Chancen und Herausforderungen: Evaluation und Erfahrungen aus der Praxis*. Berlin: Cornelsen Scriptor.

Fidler, S. (2006) Awakening to languages in primary school. *ELT Journal* 60 (4), 346–354.

Glaser, B.G. and Strauss, A.L. (1967) *The Discovery of Grounded Theory: Strategies for Qualitative Research*. Chicago, IL: Aldine Publishing Company.
Gogolin, I. (1994) *Der Monolinguale Habitus der Multilingualen Schule*. Münster: Waxmann.
Guarda, M. (2013) Negotiating a transcultural place in an English as a lingua franca telecollaboration exchange. Unpublished PhD thesis. See http://paduaresearch.cab.unipd.it/5337/1/guarda_marta_tesi.pdf (accessed 6 January 2016).
Haukås, Å. (2016) Teachers' beliefs about multilingualism and a multilingual pedagogical approach. *International Journal of Multilingualism* 13 (1), 1–18.
Hawkins, E. (1984) *Awareness of Language: An Introduction*. Cambridge: Cambridge University Press.
Hesse, H.G. and Göbel, K. (2009) Mehrsprachigkeit als Kapital: Ergebnisse der DESI Studie. In I. Gogolin and U. Neumann (eds) *Streitfall Zweisprachigkeit: The Bilingualism Controversy* (pp. 281–288). Wiesbaden: VS Verlag.
Horst, M., White, J. and Bell, P. (2010) First and second language knowledge in the language classroom. *International Journal of Bilingualism* 14 (3), 331–349.
Jessner, U. (2006) *Linguistic Awareness in Multilinguals: English as a Third Language*. Edinburgh: Edinburgh University Press.
Kramsch, C. (1998) *Language and Culture*. Oxford: Oxford University Press.
Lewis, T., Chanier, T. and Youngs, B. (2011) Special issue commentary: Multilateral online exchanges for language and culture learning. *Language Learning & Technology* 15 (1), 3–9.
Lohe, V. (2015) Entwicklung von language awareness bei Grundschulkindern durch mehrsprachige digitale Bilderbücher. In M. Koetter and J. Rymarczyk (eds) *Englischunterricht auf der Primarstufe* (pp. 101–122). Frankfurt: Peter Lang.
Mehlhorn, G. (ed.) (2010) *Werbestrategien für Polnisch als Fremdsprache an Deutschen Schulen*. Hildesheim: Georg Olms Verlag.
Mueller-Hartmann, A. (2006) Learning how to teach intercultural communicative competence via telecollaboration: A model for language teacher education. In J.A. Belz and S.L. Thorne (eds) *Internet-Mediated Intercultural Foreign Language Education* (pp. 63–84). Boston, MA: Thomson Heinle.
O'Dowd, R. (2006) *Telecollaboration and the Development of Intercultural Communicative Competence*. München: Langenscheidt-Longman.
Oliveira, A.L. and Anca, M.H. (2009) 'I speak five languages': Fostering plurilingual competence through language awareness. *Language Awareness* 18 (3/4), 403–421.
Piccardo, E. (2013) Plurilingualism and curriculum design: Toward a synergic vision. *TESOL Quarterly* 47 (3), 600–614.
Schroeder, C. and Stölting, W. (2005) Mehrsprachig orientierte Sprachstandsfeststellungen für Kinder mit Migrationshintergrund. In I. Gogolin, U. Neumann and H.J. Roth (eds) *Sprachdiagnostik bei Kindern und Jugendlichen mit Migrationshintergrund: Dokumentation einer Fachtagung am 14. Juli 2004 in Hamburg* (pp. 59–74). Münster: Waxmann.
Stille, S. and Cummins, J. (2013) Foundation for learning: Engaging plurilingual students' linguistic repertoires in the elementary classroom. *TESOL Quarterly* 47 (3), 630–638.
Thomas, J. (1992) Metalinguistic awareness in second- and third-language learning. In R. Harris (ed.) *Cognitive Processing in Bilinguals* (pp. 531–545). Amsterdam: North Holland.
Volgger, M.-L. (2010) Wenn man mehrere Sprachen kann, ist es leichter, eine weitere zu lernen... Einblicke in die Mehrsprachigkeitsbewusstheit lebensweltlich mehrsprachiger FranzösischlernerInnen. *Zeitschrift für Interkulturellen Fremdsprachenunterricht* 15 (2), 169–198.

Whyte, S. and Cutrim Schmid, E. (2014) A task-based approach to video communication with the IWB: A French-German primary EFL class exchange. In E. Cutrim Schmid and S. Whyte (eds) *Teaching Languages with Technology: Communicative Approaches to Interactive Whiteboard Use* (pp. 50–79). London: Bloomsbury.

Wilden, E. and Porsch, R. (2015) Die Hör- und Leseverstehensleistungen im Fach Englisch von Kindern am Ende der Grundschulzeit unter besonderer Berücksichtigung von lebensweltlicher Ein- und Mehrsprachigkeit. In M. Kötter and J. Rymarczyk (eds) *Englischunterricht auf der Primarstufe: Neue Forschungen – Weitere Entwicklungen* (pp. 59–80). Frankfurt am Main: Peter Lang.

Ziegler, G. (2013) Multilingualism and the language education landscape: Challenges for teacher training in Europe. *Multilingual Education* 3, 1–23.

11 Advanced Language Learners as Autonomous Language Users on Facebook

Antonie Alm

Introduction

The conditions for autonomous language learning have significantly changed since Holec introduced the concept in 1981. His frequently quoted definition of learner autonomy as 'the ability to take charge of one's own learning', however, is as relevant as ever in times when foreign language learners are able to communicate with native speakers and follow their activities regardless of their geographical location. Social media have opened new avenues of communication that have affected the ways we interact and use language in our daily lives, both in our first (L1) and second (L2) language (Jones, 2016). The global social networking site (SNS) Facebook is one of the key features in the current landscape of social media. 'Particularly well-suited for relationship maintenance' (Ellison & Vitak, 2015: 205), it enables an increasingly mobile student population (OECD, 2013) not only to stay in touch with friends and family while traveling (Godwin-Jones, 2016) but also to build new social networks during their time abroad (Reinhardt & Chen, 2013) and to maintain friendships with native speakers once they return home (Sockett, 2014).

This chapter discusses the impact of these developments on learner autonomy and investigates the L2 Facebook practices of advanced language students.

Learner Autonomy

Access to personal L2 networks changes the language learning context for many language students and further diversifies the already complex concept of learner autonomy. The theory of learner autonomy has evolved over the years in response to changing conditions of language learning (Benson, 2013). Autonomy scholars Holec (1981),

Little (1991) and Benson (2001) have conceptualised learner autonomy at different levels (Cotterall, 2008). Holec focused primarily on the more technical and methodological skills of learning management, such as determining learning objectives, defining contents, selecting methods, and monitoring and evaluating acquisition, whereas Little (1991: 3) stressed the psychological dimension of autonomy, describing autonomy as a 'capacity – for detachment, critical reflection, decision-making, and independent action'. Benson maintained furthermore that learners should not only control how they learn but also what they learn and determine freely the content of learning. The ability to create language situations based on personal connections adds a new level of complexity to these established concepts. As participants – friends or followers – in online environments, language learners are able to act as autonomous language users beyond the boundaries of formal education. Chatting on Facebook, reading and commenting on status updates, watching L2 videos shared by native speaker friends are some examples of informal digital everyday practices of networked language learners. Toffoli and Sockett (2013: 1), who coined the term OILE (Online Informal Learning of English), found that many learners not only 'spend more time learning English informally than they do in the classroom' but that they also benefit linguistically from their out-of-class L2 engagement. This argument is only starting to find acceptance in the L2 acquisition research community (Benson *et al.*, 2016), and rather than abandoning the concept of learner autonomy, as suggested by Sockett and Toffoli (2012), it seems preferable to include this informal dimension and to extend the definition of learner autonomy as 'a capacity to control important aspects of one's language learning (...) that takes place outside the context of formal instruction' (Benson, 2013: 839–840) and to accordingly revise the tenets of learner autonomy.

Shifting grounds in learner autonomy

The shift towards self-initiated forms of L2 engagement is leading to new trends in learner autonomy.

Shift from training to self-initiated learning

Earlier concepts of learner autonomy 'placed high priority on the collection and provision of resources through self-access and on programmes to train learners in their use for self-directed learning' (Benson, 2013: 840). The range of resources was carefully selected according to their pedagogical value and adjusted to specific learner needs. The uniformity of the mainstream materials available to language learners is in stark contrast to the range of 'legal, tolerated and illegal sources' (Sockett, 2014: 13) that are now accessible to language learners. Without being tied to a place (class, self-access centre) or person (teacher, adviser), this new form of autonomous language learning is likely to be self-initiated and carried out in the personal space of the learner.

Shift from learning goal to social goals and exploration

The process of guided autonomy is typically oriented towards agreed predefined learning goals, unlike self-initiated and self-directed language use that 'emerges through exploration' (Ito *et al.*, 2008: 2). Informal autonomous learners are more likely to be led by social than by pedagogical goals (such as the communication with a friend) (Jones, 2016; Sockett, 2014).

Shift from organisational skills to social skills

The organisational skills of planning, monitoring and evaluating are the traditional core features of learner autonomy. Little (2015: para 23) suggests that the capacity to 'receptively, interactively and productively' participate in online communications presupposes 'reflective control' and infers that successful engagement in such conversation perpetuates the desire to engage in further communications. Benson (2013: 841) further proposes that 'attributes such as sociability, self-initiative, and an ability to create learning opportunities are [now] equally if not more important'.

Shift from individualistic self-orientation to holistic other-orientation

In a traditional autonomy setting, the focus tends to be on the capacities of the learner as an individual (Jones, 2016). The informal autonomous learner, however, often operates in a wider social context, drawing on L2 experiences of peers, interactions with native speaker friends (Eaton, 2010) or observation of their engagement with others and cultural materials (Sockett, 2014). This shift from an individualistic notion of autonomy to a more holistic perspective acknowledges this broader context in which learning can take place (Jones, 2016: 289).

Shift in emphasis from language learning to language use

When language learners engage in personal interactions with native speakers, or seek out exposure to L2 materials for entertainment, the L2 becomes the 'tool to gain access to other skills and information' (Sockett, 2014: 119) and language learning takes place as a by-product of these activities. Even if the intention of language learning is at the origin of their actions, 'once engaged in the situation, switches the focus of attention to communication, enjoyment or learning something other than the language itself' (Benson, 2011: 139).

SNSs are one of the tools available to autonomous language learners to access L2 material and to engage in L2 interactions.

Autonomy and social networking sites

There is growing evidence that many language learners use their L2 to communicate in online social networks. Cole and Vanderplank (2016), Lantz-Andersson *et al.* (2013) and Sockett and Toffoli (2012) have reported on the L2 online engagement of English learners in France, Sweden and Brazil, and remarked on the positive effects of informal learning on language development. Social networking involvement by learners of other languages has received less attention, yet there is no reason to believe that learners of German, French or Japanese are not equally seeking L2 exposure through their SNSs. Since national SNSs such as StudiVZ in Germany have been substituted by local versions of Facebook, the now truly global SNS enables people from all geographical locations to connect and share their experiences.

From an autonomy perspective, however, it is not only important to understand the extent to which language learners, regardless of English or other languages, participate in social networks and improve their L2, but also to identify what kinds of practices (in the sociological meaning of the term) they engage in and which competencies they develop as they 'strategically navigate, respond, and incorporate multiple communication channels' in their online communications (Chen, 2013: 163). Digital technologies have, as Jones (2016: 286) points out, 'dramatically changed the way people use language in their daily lives'. Language learners will often be familiar with new literacy practices (Lankshear & Knobel, 2006) from their first language (L1). However, the participation in L2 online environments assumes an understanding of 'cultures-of-use' (Thorne, 2003) that goes beyond linguistic proficiency. The language is the tool that enables language learners to engage in practices with more far-reaching consequences than language learning, namely the maintenance of their social relationships (Jones, 2016: 286).

Early studies into the digital practices of university students, such as Madge *et al.*'s (2009) article 'Facebook, Social Integration and Informal Learning at University: "It is More for Socialising and Talking to Friends about Work than for Actually Doing Work"', highlighted the widespread perception that students are often not able to apply their digital knowledge in educational contexts. Scholars in computer assisted language learning (CALL) have made similar observations (Winke & Goerther, 2008) and also found that the personal and academic use of Facebook varied greatly (Blattner & Lomicka, 2012); some concluded that language learners should be trained to use Facebook 'appropriately and effectively' (Prichard, 2013). This view stems from a long tradition of learner training in the discipline (Hubbard, 2004; Stockwell & Levy, 2001). From a digital literacies perspective, however, which shares some common ground with the more recent research on learner autonomy, language learners are positioned as agentic L2 social network users who develop their individual literacy practices. An understanding of the everyday digital practices of individuals and their participation in their social contexts is crucial to understand how people learn in digital environments (Lang, 2012).

The gap between L2 autonomous social network use and classroom practices has also been noted by Lantz-Andersson *et al.* (2013: 294), who assert that language education has yet 'to increase the understanding of changing conditions for languages to make more informed use of the language-learning potentials in this new arena'. The authors criticise studies that are grounded in linguistic research traditions, which focus on 'assessing, grading, quantifying participation and investigating the use of language regarding vocabulary or grammar', and support in their own study the exploration of 'new spaces that might occur when SNSs are implemented as part of schooling when students use English for communication and consequently grading and assessment have been omitted' (Lantz-Andersson *et al.*, 2013: 299).

This present study is concerned with the digital practices of advanced language students and investigates their autonomous use of Facebook in their L2. The data of this investigation derives from a larger data set, which included information about university language students from beginner to advanced levels (for more details, see Alm, 2015). The analysis of combined language levels indicates that advanced language learners are more likely to have been on exchange, have more native speaker friends on Facebook and use Facebook generally more extensively than learners of lower levels. It is the aim of this study to obtain a clearer understanding of the self-initiated and self-directed L2 engagement and the communication practices of advanced language learners, which in turn should inform the use of Facebook in educational settings.

To guide this investigation, two research questions were asked:

(1) To what extent do advanced language students use Facebook to create their personal L2 environment?
(2) In what type of digital practices do they engage when interacting on Facebook?

Method

Participants

Questionnaire

The participants in this study were 71 advanced (third-year) language students (57 female/14 male) of French (23/1), German (13/8), Japanese (8/3) and Spanish (13/2) at a tertiary institution in New Zealand. The average age was 20–22 years; 70.4% indicated that they had been on a high school or university exchange (or both). Six participants did not have a Facebook account.

Table 11.1 Interview participants

Name (pseudonyms)	Age	Background
Alice	20	Exchange to German (two months high school, six week university language course)
Ben	21	Exchange to Japan (six months high school, one semester university)
Victoria	21	Exchange to German (two month high school)
Lily	22	On university (one semester) exchange in Spain at the time of the interview
Tristan	21	German mother, grew up in New Zealand
Till	20	German parents, grew up in New Zealand
Sean	19	No exchange

Interviews

Seven participants provided additional information about their L2 Facebook use (Table 11.1).

Instruments

The questionnaire examined the multilingual appearance of the participants' Facebook profile, their digital practices and the participants' views on the usefulness of their online engagement for language learning. A range of answer choices (multiple-choice, Likert-type scale and open-ended) were selected to enable participants to indicate preferences and to elaborate on their views and practices. In addition, demographic data was collected about gender, age, enrolment in language courses and participation in language exchange programmes.

Interviews were conducted with seven advanced language students. Four participants (Alice, Sean, Tristan and Till) were interviewed together as a group, one over Facebook chat (Lily) and the other two individually in person (Ben and Victoria). The questions related to the questionnaire items and participants were prompted to provide additional examples from Facebook for language learning and to elaborate on their individual online practices.

Data collection and analysis

The responses of 71 advanced language students were extracted from the original data set (n = 190) presented in Alm (2015). The data files were exported to Excel and the open-ended answers thematically coded. For further analysis, the data file was cleaned and exported to SPSS. Frequencies (counts and percentages) and descriptive statistics (means and standard deviations) of the relevant items of the questionnaire were established for all Likert-type questions. The items on the usefulness of Facebook for L2 exposure and L2 use (Useful-items) were cross-tabulated with the other items of the questionnaire in order to establish correlations between perceived usefulness and reported use. The Likert-type items were reduced from a 5-point scale (*never*, *rarely*, *sometimes*, *frequently*, *all the time*) to a 3-point scale, combing the two points on either side (*never/rarely* on the one hand, and *frequently/all the time* on the other hand), resulting in 3 × 3 tables. A test of association (Pearson Chi-Square) was conducted between the usefulness variable and reported use variables.

The qualitative data from the comments of each item and from the open-ended questions were also cross-tabulated with the Useful-items (as above). The data within the three categories (*useful*, *somewhat useful* and *not useful*) was then sorted into themes. Each item (quote) was labelled with the language of the participant (FRE, GER, JAP, SPA), and level of *usefulness*, Level 1 standing for *not useful or not useful at all*, Level 2 for *somewhat useful* and Level 3 for *useful* or *very useful*.

The interview data was transcribed verbatim and inductively coded. The emerging themes were compared with the themes of the qualitative data from the questionnaire and combined in one file. The interview quotes were labelled with the name (pseudonym) of the participant and their language (name/language). Typos occurring in the data were not corrected.

There are some limitations in the research design of this study. Firstly, there was no random selection of participants. The analysis includes the data from all participants who returned the questionnaire and volunteered to participate in the interview. However, the invitation to take the questionnaire was phrased in such a way that students, regardless of their positive or negative attitude towards the subject of the study, would be encouraged to take part in the study. This has also been confirmed by the data, which included six non-users. Secondly, the quantitative and qualitative data presented in this chapter are self-reported data. The reliability of some of the responses may therefore be questioned due to participants' inaccurate statements or deliberate misrepresentation. To gain a more complete understanding of L2 Facebook use, direct observation of actual language behaviour would have been useful. There is, however, significant ethical and methodological complexity involved in conducting a study that deals with people's personal communications (Cunliffe *et al.*, 2013: 342). This approach was preferred for this initial exploratory study that will hopefully provide insight and direction for future research

Findings

Language exchange and online friendships

Most participants (70.4%) had taken part in a language exchange programme, during which they formed friendships with native speakers and connected on Facebook. Only two older participants (over 35 years) had no native speaker Facebook friends (NSFBF) and neither of them had been on exchange. Participants also met native speakers who came as international students or visitors to New Zealand in educational or social settings.

Two of the interview participants described the impact of the friendships made during exchange on their online L2 use once they returned home. Ben, an advanced Japanese learner explained:

> [...] after returning from a 6-month exchange in Yokohama, Japan, I ended up with hundreds of new Japanese friends, many of whom were keen to keep in touch afterwards. [...] Needless to say, I have spent many days and nights online chatting with my exchange friends in Japanese (our base language for communication) as a means of further extending my language skills and intercultural understanding. (Ben/JAP)

Victoria, who spent a shorter period in Germany, also felt that her contacts gave her additional L2 exposure and support during her university language study.

> [...] while I was in school I went on exchange to Germany, living with a German family for 2 months [...] This exchange provided me with contacts in Germany, which meant that when I was at university I could talk to them outside of the classroom through Facebook or Skype, and they could help me with what I was doing, and I could help them as well. (Victoria/GER)

A total of 40.5% of students who had been on exchange valued Facebook as useful to apply and practice their L2, as opposed to 25% who had not been on exchange. Some of their Facebook practices already developed during the exchange where the SNS was used to communicate with new native speaker friends, or, if they were already users, to organise their social life. In the following section, we will look in more detail at the features that were used by advanced language learners to create L2 exposure.

Creating an L2 environment on Facebook

There are a number of ways to transform Facebook into an L2 environment. Users can, for example, set up the Facebook interface in their L2. Changing the language settings from English to Spanish translates the standard text that appears on the Facebook page into Spanish. The familiar prompt 'What's on your mind?' will then read '*¿Qué estás pensando?*'. To 'like' a post, one has to click on *me gusta*, and the user will be encouraged to *escribe un comentario* (write a comment). Friends will be *amigos*, events can be found under *eventos* and, on the top right column where the ticker displays the activities of Facebook friends, users can see what they liked, shared, commented on (*A Maria le gusta el video de..., John compartío la foto de..., Lisa comentó su publicación*) and so on. Language learners who are familiar with the Facebook set-up in their native language are likely to figure out the meaning of these words and expressions without too much difficulty.

'Liking' Facebook pages and joining Facebook groups expose learners to more creative language. By 'liking' a Facebook page (not a post), users receive updates of that page in their newsfeed. However, in order to 'like', or in conventional terms to 'subscribe to', a page, one has to find suitable pages of newspapers, TV programmes, famous people or others. Once located and 'liked', users can then also read the comments and replies that develop between native speakers about the topic of a specific post. Facebook groups on the other hand are often common interest groups, allowing group members to post and comment without being Facebook friends. Language learners can join groups of their personal interest and be active or passive participants in these spaces.

Most participants of this study were aware of these features and their self-reported use of language settings, L2 Facebook pages and Facebook groups correlated with the level of perceived usefulness of Facebook as a tool for L2 exposure.

Language settings, likes and Facebook groups

Language settings

Level 1 users (who found Facebook not useful for L2 exposure) had very little experience of changing language settings. A German student commented: 'I've never really thought about changing it to german' (GER/2). Most Level 2 and Level 3 users, who perceived Facebook as somewhat useful or (very) useful, had changed the setting to the L2. The preferred option was to switch back and forth between the L1 and L2. Lily explained: 'If im tired i flick back to english – And if i feel like iv been deprived ... for a while i flick it on'. Only 19% consistently used the L2 display, and about a third chose to keep the Facebook interface in English.

Likes

Over half of all participants used L2 Facebook pages. Level 3 users had a preference for pages relating to social and cultural aspects of the target culture such as restaurants, film, dance and travel. Comments from Level 2 users were mostly about 'funny pages', and Level 1 users only rarely liked pages, claiming they 'never thought about it' (GER/1).

Facebook groups

A total of 59% of participants belonged to L2 Facebook groups. Two Japanese students reported that they set up study groups for their classes, groups for social events and informal chat. Others indicated that they were members of the university's non-academic Japanese language groups. Some Level 1 users also belonged to L2 groups, yet the nature of these groups was more organisational and not aimed at L2 interaction (Table 11.2).

Table 11.2 Useful to be exposed * reported use of L2 Facebook features

	Language setting			Likes		Groups	
	L1 (%)	L2 (%)	L1/L2 (%)	No (%)	Yes (%)	No (%)	Yes (%)
Not (at all) useful (14)	*57.1*	0.0	42.9	92.9	7.1	57.1	42.9
Somewhat useful (25)	32.0	20.0	*48.0*	36.0	64.0	44.0	56.0
(very) Useful (19)	26.3	31.6	*42.1*	15.8	84.2	26.3	73.7
Total	36.2	19.0	44.8	43.1	56.9	41.4	58.6

Attention to L2 items on newsfeed

All participants, but in particular Level 3 users, paid close attention to L2 items on their newsfeed. They were especially interested in the posts from their native speaker friends. Reading their status updates and comments was most popular with a mean of 3.57 (SD 1.05), followed by looking at photos (*M* 3.32, SD 1.02), watching video clips (*M* 2.6, SD 0.995) and reading articles they shared (*M* 2.6, SD 1.04).

A significance test (Pearson Chi-Square) suggests an association between the useful levels and reported use for reading L2 status updates and comments $\chi^2(4) = 19.9$, $p = 0.001$, looking at photos $\chi^2(4) = 14.3$, $p = 0.006$, videos $\chi^2(4) = 10.4$, $p = 0.034$ and articles $\chi^2(4) = 19.4$, $p = 0.001$ their NSFBFs shared.

The interview data also confirmed the importance of NSFBF activity for meaningful L2 exposure. Participants read their friends' status updates and comments on photos, their shared items, such as quotes and videos, and also followed their friends' activities through the ticker. Alice reported that she found interesting Facebook pages through her friends' activities.

> I got to know quite a few German comedians and German musicians because my friends post this. So if they link it, I go and watch the video [...]. Without them posting those things I would never searched it myself. (Alice/GER)

Checking one's newsfeed for L2 posts provided the participants with valuable L2 resources, which they processed as language *users*, rather than language *learners* (Table 11.3). This was clearly expressed by a Spanish

Table 11.3 Useful to be exposed * Attention to L2 features on Facebook newsfeed

	Attention to L2 items on newsfeed		
	No (%)	Sometimes (%)	Yes (%)
Not useful (14)	28.6	50.0	21.4
Somewhat useful (25)	4.0	44.0	52.0
Useful (19)	0.0	0.0	100.0
Total (58)	8.6	31.0	60.3

student, 'Often I don't think of it as studying the language though, simply using facebook to communicate with people who happen to speak other languages' (SPA/2).

Sharing, L2 status updates and comments

Sharing

Participants of all levels were reluctant to share L2 items on their timeline (*M* 2.11, SD 0.985). Even Level 3 users perceived sharing L2 posts as inappropriate practice. A German student admitted: 'I would like to share more videos, articles, or quotes in one of the languages I study, however I find that my friends who don't speak those languages, find anything I post in those languages annoying' (GER/3).

L2 status updates

Some participants were 'too embarrassed' to post L2 status updates in front of a native speaker audience, but they mainly felt that posts in a foreign language 'alienated' (GER/3) them from their L1 friends (*M* 2.03, SD 1.02). Writing in a different language was perceived as 'weird' (FRE/2) and 'rude' (FRE/2). L2 posts seemed only to be acceptable when staying in the target language country.

These reservations were also expressed in the interviews. Participants also noted that 'no one does status updates at all' (Alice/GER). However, they also pointed out that their German friends often wrote English status updates, using their L2. This indicates that L2 use might be handled differently in Germany than in New Zealand, and suggests that it is more acceptable for non-native speakers to post in English than in other languages (Table 11.4).

Comments

Commenting was more common among Level 3 users who indicated that they frequently commented on their friends' updates and photos and left birthday messages. In addition, they were interested in the conversations between native speakers. Reading native speaker

Table 11.4 Useful to apply and practice * Share/status updates

	Share L2 items on timeline			Status updates		
	Never/ rarely (%)	Sometimes (%)	Frequently/ all the time (%)	Never/ rarely (%)	Sometimes (%)	Frequently/ all the time (%)
Not useful (14)	100.0	0.0	0.0	100.0	0.0	0.0
Somewhat useful (23)	65.2	34.8	0.0	69.6	30.4	0.0
Useful (21)	38.1	42.9	19.0	42.9	33.3	23.8
Total (58)	63.8	29.3	6.9	67.2	24.1	8.6

Table 11.5 Useful to apply and practice * Commenting

	Comments		
	Never/rarely (%)	Sometimes (%)	Frequently/all the time (%)
Not useful (14)	64.3	35.7	0.0
Somewhat useful (23)	30.4	56.5	13.0
Useful (21)	9.5	42.9	47.6
Total (58)	31.0	46.6	22.4

comments and replies allowed them to pick up colloquial words and phrases which they felt native speakers tend to avoid when addressing L2 speakers. Reading the conversations 'between two native speakers not making the language easier for u to understand' (SPA/3) provided these participants with an insider perspective of the literacy practices of their L2 (Table 11.5).

Private message and chatting

Rather than writing public posts, participants used the private message system to write to their NSFBFs. It is not clear from the data if participants differentiated between the asynchronous private message and the synchronous chat feature. Their responses indicate, however, that they were looking for opportunities to chat rather than leaving messages for each other (Table 11.6).

The appeal of Facebook chat is that friends are concurrently online and are able to spontaneously talk to each other. This spontaneity is reduced if interlocutors live in different time zones. A German student commented that she only chatted a couple of times a week 'when we are both awake, so either very early or late' (GER/3). Lily, a student of Spanish, managed to increase her contact with native Spanish speakers by configuring a Spanish chat group:

> Theres also a useful función in chat. You can créate [...] groups within ur friends. So ive got a group with everyone i know in Spain [...]. So if i feel like practising Spanish I just go into my advanced chat settings and select

Table 11.6 Useful to apply and practice * Private message

	Private message		
	Never/rarely (%)	Sometimes (%)	Frequently/all the time (%)
Not useful (14)	71.4	28.6	0.0
Somewhat useful (23)	21.7	43.5	34.8
Useful (21)	4.8	38.1	57.1
Total (58)	27.6	37.9	34.5

> to only appear online to my spanish friends. And it filters it for you so any other friends online dont show up/ Actually came across it when a friend told me she has a group called 'annoying people' and selects for them to not see shes on chat haha. (Lily/SPA)

Lily displays the attributes of an autonomous online language learner as described by Benson (2013). She is able to create a space for Spanish practice by adapting a friend's practice to her own purpose (self-initiative) and by drawing on her Spanish friends (sociability).

Regardless how they connected with NSFBFs, Level 3 described their chatting sessions as *conversations*. Level 1 users had fewer chatting experiences, which were also of a more utilitarian nature, often taking the shape of *requests*. A Japanese student wrote: 'If I do, its to ask a question about how to say something in the language' (JAP/1).

The following section will look more closely into the self-reported L2 writing practices of the participants' chat sessions.

Online writing practices

L2 use

Level 3 participants tried to consistently use their L2. However, the language choice also depended on their interlocutors and their intentions. A German learner explained, 'I will try my best to speak in German at all times, unless the other person is speaking English to me'. At other times, they followed the language choice of their friends, because of their preference, as a French student said, 'It depends if they're messaging me in French or English', or their language proficiency, 'If we are a similar [language] level we take turns. Otherwise we normally chat in the language which is easiest for both people' (GER/3).

Error correction

Level 3 users had individual attitudes towards errors and error correction. One German student felt that corrections would stop the flow of a conversation and preferred to ignore them, 'I generally chat with foreign friends in German as I do with english-speaking friends. But if i make a mistake, friends don't usually bother to correct me because it's not really necessary and not nice to constantly be corrected when chatting with a friend' (GER/3), whereas another German student was happy to receive implicit corrective feedback, 'My friends use text language to me but when I have used a word wrong they will reply in full using the correct word or the word in the correct way to show me (indirectly) what I did wrong' (GER/3). Another student saw his errors as part of the conversation. 'I enjoy talking to my mates and the mistakes i make when i speak to them actually contribute to the conversation; it is funny for them and me' (GER/2). Self-correction seemed to be a common practice at both Levels 3 and 2 but depended on the situation, 'if i am in a rush i dont bother' (FRE/2). In general, they described their language use as informal, with little attention given to accents and frequent use of colloquial terms.

Colloquial language

Colloquial terms and phrases created a cultural connection between participants and their interlocutors. A Spanish student explained, 'I use Chilean slang as per how I learnt while on exchange' (SPA/3). Level 3 users expressed that they felt 'comfortable' (FRE/3) with the 'set phrases, idiomatic and colloquial expressions picked up from both native and other foreign speakers in conversation face to face and fb chat or what iv read on fb on my news feed etc' (SPA/3).

Native speaker phrases vs dictionaries

Native speaker phrases provided students with more support in their writing than dictionaries, translators or Google searches. Level 3 users in particular relied on the input of their friends to make a conversation flow and some used Google search to double-check their output. A Level 3 student of Spanish commented: 'I use simple phrases that people say all the time, if they are harder, then I will check on google if it's correct' (SPA/3), and a German student explained, 'to check that the word of phrase is idiomatic, I then look at the number of hits in Google' (GER/3).

Emoticons

Some participants resorted to emoticons to better express their feelings. The majority, however, used emoticons as in their L1. Difference in use was only reported by Japanese students. Four Japanese Level 3 users explained that they used more emoticons (which also differed from English emoticons) when chatting with Japanese native speakers, 'as this is very common in Japanese' (JAP/3).

Discussion

The data suggests that L2 engagement on Facebook is closely related to the usefulness that participants attribute to Facebook as a place for L2 exposure and L2 use.

In response to Research Question 1, which focused on the self-initiatives of the participants, it has been found that self-reported L2 use increased with the level of perceived L2 Facebook usefulness. Participants who found Facebook not useful for L2 exposure, hardly used any features and some admitted that they 'never thought of it'. Those who found Facebook somewhat useful had changed language settings into the L2, joined groups, liked L2 pages and also paid attention to L2 items on their newsfeeds. The L2 activities of participants who perceived Facebook as a useful tool for L2 exposure showed active engagement by participating in chat groups, liking L2 pages that they noticed their native speaker friends had liked; they followed their friends' conversations, picked up new words and phrases and found ways of maximising exposure and opportunities to interact, as with Lily's set-up of a chat group with her Spanish friends. Also, the level of engagement was socially motivated. Active users had established contact with native speakers, which they had mainly gained from a language exchange. The close social ties to friends and host families are the 'social capital' (Ellison *et al.*, 2007) of these L2 learners and the maintenance of these ties is a *social goal*.

The second research question investigated the digital writing practices of the participants. The data presented has shown that L2 engagement was highly dependent on others and the social context of their interactions. For example, participants of all levels were reluctant to share or to post status updates in their L2 mainly because of its perceived negative impact on their L1 relationships, but also to avoid the embarrassment of inappropriate or incorrect L2 messages. Some participants used their L2 while on exchange, possibly with the primary goal of building relationships with native speakers (rather than practicing the language). Language choice also depended on the interlocutor, as did the use of emoticons in the case of Japanese learners. Participants were interested in the interactions of and with native speakers and also relied more on phrases they observed in these interactions than on dictionaries to find their own ways of expressing themselves. Finally, it was through the observation of the online activities of their native speaker friends, and the recommendations made by them, that they were able engage in L2 activities (such as watching L2 music videos).

This study has shown that L2 Facebook use is more socially than linguistically motivated. Participants who had taken part in a language exchange programme had developed social ties to native speakers and used Facebook to maintain their friendships. These close connections are also referred to as *bonding* social capital, the advantages one gains from close relationships (McMahon, 2015: 724). *Bridging* social capital describes a relationship based on weak social ties, acquaintances or people we add on Facebook without really knowing them. Facebook makes it easy to nurture these superficial friendships, by letting people *like* status updates and reminding them of their birthdays. It seems, however, that this type of relationship maintenance behaviour is secondary for L2 Facebook engagement. In other words, language learners don't use their native speaker contacts to practice the language for practice's sake. This has only been observed with some Level 1 users who did not have established L2 friendships.

Another point that has to be taken into consideration is the personal attitudes that language learners have towards social media and Facebook. Six out of the 71 participants were not Facebook users and several participants expressed their dislike of the site or some of its features. They used the words 'jargon' and 'social media-specific terminology' to describe the informal language they encountered on Facebook, whereas others used the positive terms 'knowledge' and 'skills'. This range of responses illustrates the difference in personal attitudes towards the SNS, suggesting different levels of preparedness (or reluctance) to use Facebook in the L2. Language educators have to take these attitudes into account if they want to use the SNS for formal language education. Further research will have to explore the role of learner technobiographies (Barton & Lee, 2013) in L2 Facebook use and how individual practices and pedagogical agendas can be negotiated in formal L2 learning contexts.

Conclusion

It was the aim of this chapter to illustrate the changing conditions for language learning and its impact on learner autonomy with examples from L2 Facebook use. This study has shown that advanced language students vary in their perception of Facebook as a useful tool for L2 exposure and L2 use. Those who view Facebook as *useful* for language practice display a capacity for taking charge of their learning, or as it has been argued in this chapter, for language use. Language students who rate Facebook as only *somewhat useful* or *not useful* – a good two thirds of the participants – are less inclined to explore the SNS for L2 use. This finding differs from Toffoli and Sockett (2013) who observed a general increase in informal learning of English in online environments. However, this might be explained by the global dominance of English and the stronger appeal of learning English generally. The study indicates that the majority of English-speaking university language students are either not aware of the potential of SNSs for L2 practice, or are not willing to use it. This reluctance and the social, rather than linguistic, focus of Facebook interactions has to be taken into consideration when language educators want to integrate Facebook or other social media tools into their courses, and should not be downplayed as an inability to transfer digital literacy skills from personal to educational spheres. The creative use of Facebook features by autonomous students, however, supports the idea that informal language learning is indeed increasing, and that the emerging digital practices will shape the needs of future language learners.

References

Alm, A. (2015) Facebook for informal language learning: Perspectives from tertiary language students. *Eurocall Review* 23 (2), 3–18.

Barton, D. and Lee, C. (2013) *Language Online: Investigating Digital Texts and Practices.* New York: Routledge.

Benson, P. (2001) *Teaching and Researching Autonomy in Language Learning.* Harlow: Pearson.

Benson, P. (2011) *Teaching and Researching Autonomy.* London: Pearson.

Benson, P. (2013) Learner autonomy (Symposium on digital literacies, globalization and language learning). *TESOL Quarterly* 47 (4), 839–843.

Benson, P., Chávez Sánchez, M., McLoughlin, D., Mynard, J. and Peña Clavel, M. (2016) New scenarios in autonomy for foreign language learning: Conference summary and reflections. *Studies in Self-Access Learning Journal* 7 (3), 287–296.

Blattner, G. and Lormicka, L. (2012) Facebook-ing and the social generation: A new era of language learning. *Alsic* 15 (1). See http://journals.openedition.org/alsic/2413 (accessed 5 April 2018).

Chen, H.I. (2013) Identity practices of multilingual writers in social networking spaces. *Language Learning & Technology* 17 (2), 143–170.

Cole, J. and Vanderplank, R. (2016) Comparing autonomous and class-based learners in Brazil: Evidence for the present-day advantages of informal, out-of-class learning. *System* 61, 31–42.

Cotterall, S. (2008) Autonomy and good language learners. In C. Griffiths (ed.) *Lessons from Good Language Learners* (pp. 110–120). Cambridge: Cambridge University Press.

Cunliffe, D., Morris, D. and Prys, C. (2013) Young bilinguals' language behaviour in social networking sites: The use of Welsh on Facebook. *Journal of Computer-Mediated Communication* 18 (3), 339–361.

Eaton, S. (2010) *Formal, Non-Formal and Informal Learning. The Case of Literacy, Essential Skills and Language Learning in Canada.* Canada: Eaton International Consulting Inc.

Ellison, N.B. and Vitak, J. (2015) Social network site affordances and their relationship to social capital processes. In E. Sundar (ed.) *The Handbook of the Psychology of Communication Technology* (pp. 205–227). Hoboken, NJ: Wiley-Blackwell.

Ellison, N., Steinfield, C. and Lampe, C. (2007) The benefits of Facebook 'friends': Social capital and college students' use of online social network sites. *Journal of Computer-Mediated Communication* 12 (4), 1143–1168.

Godwin-Jones, R. (2016) Integrating technology into study abroad. *Language Learning & Technology* 20 (1), 1–20.

Holec, H. (1981) *Autonomy and Foreign Language Learning.* Oxford: Pergamon.

Hubbard, P. (2004) Learner training for effective use of CALL. In S. Fotos and C. Browne (eds) *New Perspectives on CALL for Second Language Classrooms* (pp. 45–68). Mahwah, NJ: Lawrence Erlbaum Associates.

Ito, M., Horst, H., Bittanti, M., Boyd, D.M., Herr-Stephenson, B., Lange, P.G., Pascoe, C.J. and Robinson, L. (2008) *Living and Learning with New Media: Summary of Findings from the Digital Youth Project.* Chicago, IL: The John D. and Catherine T. MacArthur Foundation.

Jones, R. (2016) Digital literacies. In E. Hinkle (ed.) *Handbook of Research into Second Language Teaching and Learning* (Vol. 3; pp. 286–298). London: Routledge.

Lang, A. (2012) Exploring the potential of social network sites in relation to intercultural communication. *Arts and Humanities in Higher Education* 11, 120–139.

Lankshear, C. and Knobel, M. (2006) *New Literacies: Everyday Practices and Classroom Learning* (2nd edn). Milton Keyes: Open University Press.

Lantz-Andersson, A., Sylvi, V. and Bowen, R. (2013) Crossing boundaries in Facebook: Students' framing of language learning activities as extended spaces. *Computer-Supported Collaborative Learning* 8, 293–312.

Little, D. (1991) *Learner Autonomy 1: Definitions, Issues and Problems.* Dublin: Authentik.

Little, D. (2015) University language centres, self-access learning and learner autonomy. *Recherche et pratiques pédagogiques en langues de spécialité* XXXIV (1), 13–26.

Madge, C., Meek, J., Wellens, J. and Hooley, T. (2009) Facebook, social integration and informal learning at university: 'It is more for socialising and talking to friends about work than for actually doing work'. *Learning, Media and Technology* 34 (2), 141–55.

McMahon, C. (2015) Why do we 'like' social media? *The Psychologist* 28 (9), 724–728.

OECD (2013) *How Many Students Study Abroad and Where Do They Go? Education at a Glance 2013: Highlights*. OECD Publishing.

Prichard, C. (2013) Training L2 learners to use Facebook appropriately and effectively. *CALICO Journal* 30 (2), 204–225.

Reinhardt, J. and Chen, H.-I. (2013) An ecological analysis of social networking site-mediated identity development. In M.-N. Lamy and K. Zourou (eds) *Social Networking for Language Education* (pp. 11–30). Basingstoke: Palgrave Macmillan.

Sockett, G. (2014) *The Online Informal Learning of English*. Basingstoke: Palgrave Macmillan.

Sockett, G. and Toffoli, D. (2012) Beyond learner autonomy: A dynamic systems view of the informal learning of English in virtual online communities. *ReCALL* 24 (2), 138–151.

Stockwell, G. and Levy, M. (2001) Sustainability of e-mail interactions between native speakers and nonnative speakers. *Computer Assisted Language Learning* 14 (5), 419–442.

Thorne, S.L. (2003) Artifacts and cultures-of-use in intercultural communication. *Language, Learning and Technology* 7 (2), 38–67.

Toffoli, D. and Sockett, G. (2013) University teachers' perceptions of online informal learning of English (OILE). *Computer Assisted Language Learning* 28 (1), 7–21.

Winke, P. and Goertler, S. (2008) Did we forget someone? Students' computer access and literacy for CALL. *CALICO Journal*, 25 (3), 483–509.

Appendices

Appendix 1

	n	Yes (%)	No (%)
Have you been on exchange?	71	70.4	29.6
Are you on Facebook?	71	91.5	8.5
Do you have NSFBFs?	71	83.1	2.8

Appendix 2

		Frequencies						
Item	n	Never	Rarely	Sometimes	Frequently	All the time	Mean	SD
Attention to L2 items in newsfeed	61	1	4	19	24	13	3.72	0.933
• Status updates and comments	60	1	6	23	17	13	3.57	1.05
• Photos	60	1	10	25	16	8	3.32	1.02
• Videos	60	7	19	21	12	0	2.6	0.995
• Articles	60	10	13	24	12	0	2.6	1.04
Share L2 items	61	20	19	18	3	1	2.11	0.985
Status updates	60	23	18	14	4	1	2.03	1.02
Comments	60	8	11	28	10	3	2.82	1.03
Private message	60	5	11	24	14	6	3.08	1.08
Chat	58	15	13	18	9	3	2.52	1.19
Use dictionary	59	14	17	20	6	1	2.32	1.06
Use Google	60	6	9	21	18	5	3.07	1.16
NS phrases	59	3	4	27	18	5	3.2	1.1

Appendix 3

		Frequencies						
Item	**n**	**Not useful at all**	**Not very useful**	**Somewhat useful**	**Useful**	**Very useful**	**Mean**	**SD**
Useful to be exposed	58	1	13	25	13	6	3.17	0.958
Useful to apply and practice	58	5	9	23	13	8	3.17	1.13

Part 5
MCALL and Professional Development of Teachers

12 Multilingual Digital Translanguaging and Storying with New Zealand Pasifika Learners

Rae Si'ilata

Introduction

Current notions of effective practice for linguistically diverse learners within digital learning environments in Aotearoa New Zealand (NZ) are often restricted to the production of digital output or 'products' in the dominant language (English) only, and do not include the incorporation of learners' heritage language resources, or even of their particular English language varieties. In Aotearoa/NZ, the indigenous language, Te Reo Māori, is spoken by a linguistic (predominantly indigenous) minority, while other linguistic minorities, including those from the Pacific Islands, speak the languages of their island nation homes. This chapter focuses on NZ Pacific (Pasifika) learners within primary contexts, where teachers and educational leaders in English medium classrooms need to move beyond practices that rest on Pasifika learners adopting majority culture English language, literacy and identity in order to achieve academic and digital goals. This chapter explores the process and outcomes of transforming computer assisted language learning (CALL) in multilingual contexts to better meet both the learning and cultural aspirations of Pasifika peoples in Aotearoa NZ. A Pasifika metaphor of the Va'atele (double-hulled deep-sea canoe) is offered as a framework for Pasifika learners' success in order that schools and educators might understand how it is possible to both privilege and utilise students' linguistic and cultural resources within the digital learning space at school. In this way, Pasifika learners can make meaningful connections between home and school funds of knowledge (Gonzalez *et al.*, 2005), and are able to experience success in both domains. Evidence is presented from a case study that draws attention to the central roles teachers play in enabling Pasifika learners to connect, rather than replace, the world views, languages, literacy practices and experiences of their homes with the digital language and literacy practices of school. The enactment of linguistically and culturally responsive pedagogies within digital learning spaces improves students' linguistic and literacy achievement in English and heritage languages, while also enabling stronger connections between home and school domains.

Pasifika peoples in NZ

Pacific peoples began migrating from their island homes into a prevailing 'English NZ post-colonial environment' in the 1940s. In particular, island nations that were part of NZ's Pacific colonial administration, such as Western Samoa, Niue, Tokelau and the Cook Islands, comprised a significant proportion of the migrating diaspora. Children of those Pacific language communities that had been under NZ administration for a longer time period, tended to experience greater degrees of first/heritage language loss. As a consequence, many NZ-born Pacific children today, now speak Pacific varieties of English, and possess varying degrees of receptive or productive competence in their Pacific heritage language. A feature of NZ's existing Pacific population includes a growing proportion with multiple heritages or identities: 37.2% according to Statistics NZ (2013), resulting in increasing levels of cross-cultural relations within NZ society. Also, the Cook Islands, Niue and Tokelau have more community members living in NZ than in their island home nations, resulting in the resident communities within NZ becoming critical sites of language revival and 'cultural knowledge' transmission for their respective Pacific diaspora.

Pacific peoples in NZ form the third largest ethnic minority group after Māori (14.9% or 598,605 people) and Asian (11.8% or 471,708 people) (Statistics NZ, 2013). The number of Pasifika peoples in NZ is increasing, with 6.9% (265,974 people) in 2006, and 7.4% (295,941 people) of the total population identifying as Pasifika in 2013. NZ-born Pacific peoples (rather than migrant peoples) now comprise 62.3% of the total Pacific population in NZ (Statistics NZ, 2013). Although Pasifika peoples trace their heritage to distinct Pacific Island nations, they are identified by NZ government institutions under the blanket Pacific/Pasifika categories. The terms 'Pasifika peoples' or 'Pasifika' are used by the Ministry of Education (2009b), while the Ministry for Pacific Peoples uses the terms 'Pacific peoples' and 'Pacific population'. These 'masking' labels, while somewhat problematic for individual Pacific nation peoples, could also be said to represent the multiple identities and language resources of mixed heritage Pasifika peoples. 'Pasifika education' is the term used in the remainder of this chapter to refer to the education and development of the Pacific diaspora resident within NZ.

What constitutes Pasifika success?

Success for Pasifika peoples and their children should be considered holistically, relative to the multiple worlds they live in. Generally for Pasifika communities, academic success is not only about the success of the individual but is also reflective of the success of the family and the community from which they come. To be deemed fully successful in Pasifika contexts, Pasifika children are encouraged to strengthen and build capability in the 'valued knowledges' and 'ways of being' of their family/community domains, as well as the valued knowledge of school. Ideally, success achieved in one domain should have benefits or 'capital' in the other domains in which learners are socialised.

Education that enables Pasifika learners in classrooms in Aotearoa NZ to see their languages, cultures and identities represented in the 'valued knowledge of school', and to be utilised as a normal part of language and literacy learning in their classrooms suggests that their perceptions of success will include, rather than exclude, their linguistic and cultural identities. The continued development of Pasifika languages and literacies not only enables learners to be successful in the worlds of their families and communities, but also has direct impact on their successful acquisition of English language and literacy (Baker, 2011; Cummins, 2008; Si'ilata, 2014).

Pasifika Languages Policy

Within English medium education, the Ministry of Education promotes the utilisation of family language resources to support successful transition to English. There is minimal systemic support for ongoing Pasifika language maintenance, or for biliteracy development through Pasifika bilingual/immersion education. As stated in a Ministry of Education (2014: 6) 'request for proposals' for teacher professional learning and development (PLD) in the utilisation of dual language texts in English medium education, '[t]eachers need to build on all of the Pasifika children's language knowledge, skills and experiences to support English language learning and literacy'. Language shift and loss among NZ Pasifika communities is occurring at an alarming rate. Concerns about Pasifika language loss have been expressed within educational forums for many years: 'According to NZ Census data (2006), all Pasifika languages in the Realm of Aotearoa NZ are showing significant signs of language shift and loss' (Post Primary Teachers Association, 2010: 1).

Historically, the Ministry of Education has provided Pasifika language texts (Tupu Readers) in the five main language groups of Reo Maori Kuki 'Airani (Cook Islands Maori), Vagahau Niue (Niuean), Gagana Samoa (Samoan), Gagana Tokelau (Tokelauan) and Lea Faka-Tonga (Tongan); online support through the LEAP (Language Enhancing the

Achievement of Pasifika) website (McComish *et al.*, 2008); language learning material for new learners of those languages, but not necessarily speakers or members of those speech communities (Ministry of Education, 2009a); and PLD provision for Pasifika bilingual teacher aides (Ministry of Education, 2007). Recently, Pasifika dual language texts for shared reading purposes in English medium classrooms have also been developed (Ministry of Education, 2016a); however, there is currently no further development of instructional reading material in Pasifika languages to enable biliteracy development within bilingual learning contexts within schools. It is necessary, therefore, to consider notions of 'Pasifika success' within English medium education, where the majority of Pasifika learners are schooled.

Biliteracy Development

Pasifika bilingual learners are able to draw on language resources that include their receptive and productive capabilities in their Pasifika heritage languages, as well as a repertoire of sociolinguistic registers in their English language proficiency. When students are supported to access their common underlying proficiency (Cummins, 1980, 2000), their bilingualism, biliteracy and academic development can develop simultaneously rather than sequentially (Baker, 2011; García, 2009). The implications of the common underlying proficiency construct require teachers to actively *teach for transfer* of linguistic, meta-cognitive and meta-linguistic knowledge. The theoretical rationale for this teaching for crosslinguistic transfer originates from several sources. Hornberger (2003) proposed a 'continua of biliteracy' where both literacies are interconnected in the unconscious mind of the learner, cannot be separated and have to be viewed as a single biliteracy system. This means that rather than ignoring what students know in their heritage language, teachers in English medium contexts should draw on, make links to and build on students' language, literacy and curriculum content knowledge in their heritage languages and show students how to transfer skills, strategies and content learned in English to their other language (Cummins, 2007, 2008, 2011).

In English medium and immersion/bilingual classrooms, the 'monolingual principle' has dominated, meaning that students' first languages are often ignored and are kept rigidly separate from the learning of English and content (Cummins, 2008; Si'ilata, 2004) and, in immersion classrooms, students are prohibited from using their stronger language if it is not the medium of instruction of the immersion programme. Cummins (2008: 65) argues that when educators are freed 'from exclusive reliance on monolingual instructional approaches, a wide variety of opportunities arise for teaching bilingual learners by means of bilingual instructional strategies that acknowledge the reality of, and strongly promote, cross-language transfer'. Creative translation activities and 'translanguaging' have a role to play within communicative approaches to language and literacy learning, 'as a means of enabling learners to create multimedia texts that communicate in powerful and authentic ways with multiple audiences in both L1 and L2' (Cummins, 2008: 65). 'Translanguaging' originated with Williams (1996, 2000), who used it in Welsh medium education to name a pedagogical practice that switches the language mode – for example, reading is done in one language and writing in another. In essence, it teaches students to receive curriculum content input in one language and output it in another mode or genre in another language. It is not simply a translation of the same text form or mode of expression (García, 2009; García & Kleifgen, 2010):

> Translanguagings are *multiple discursive practices* in which bilinguals engage in order *to make sense of their bilingual worlds*. Translanguaging therefore goes beyond what has been termed code switching although it includes it, as well as other kinds of bilingual language use and bilingual contact. (García, 2009: 45)

Translanguaging extends what Gutierrez and her colleagues have called 'hybrid language use', that is, a 'systematic, strategic, affiliative, and sense-making process' (Gutierrez *et al.*, 2001: 128). Creating opportunities for students to translanguage is one way to utilise the idea of teaching for transfer across languages. Cummins (2008) proposed five possible types of transfer across languages, including transfer of conceptual elements, transfer of meta-cognitive and meta-linguistic strategies, transfer of pragmatic aspects of language use, transfer of specific linguistic elements and transfer of phonological awareness. Research into the connection between transfer, translanguaging and the discourse practices of bilinguals, has been investigated by other researchers who argue that translanguaging as a pedagogic process can be used to develop the linguistic repertoire and academic identities of emergent bilinguals in a range of ways (Celic & Seltzer, 2011; Champlin, 2016; García & Kleyn, 2016; Hesson *et al.*, 2014; Lee *et al.*, 2011). In providing planned and deliberate translanguaging opportunities for these learners, emergent bilinguals are able to 'adapt their language practices to the particular communicative situation in which they find themselves in order to optimize communication and understanding. That is, bilinguals learn to self-regulate to maximize their language use' (Celic & Seltzer, 2011: 2). These authors argue further that translanguaging supports emergent bilinguals to develop and transfer their linguistic flexibility within additional language learning, while validating their home language practices and enabling the rigorous teaching of both content and language.

Many researchers in the area of language and literacy development emphasise the importance of utilising learners' linguistic and cultural resources in teaching and learning interactions in schools (Cummins, 2001; McCaffery, 2014; Ruíz, 1984; Si'ilata, 2014). Dickie (2010: 25), for example, described the 'out of school' literacy experiences of Samoan children 'reading passages of the Bible aloud with perfect accuracy; and *tauloto*, which are passages from the Bible to be memorised'. Dickie argued that Samoan church literacy practices maintained a strong focus on comprehension, as well as memorisation, and that being informed about these practices could enable teachers to link to and build on these strengths in their classrooms.

Subtractive bilingual contexts for Pasifika learners were identified by McComish *et al.* (2008) as being those where bilingualism is seen as a negative phenomenon in wider society; the learner's first language is not valued and encouraged, and is replaced by the dominant language (English). In these contexts, bilinguals will not learn to use both languages extensively and are unlikely to have high proficiency in both languages (McComish *et al.*, 2008: 17). These authors maintain that, regardless of the language skills of bilingual (and other) learners, teachers should build on those competencies as a basis for further teaching and learning. The need for teachers to utilise linguistically and culturally responsive pedagogies when teaching Pasifika learners is highlighted in Chu *et al.*'s (2013) summary of Pasifika education research literature. Despite the research and policy emphasis on the value of utilising linguistically and culturally responsive pedagogies, the NZ Ministry of Education has tended to provide systemic support for digital technology development in schools through the medium of English only, rather than promoting the utilisation of students' language resources in both English and their heritage languages.

Digital Technologies for Teaching and Learning

A significant focus of the NZ Ministry of Education's work programme is concentrated on supporting schools to utilise digital technologies. The ministry's website states that by the end of 2016, 'all schools will have access to the technology available to provide high quality, high capacity, ultrafast internet access for teaching and learning' (Ministry of Education, 2016b: 1). The ministry's focus on the development of connected classrooms, utilisation of digital devices and connecting students with educational resources and 'subject-matter experts' over the internet, is premised on the default position of English medium digital teaching and learning. However, there is some evidence of strong connections being made between schools and families through the use of digital services such as social networks and websites and the development of digital resources such as ebooks. Most of the ebook development to date has been in English, with some parallel development in Te Reo Māori, and more recently the production of 20 dual language early reading texts, mentioned above, in the five main Pasifika languages in school: Cook Islands Maori, Niuean, Samoan, Tokelauan and Tongan to support transition to English medium schooling (Ministry of Education, 2016a). Digital media are becoming increasingly relevant tools in multilingual classrooms in Aotearoa NZ, enabling students and families to access learning tools and digital storybooks outside of classroom hours, thus enabling digital 24/7 learning. Audio sound files of digital storybooks are of particular use to classroom teachers who may not be speakers of children's languages, and also for enabling children to read stories in their own languages independently, supported by a 'digital listening post'.

One network of schools: Manaiakalani (http://www.manaiakalani.org/home) has led the development in the digital learning space in NZ. An evaluation by University of Auckland researchers on the impact of these digital pedagogies on student learning revealed significant impact on student engagement, while also highlighting the possibility of extending instruction to incorporate language choice:

> Vocabulary strategies and word consciousness are areas where there was less instruction and appears likely to be catalytic for supporting comprehension and thinking, supported by multimedia. Similarly, critical skills, perspective taking and language choices are all areas where there is opportunity to extend instruction. (Jesson *et al.*, 2016: 8f)

Dimensions of Effective Practice for Pasifika Learners

The six 'dimensions of effective practice' for learners in general, are described in *Effective Literacy Practice in Years 1 to 4* (Ministry of Education, 2003: 12, 2005). These six generic dimensions of effective literacy practice were modified to make them more specific to Pasifika learners and to validate the utilisation of learners' linguistic and cultural resources within the NZ education space (Si'ilata, 2014). The 'Pasifika-specific' dimensions of effective practice for Pasifika learners were developed from the literature on linguistic and cultural responsiveness, and the findings of a prior PLD and research project (Si'ilata, 2014; Si'ilata *et al.*, 2012). The Va'atele framework, which incorporated the dimensions of effective practice for Pasifika learners, was developed by Si'ilata (2014), as a metaphor and model for Pasifika success within language and literacy teaching practices in primary schools. This set of six 'Pasifika-specific' dimensions of effective classroom practice for Pasifika learners, each elucidated by two indicators, was used as a framework to consider all of the evidence collected (Table 12.1). The dimensions included:

- Knowledge of Pasifika learners.
- Expectations of Pasifika learners.
- Knowledge of Pasifika bilingualism, second language acquisition and literacy learning.
- Instructional strategies, including Pasifika languages as resources for learning.
- Pasifika connections with texts, world, language and literacy knowledge.
- Partnerships with Pasifika families/aiga and community knowledge holders (Si'ilata, 2014: 255–258).

Table 12.1 Dimensions of effective practice for Pasifika learners (Si'ilata, 2014)

Dimensions of effective practice for Pasifika learners	Indicators
Knowledge of Pasifika learners	(1a) Teachers analyse and use English language and literacy data in their practice. (1b) Teachers analyse and use Pasifika home language data and family/cultural funds of knowledge.
Expectations of Pasifika learners	(2a) Teachers set high, informed expectations for student learning which build on Pasifika learners' aspirations and values. (2b) Teachers build effective teacher-student relationships that focus on learning and build Pasifika learner agency.
Knowledge of Pasifika bilingualism, second language acquisition, and literacy learning	(3a) Teachers know about Pasifika bilingualism, second language acquisition, and literacy learning. (3b) Teachers use evidence from student data and from practice to design learning sequences, and monitor progress in relation to Pasifika learners' language and literacy needs.
Use of instructional strategies including Pasifika languages as resources for learning	(4a) Teachers explicitly teach English language and vocabulary by building on Pasifika home languages and oral practices. (4b) Teachers explicitly teach strategies for written language, including use of Pasifika literacy practices.
Supporting Pasifika connections with text, world, language, and literacy knowledge	(5a) Teachers support Pasifika learners to make meaningful connections with Pasifika cultures, experiences, languages, literacies, texts and worldviews. (5b) Teachers provide opportunities for Pasifika learners to transfer knowledge, languages and literacies from one context to another.
Partnerships with Pasifika families/aiga and community knowledge holders	(6a) Teachers collaborate with Pasifika families/aiga in identifying student learning needs and valued outcomes. (6b) Teachers build reciprocal relationships with Pasifika families/aiga and community experts to utilise their knowledge at school.

Source: Adapted from 'The Dimensions of Effective Practice' Ministry of Education (2003: 12).

These six dimensions were utilised with teachers in a PLD and research project that focused on supporting teachers to employ dual language texts with Pasifika learners, including digital learning technologies (Si'ilata *et al.*, 2015a). Teachers were encouraged to support students and their families 'to story' in their own languages, using the digital and hard copy books as catalysts for the promotion of 'translanguaging storying' and the creation of their own multimedia texts. Teachers were encouraged to make links between learners' home and school contexts 'in ways that were visible and significant for the child' (Ministry of Education, 2003: 117). These Pasifika-specific dimensions were used as the overarching framework for the analysis of teaching practice, and form the lens through which the data from teachers and the observations of their practice have been analysed and the results articulated. The way in which teachers demonstrated aspects of these dimensions are described in two case studies below.

The first case study is situated within a research project that examined the language and literacy outcomes of Samoan children in the classes of 24 teachers who participated in the PLD pilot. The classroom practices of six teachers were investigated by gathering in-depth data based on audio-recorded and transcribed classroom lessons and post-observation interviews with each teacher. The design team of early literacy, *English for speakers of other languages* (ESOL) and bilingual experts had been contracted by the Ministry of Education to design and deliver a six-month teacher PLD and family meeting pilot programme to a cluster of seven schools (including 24 Year 1–2 teachers). These schools had significant numbers of Samoan bilingual children, with the pilot's focus being on the development of continuity between home and school language/literacy practices. The ministry's goal for the pilot was to support the development of smooth transitions between home/early-childhood contexts and schooling by supporting teachers and parents to utilise dual language Samoan–English texts with their students/children. Through the PLD programme, teachers were supported to use communicative translanguaging approaches to language and literacy learning, and to foster connections between children's Samoan and English language and literacy resources. They were encouraged to incorporate the trialling of dual language text utilisation within their existing language, literacy and digital programmes. Through the family meeting programme, parents were encouraged to 'talanoa' (talk) with their children, to maintain their Samoan language in the home and to 'story around the text' by connecting their own stories with the schema of the book. Teachers participating in the PLD programme attended four full-day workshops over four months, and the parents of the Samoan children in the teachers' classes attended three parent meetings/fono over the same time period. Teachers were also visited by PLD facilitators who observed their practice and engaged in co-constructed learning conversations following their lessons. Meetings with senior managers were held prior to, and following the PLD workshop programme in order to provide information, share outcomes, present opportunities for feedback and support systemic change within schools. Data were based on audio recordings and transcriptions from the pilot workshops; from the observations of the teacher lessons; and from the lead facilitator's post-observation interviews with the teachers. The participating teachers were drawn from seven schools with significant numbers of Samoan children. The pilot preceded subsequent development in the four other Pasifika languages afforded with resource development by the Ministry of Education (Te Reo Māori Kuki Airani/Cook Islands Maori, Vagahau Niue/Niuean, Lea Faka Tonga/Tongan and Gagana Tokelau/Tokelauan). A case methodology was utilised, supported by both quantitative and qualitative research methods in order to answer the research questions. The questions were:

(1) What is the impact on classroom teachers' practice following participation in a PLD pilot programme focused on the utilisation of Samoan dual language texts?
(2) What is the impact of teacher utilisation of dual language texts on Samoan children and their families?
(3) What does effective teaching that is focused on the development of bilingual, translanguaging and biliteracy pedagogies with Pasifika children look like?
(4) Within multilingual classrooms, how might teachers synthesise translanguaging pedagogies with students' production of bilingual multimedia products?

The PLD pilot took a co-constructed approach with teachers to enable them to connect new professional learning with their existing classroom practice. They had opportunity to consider classroom implications for ongoing bilingual and biliteracy development; they learnt about utilising students' prior linguistic and literacy knowledge through employing translanguaging pedagogies; they learnt how to integrate receptive and productive modes, accelerate vocabulary acquisition and synthesise dual language text utilisation with existing classroom digital tools.

Case Study 1 highlights the beliefs and practices of effective teachers who demonstrated dimension (4a) within the digital learning space: Teachers explicitly teach English language and vocabulary by building on Pasifika home languages and oral practices. It is drawn from research undertaken with Years 1–2 teachers of Samoan learners who participated in a Ministry of Education PLD pilot programme that was focused on the utilisation of Samoan dual language texts to support language and literacy learning at school (Si'ilata *et al.*, 2015a, 2015b). The second case study provides a brief account of an exemplary teacher, Teacher K, who worked within Manaiakalani (the digital learning network of schools), where teachers taught in digital classrooms, and supported their Pasifika learners to create multimedia digital products. Only a few of these teachers, however, were synthesising translanguaging and digital pedagogies in systematic ways. Case Study 2 highlights the practice of Teacher K, who demonstrated dimension (4b): Teachers explicitly teach strategies for written language, including use of Pasifika literacy practices. Her work was shared with teachers who participated in the dual language text PLD programme described in Case Study 1, to provide them with actual examples of translanguaging pedagogies being used within digital learning spaces.

Through these cases, illustrative narratives of the Va'atele dimension: Instructional strategies, including Pasifika languages as resources for learning, are presented.

Case Study 1

Dimension 4: Instructional strategies, including Pasifika languages as resources for learning

Indicator (4a) Teachers explicitly teach English language and vocabulary by building on Pasifika home languages and oral practices

This case illustrates the importance of surfacing and changing teacher beliefs before endeavouring to change teacher practice. It includes the voice of Teacher A who talked about what enabled her to change her beliefs and practices in relation to the use of Pasifika languages as resources for learning. It also includes a short classroom excerpt from Teacher D that provides an example of a teacher endeavouring to synthesise translanguaging pedagogies with multimedia digital product production by her Pasifika learners.

The pre-eminence of the role of pre-existing knowledge as a foundation for learning has been well documented by Bransford *et al.* (2000) who emphasise three requirements for effective learning: (a) engaging prior understandings, (b) integrating factual knowledge with conceptual frameworks and (c) taking active control over the learning process through meta-cognitive strategies. The inquiry and knowledge building cycle from the best evidence synthesis on teacher PLD (Timperley *et al.*, 2007) connects strongly with Bransford *et al.*'s thinking about how people learn. The synthesis identified how cycles of teacher inquiry and knowledge building can improve learners' engagement, learning and well-being. The stages of the inquiry cycle focus on teacher inquiry in order to meet student learning needs: identifying valued outcomes and student learning needs; identifying professional learning needs; engaging in professional learning to deepen knowledge and refine skills; engaging in new learning experiences and assessing the impact and re-engagement in the next cycle.

In order for teachers to learn effectively, it is vital that their existing beliefs in relation to their students' learning are surfaced and engaged (Bransford *et al.*, 2000). If teachers' existing beliefs about their students' ability to learn, and about what is important for their students' learning are not surfaced and challenged, it is unlikely that they will engage in the next stage of deepening their pedagogical content knowledge because their existing beliefs may prevent them from doing so. In relation to their Pasifika learners, this would mean surfacing existing teacher beliefs and assumptions about the ways in which Pasifika learners learn, about what helps them to learn, about their families' aspirations for their learning, about their abilities and experiences outside of school and particularly about their languages, family and cultural backgrounds.

The overarching principle of the PLD programme, encapsulated in each of the workshop underpinning principles and outcomes, was the integration of home and school 'funds of knowledge' and the utilisation of Samoan children's language and literacy resources. This focus on utilising Samoan children's funds of knowledge, rather than maintaining a focus solely on student needs as a basis for effective teacher PLD, meant that teachers were supported to view their Samoan (and other linguistically diverse learners) through an appreciative lens. Teachers were encouraged to engage in communicative bilingual approaches to language and literacy learning within the digital learning space, throughout the PLD programme, which prompted reflection on their current practice and classroom environment.

Teachers' existing beliefs

Before endeavouring to change teacher practice, it was first necessary to surface teachers' existing beliefs about how Pasifika bilingual children learn, and about what it means to 'tap into students' funds of knowledge'. Teachers needed to surface and understand their own tacit beliefs about the perceived value of making connections with bilingual students' funds of knowledge to support teaching and learning in the classroom. Through conversations with teachers during workshops, there was evidence that some teachers knew little about the out-of-school lives and experiences of Pasifika children and their families. Some teachers expressed that they had previously taken a deficit view of Pasifika children's and families' lives and experiences, primarily their language/s, dialects, registers of English and their particular literacy practices (for example, church literacy knowledge and practices). They were provided with opportunities to discuss how their beliefs about what works in classrooms for bilingual learners had been challenged, the impact on their practice and the changed outcomes:

> Teacher A:
> The bottom line is I failed this child and I have changed. Now I am really emotional about this because if I failed him how many other children have I? And I've noticed that every single one of my children is now moving… I was given two children that haven't moved at all in another class, and then I got them. They are now moving. And this has all taken part in the last month or so… It's happened. I am proof of that and I am such a happy person because of that… And often we think we know it all. Actually we don't. I used to think I was a damn good teacher and you woke me up on that day. I had to have a really good check of myself and my teaching practices and what was working and what wasn't, and how I could change it and to this day it has affected me so greatly…

Many teachers expressed that they already made connections with students' prior knowledge, but the connections made were often limited to a brief discussion about children's prior 'world knowledge' prior to reading. Few monolingual teachers were making connections with children's existing linguistic or first language knowledge. Some teachers expressed the belief that it was better to keep the first language separate from the learning of English and that five-year-olds would get confused if teachers tried to teach more than one language at a time, especially while endeavouring also to teach mastery of digital tools.

Utilising digital tools to promote language and literacy learning

A number of (non-Samoan) teachers read Samoan texts with their students using digital sound files of the texts that provided models of correct pronunciation. Teacher D supported her learners to connect their own schema with the schema in the book, and enabled them to utilise the text structure to tell and write their own bilingual digital stories using iPads:

> [Teacher with new entrant five-year-olds creating their own digital stories about themselves using the dual language Samoan text as a structure]:

Teacher:	Off you go, you guys carry on.
Children:	Yay! (Reading the story they have written on their iPad): 'O la'u 'ato ā'oga lea. Here is my school bag.
Teacher:	Okay do you maybe need to record that one again if you can't really hear it?
Child 1:	You need to delete it.

Teacher:	Okay so delete that one. You guys have another go at the sound file.
Teacher and child together:	‘O la‘u ‘ato ā‘oga lea. (Here is my school bag).
Teacher:	Want to play it and see what it sounds like?
Children play their sound recording:	‘O la‘u ‘ato ā‘oga lea. Here is my school bag. ‘O la‘u pusa mea‘ai lea. Here is my lunch box. ‘O la‘u tusi lea. Here is my book.
Teacher:	Let’s see if they’ve got their sound file (plays the file). Awesome. You guys are way ahead. Let’s read it together (uses the digital text on the interactive whiteboard to read with students):
Teacher and children:	What’s this one? We can read this one; we’re clever. ‘O la‘u tusi lea. And what does that one mean? Here is my book.
Child:	How do you know how to do it?
Teacher:	Because Mrs R_____ has been practising at home!
Child:	Are you Samoan?
Teacher:	No sweetie, but I’m learning.
Child 2:	She’s English. She’s from England…
Teacher:	Yes, cos even though I’m a teacher, I never stop learning either. I have to go home and do homework too.
Child:	Cos you’re a English. You’re from England.
Teacher:	I am from England, yes.

It was evident that the teacher’s willingness to put herself in the position of the learner, to privilege the linguistic knowledge of the children and to create opportunities for them to connect their Samoan linguistic and conceptual knowledge with their English language and literacy acquisition had a major impact on the children’s willingness to utilise their linguistic resources at school. The use of their linguistic resources had a direct impact on their English language acquisition, their biliteracy development and their meaningful use of digital tools for multilingual storying within the translanguaging space. They were also prompted to consider their teacher’s and their own linguistic and cultural identities as a result of reading digital dual language texts together. The teacher’s deliberate use of translanguaging as a pedagogical tool enabled the Samoan children in her class to develop greater bilingual and biliterate capability.

Another junior school teacher (Teacher N) who participated in the same PLD programme, decided to call on the older siblings of the children in her class to record their own bilingual versions of the digital storybooks because their younger siblings struggled to keep up with the speed of the commercially produced sound files. The outcome of this choice by the teacher resulted in the younger children exhibiting greater reading engagement, evidence of accelerated achievement in English and enhanced maintenance and production of their heritage language (Samoan).

Case Study 2

Dimension 4: Instructional strategies, including Pasifika languages as resources for learning

Indicator (4b) Teachers explicitly teach strategies for written language, including use of Pasifika literacy practices

This case study draws on the work of an exemplary teacher within the translanguaging/digital teaching and learning space. Teacher K's work and personal reflection were provided via her online blog. As one of the lead teachers in the digital learning community, her online blog described her professional inquiry into her own practice. She sought to combine the Manaiakalani digital learning community's approach of *Learn, Create, Share* with translanguaging pedagogical approaches to enable her Tongan learners to create multimedia digital texts in both English and Tongan. Teacher K had recently completed studies in teaching English in schools to speakers of other languages (TESSOL), and having learnt about translanguaging pedagogies, she endeavoured to utilise these approaches with the Tongan children in her class. The children engaged in bilingual reading and discussion about an ancient Tongan story that was familiar to them, and which was then used as a basis for bilingual multimedia text production. The following example demonstrates the children negotiating their understandings of the Tongan text using both Tongan and English. Teacher K supported them to read a text about the heilala flower, and to find out how it was created, according to an ancient Tongan love story. The children worked collaboratively and bilingually to make connections to the text using all of their language resources to do so. Teacher K explains:

> This is a quick post about another example of translanguaging I have tried. The setting was Reading. Students needed to read a Tongan text and make connections to the text to infer what was happening in the pictures… I hope that when completing this, they use some of the key Tongan language phrases that we learned/discussed while reading this today. This text was very simple and prompted a lot of discussion. I did not need any prior translating of the text before teaching, so this could be an ideal text for any teacher wanting to begin this journey, or a teacher who has a student new from Tonga and who needs support from texts written in their first language.

> Tongan children reading together:

> Kakala faka'ofo'ofa! Ko e heilala, ko e huni, pea mo e fa'. 'Oku faka'ofo'ofa 'aupito. 'Oku ou sa'ia hono lanu'. Lanu kulokula lelei.

English translation:

What beautiful flowers! They're heilala, huni, and fa'. The flowers are really beautiful. I love the colour. It's a great red.

Teacher K described this as the 'learn' stage of '*Learn, Create, Share*', connecting it with 'linguistic input in one language', where students were receiving and negotiating input in Tongan and producing oral 'output' in English, using a Tongan medium text. At the 'create' stage, she linked this with 'linguistic and cognitive processing', aimed at extending learners' oral and written output using a range of digital tools, including Google apps, Google images and the children's independent online research about the heilala flower. The following is an example of their written output:

What types of Heilala are there? There is more than one colour of Heilala. The colours of the heilala are red and yellow. They wear heilala flowers to weddings, birthdays and funerals.

The children used these input and cognitive processing modes to create their own digital multimedia texts using a movie app to tell their audience about the origins of the heilala flower. It was apparent that the students were drawing on prior learning by making connections to a story they had explored before. They also utilised Pasifika literacy practices including oratory techniques such as memorisation, recitation, choral reading, music and song to create their version of the Tongan myth in a digital format using both Tongan and English. At the 'share' stage, the children posted their digital products on their class blog to share with others.

Understanding the Va'atele metaphor

The dimensions of effective practice for Pasifika learners were applied to the metaphor or model for Pasifika learner success: the *va'atele*, or double-hulled canoe. The analogy of the Va'atele framework may be applied to Pasifika learners as they navigate their way through the education system, enabled by teachers and leaders who employ the dimensions of effective practice for Pasifika learners in their practice. To understand the metaphor in relation to Pasifika learners and their experiences at school, the double hulls and the voyaging of the deep-sea canoe are compared with Pasifika learners' passage or journey through the schooling system as bilingual/bicultural people. Ideally, Pasifika learners would be in school settings that support the development of their bilingualism, biliteracy and biculturalism, enabling success not only in the world of school, but also in the world of home and community. One hull may be seen to represent the language, literacy, culture and world view of home, while the second hull is representative of the language, literacy, culture and world view of school. The platform/fata built over the two hulls is a bridge that helps to hold the whole *va'atele* together, thus enabling the hulls/va'a to move through the water as one vessel, while also providing the stability needed to sail through any storm.

For Pasifika learners at school in Aotearoa NZ or throughout the Pacific, enacting the metaphorical double-hulled canoe (or linguistically and culturally responsive environment that privileges bilingual and biliterate goals over monolingual ones), is more likely to elicit effective outcomes than the single-hull metaphor – whether the single-hull be 'English-only' language, literacy and cultural knowledge, or single-hulled Pasifika-only language, literacy and cultural knowledge. In order for Pasifika learners to be successful in these two worlds, they need to strengthen and build capacity and capability in both, and to have opportunity to use their full linguistic resource within the digital learning space.

Conclusion

This chapter began by providing an overview of the educational landscape for Pasifika learners in Aotearoa NZ, followed by an explanation of the Va'atele framework and two case studies that illustrate one of the dimensions, as a suggested way to modify practice to incorporate multilingual approaches with Pasifika learners in digital language and literacy teaching spaces at school. The case study illustrates two principles in relation to Pasifika learners' success at school. Through the development of inquiry-focused, collaborative and success-oriented relationships, the following are possible:

(1) Pasifika learners can be highly successful at school. Their utilisation of language and literacy as interactive learning tools within the digital space is fundamental to that success.
(2) Teachers can teach Pasifika learners effectively, and in particular ways that connect with and build on their specific languages, cultures and identities, to meet the demands of the curriculum, and to create bilingual/multilingual digital products.

Future directions

Successfully enacting each of these dimensions and their indicators in the classroom with Pasifika learners was not solely the province of Pasifika teachers. These indicators were enacted in classrooms to varying degrees by the teachers involved in the research studies, with only 2 of the 24 teachers being of Pasifika ethnicity (Samoan). The findings of this research illustrate that any teacher, regardless of ethnicity, can improve their practice in creating opportunities for Pasifika learners to make the timely, meaningful connections that build on their languages, cultures and identities within the digital learning space, in order to master the linguistic and cognitive demands of school. From the case studies, it was evident that the teachers who were effective at supporting children to create bilingual digital products, were those who held specific pedagogical content knowledge in bilingual/translanguaging pedagogies. They also were willing to experiment in the digital learning space, to synthesise translanguaging pedagogies with the children's use of digital tools, thus enabling them to create bi/multilingual digital products. Further research into the systemic structures and effective classroom practices that enable English medium teachers to work in linguistically and culturally responsive ways to enable their Pasifika (and other) linguistically diverse learners to utilise their bilingual and bicultural resources at school, particularly with digital tools, is urgently needed.

References

Baker, C. (2011) *Foundations of Bilingual Education and Bilingualism* (5th edn). Bristol: Multilingual Matters.

Bransford, J.D., Brown, A.L. and Cocking, R.R. (2000) *How People Learn: Brain, Mind, Experience, and School*. Washington, DC: National Academy Press.

Celic, C. and Seltzer, K. (2011) *Translanguaging: A CUNY-NYSIEB Guide for Educators*. New York: The Graduate Center, The City University of New York.

Champlin, M. (2016) Translanguaging and bilingual learners: A study of how translanguaging promotes literacy skills in bilingual students. Unpublished master's dissertation, St. John Fisher College. See http://fisherpub.sjfc.edu/cgi/viewcontent.cgi?article=1326&context=education_ETD_masters (accessed 17 April 2016).

Chu, C., Glasgow, A., Rimoni, F., Hodis, M. and Meyer, L. (2013) *An Analysis of Recent Pasifika Education Research Literature to Inform and Improve Outcomes for Pasifika learners*. Wellington, NZ: Ministry of Education. See http://www.educationcounts.govt.nz/__data/assets/pdf_file/0003/121773/An-analysis-of-recent-Pasifika-Education-research-literature-to-inform-improve-outcomes-for-Pasifika-learners.pdf (accessed 13 March 2016).

Cummins, J. (1980) The construct of language proficiency in bilingual education. *NABE Journal* 4 (3), 25–59.

Cummins, J. (2000) *Language, Power and Pedagogy: Bilingual Children in the Crossfire*. Clevedon: Multilingual Matters.

Cummins, J. (2001) Empowering minority students: A framework for intervention. In C. Baker and N. Hornberger (eds) *An Introductory Reader to the Writings of Jim Cummins* (pp. 175–194). Clevedon: Multilingual Matters.

Cummins, J. (2007) Rethinking monolingual instructional strategies in multilingual classrooms. *The Canadian Journal of Applied Linguistics* 10 (2), 221–240.

Cummins, J. (2008) Teaching for transfer: Challenging the two solitudes assumption in bilingual education. In J. Cummins and N.H. Hornberger (eds) *Encyclopaedia of Language and Education* (pp. 65–75). New York: Springer.

Cummins, J. (2011) *The Intersection of Cognitive and Sociocultural Factors in the Development of Reading Comprehension among Migrant Students*. New York: Springer Science and Business Media. See http://link.springer.com/article/10.1007%2Fs11145-010-9290-7 (accessed 25 April 2018).

Dickie, J. (2010) Proclaiming the good news: Samoan children, church literacy, and comprehension. *Set* 2, 25–31.

García, O. (2009) *Bilingual Education in the 21st Century: A Global Perspective*. Chichester: Wiley-Blackwell.

García, O. and Kleifgen, J. (2010) *Educating Emergent Bilinguals: Policies, Programs, and Practices for English Language Learners*. New York: Teachers College Press.
García, O. and Kleyn, T. (2016) Translanguaging theory in education. In O. García and T. Kleyn (eds) *Translanguaging with Multilingual Students: Learning from Classroom Moments* (pp. 9–33). New York: Routledge.
Gonzalez, N., Moll, L. and Amanti, C. (eds) (2005) *Funds of Knowledge, Theorizing Practices in Households, Communities, and Classrooms*. New York: Routledge.
Gutierrez, K., Baquedano-Lopez, P. and Alvarez, H.H. (2001) Literacy as hybridity: Moving beyond bilingualism in urban classrooms. In M. Reyes and J.J. Halcon (eds) *The Best for Our Children: Critical Perspectives on Literacy for Latino Students* (pp. 122–141). New York: Teachers College Press.
Hesson, S., Sletzer, K. and Woodley, H. (2014) *Translanguaging in Curriculum and Instruction: A CUNY-NYSIEB Guide for Educators*. New York: The Graduate Center, The City University of New York
Hornberger, N. (2003) *Continua of Biliteracy: An Ecological Framework for Educational Policy, Research, and Practice in Multilingual Settings*. Clevedon: Multilingual Matters.
Jesson, R., McNaughton, S., Rosedale, N., Zhu, T., Meredith, M. and Kegel, A. (2016) Manaiakalani whānau Capability Building and Classroom Instruction: Final Report – executive summary. Report to Manaiakalani Education Trust. Auckland UniServices, Auckland.
Lee, J.S., Hill-Bonnet, L. and Raley, J. (2011) Examining the effects of language brokering on student identities and learning opportunities in dual immersion classrooms. *Journal of Language, Identity, and Education* 10 (5), 306–326.
McCaffery, J. (2014) Simultaneous biliteracy at Richmond Road School. Unpublished PhD draft, University of Auckland.
McComish, J., May, S. and Franken, M. (2008) *Language Enhancing the Achievement of Pasifika*. Wellington, NZ: Learning Media.
Ministry of Education (2003) *Effective Literacy Practice in Years 1 to 4*. Wellington, NZ: Learning Media.
Ministry of Education (2005) *Effective Literacy Practice in Years 5 to 8*. Wellington, NZ: Learning Media.
Ministry of Education (2007) *The Pasifika Teacher Aide Handbook: Supporting Pasifika Teacher Aides in Mainstream Classrooms*. Auckland, NZ: Ministry of Education.
Ministry of Education (2009a) *Mua O! An Introduction to Gagana Samoa. Teachers' Guide and Support Materials: Learning Languages Series*. Auckland, NZ: Teuila. See http://pasifika.tki.org.nz/Media/Files/Mua-O!-An-Introduction-to-Gagana-Samoa (accessed 13 March 2016).
Ministry of Education (2009b) The Pasifika Education Plan 2009–2012. See http://www.minedu.govt.nz/~/media/MinEdu/Files/EducationSectors/PasifikaEducation/PEPKeyMessages2011.pdf (accessed 12 November 2012).
Ministry of Education (2014) *Request for Proposals – Pasifika New Entrant Pilot: The Design and Implementation of a Pilot Plan to Support New Entrant Pasifika Children into English Medium Schooling*. Wellington, NZ: Ministry of Education.
Ministry of Education (2016a) Pasifika dual language books. See http://literacyonline.tki.org.nz/Literacy-Online/Planning-for-my-students-needs/Pasifika-dual-language-books (accessed 11 Feb 2017).
Ministry of Education (2016b) Digital technologies for teaching and learning. See http://www.education.govt.nz/ministry-of-education/specific-initiatives/digital-technologies-for-teaching-and-learning/ (accessed 13 April 2018).
Post Primary Teachers' Association (2010) *'Mind Your Language': Our Responsibility to Protect and Promote Pacific Islands Languages in New Zealand as Part of a National*

Languages Policy. Wellington, New Zealand: PPTA Annual Conference Papers. See http://ppta.org.nz/dmsdocument/302 (accessed 13 April 2018).

Ruíz, R. (1984) Orientations in language planning. *NABE: The Journal for the National Association for Bilingual Education* 8 (2), 15–34. http://dx.doi.org/10.1080/08855072.1984.10668464

Si'ilata, R. (2004) Tala'aga o gagana a tamaiti mai le Pasifika: Language stories of children from the Pacific. Unpublished master's dissertation, University of Auckland.

Si'ilata, R. (2014) Va'a Tele: Pasifika learners riding the success wave on linguistically and culturally responsive pedagogies. Unpublished PhD thesis, University of Auckland. See http://hdl.handle.net/2292/23402 (accessed 1 Feb 2015).

Si'ilata, R., Dreaver, K., Parr, J., Timperley, H. and Meissel, K. (2012) *Tula'i Mai! Making a Difference to Pasifika Student Achievement in Literacy: Final Research Report on the Pasifika Literacy Professional Development Project 2009–2010*. Auckland: Auckland UniServices Ltd. http://www.educationcounts.govt.nz/publications/pasifika/literacy-professional-development-project-2009-2010 (accessed 9 June 2015).

Si'ilata, R., Gaffney, J., Stephenson, J. and McCaffery, J. (2015a) Scaffolding New Entrant Pasifika Children into English Medium Schooling – Design and Implementation of New Entrant Pilot Programme (PNEP) Gālulue Fa'atasi: Final Milestone. Report to the Ministry of Education. Auckland UniServices, Auckland.

Si'ilata, R., Le Fevre, D.M., Ell, F., Timperley, H., Twyford, K. and Mayo, S. (2015b) Adaptive Expertise in the Facilitation of Linguistic and Cultural Responsiveness. Commissioned report to the Consortium of Professional Learning.

Statistics NZ (2013) Quickstats about culture and identity. See http://www.stats.govt.nz/Census/2013-census/profile-and-summary-reports/quickstats-culture-identity/ethnic-groups-NZ.aspx

Timperley, H., Wilson, A., Barrar, H. and Fung, A. (2007) *Teacher Professional Learning and Development: Best Evidence Synthesis Iteration*. Wellington, NZ: Ministry of Education.

Williams, C. (1996) Secondary education: Teaching in the bilingual situation. In C. Williams, G. Lewis and C. Baker (eds) *The Language Policy: Taking Stock* (pp. 39–78). Llangefni, Wales: Cai.

Williams, C. (2000) Welsh-medium and bilingual teaching in the further education sector. *International Journal of Bilingual Education and Bilingualism* 3 (2), 129–148.

13 The Use of Teacher Trainees' Own and Peer Videos for the Introduction of Multilingual-Sensitive Teaching Approaches in Pre-Service Teacher Training Classes

Heike Niesen

Introduction

Pupils' increasing heterogeneity in school contexts and, more specifically, multilingualism as one dimension/aspect of that diversity highly challenges current teacher education (Trautmann, 2010; Trautmann & Wischer, 2011; Ziegler, 2013). To best enable teachers to meet this challenge, it does not come as a surprise that teacher education programmes rely on well-proven and efficient tools such as teaching videos. The merits that videos as 'artifacts of practice' (Borko *et al.*, 2008: 418) can have on teachers' education have been portrayed extensively (e.g. Brophy, 2003; Calandra & Rich, 2015; Rossi & Fedeli, 2016). In the course of various video-based professional development (PD) programmes, studies have typically investigated the effects that different video analysis settings, i.e. individual or collaborative analysis, have on the development of teachers' PD (e.g. Lefstein & Snell, 2011), and whether and how teachers' discourse about videos in collaborative settings changes over time (e.g. Borko *et al.*, 2008; Sherin & Han, 2004). The question whether the implementation of videos outperforms that of alternative presentations of teaching, such as written lesson descriptions to foster teachers' PD, has been subject to inquiry as well (Baecher *et al.*, 2013; Rosaen *et al.*, 2008). Further, an impressive number of studies have addressed the impact teachers' own and other teachers' teaching videos have on practitioners' PD (e.g. Hellermann *et al.*, 2015; Kleinknecht & Schneider, 2013; Krammer & Hugener, 2014; Zhang *et al.*, 2011).

In many of these studies, PD and 'professional vision' (Goodwin, 1994) are frequently mentioned in the same breath, since the latter is generally acknowledged as a constitutive part of the former (Lefstein & Snell, 2011; Sherin, 2007). Virtually all of these studies employ a notion of 'professional vision' (PV), which has been defined as 'the ability to see and interpret critical features of classroom events' (Sherin & Han, 2004: 179), i.e. the ability to be engaged in 'selective attention' or 'noticing' and 'knowledge-based reasoning' (Sherin & van Es, 2009; van Es & Sherin, 2008). Whereas 'noticing' refers to the 'process by which teachers identify what is relevant in a classroom', 'knowledge-based reasoning' is associated with teachers' ability to 'describe precisely what has been noticed', to 'link (observed classroom situations) to prior knowledge' and, finally, to 'evaluate and predict what might happen as a result of the observed situation' (Seidel *et al.*, 2011: 261).

Although the studies outlined above offer valuable insights into how teachers' PD/PV may be fostered via video analyses, it is important to note here that, besides a few notable exceptions (e.g. Baecher *et al.*, 2013; Zafer, 2015), these studies have been conducted almost exclusively in the context of science and mathematics teaching and learning. Of course, the implementation of videos is by no means an unrecognised issue in foreign language teaching and learning (cf. e.g. Maclean & White, 2007; Orlova, 2009; Wallace, 1979, 1981). However, none of these studies has investigated the effects different video types can have specifically on pre-service English as a foreign language (EFL) teachers' multilingual-sensitive PV development. The present chapter aims to address this gap. More precisely, it reports on the use of different types of video analysis within two university classes with a focus on teaching EFL in multilingual settings, conducted and assessed at Goethe University Frankfurt/Main. Given this focus, the two classes are henceforth referred to as 'Multilingual-sensitive-Teaching-approaches' (MsTa) classes. An overview of current findings regarding the integration of videos in teacher training will provide the theoretical background. On the basis of the latter, the conceptual design and the objectives of the courses are described, followed by a description of the in-depth course evaluations and their findings.

'Own', 'Peer' and 'Other' Videos: Possibilities and Downfalls

The majority of research on videos and their effects on teachers' PD distinguishes between 'own' and 'other' videos. In most cases, 'own' videos are those in which teachers see and analyse their own teaching, whereas 'other' videos show performances of teachers unknown to the analysts (cf. Seidel *et al.*, 2011). A more fine-grained differentiation of video types is used by Zhang *et al.* (2011: 454ff) who subdivide 'other' videos into 'video from published resources' and 'video of teachers' colleagues', also referred to as 'peer videos'.

A solid amount of research has investigated the effects 'own', 'peer' and 'other' videos have on teachers' PD. Examining the effects teaching videos have on in-service mathematics teachers' PV, Sherin and Han (2004) found that all the teachers who participated in their 'video club meetings' benefited from the fact that the videos could be analysed without the urgent demands of teaching (cf. Kleinknecht & Schneider, 2013; Sherin & Han, 2004; Sherin & van Es, 2009), no matter whether they investigated their own teaching or that of their colleagues. Not only did video discussions become increasingly complex over time, a finding similar to the one made by Borko *et al.* (2008), teachers also gradually shifted their focus of analysis from being primarily teacher-centred to more pupil-related issues (Sherin & Han, 2004).

'Own' videos

Their investigation of the effects 'own' and 'peer' videos have on middle school mathematics teachers' PD led Borko *et al.* (2008: 434) to conclude that teachers' own videos 'allowed teachers to see what they were doing well and to identify areas of improvement'. This finding is similar to the ones made by Zhang *et al.* (2011, 2015) who explored the effects of 'published', 'peer' and 'own' video analyses on in-service science teachers' PD. The authors argue that their own videos helped teachers to '(...) observe themselves from a distance', and to '(...) see things you normally don't see', thereby enabling them to 'identify their strengths and weaknesses' (Zhang *et al.*, 2015: 156).

In their experimental study on the development of German and Swiss science teachers' noticing and knowledge-based reasoning, Seidel *et al.* (2011) report higher levels of immersion and resonance for teachers watching their own videos. They further showed that teachers reacted to critical incidents in their own teaching less critically (Seidel *et al.*, 2011: 266). This corresponds to Kleinknecht and Schneider (2013: 19), who, in exploring in-service mathematics teachers' PD, state that 'the teachers observing videos of other teachers' classrooms analysed negative events in greater depth, whereas teachers in the Own Video Group often described or evaluated negative events in a more superficial way'. Interestingly, this contradicts insights gained by Borko *et al.* (2008) who found that teachers rather criticised their own teaching than their colleagues'.

Baecher *et al.* (2013: 189, 196) found 'own' videos to be powerful tools to train pre-service teachers of English to speakers of other languages (TESOL) 'self-evaluation capabilities', provided that analysis is supported by observation rubrics. The implementation of 'other' videos prior to 'own' videos counters possible dangers accompanied by the analysis of the latter, namely leniency and modesty bias, i.e. teacher training students' tendency to under- or overrate their own teaching performance, respectively (Baecher *et al.*, 2013: 191).

'Peer'/'colleagues' video

One of the possibilities offered by 'peer' videos lies in their potential to offer teachers the opportunity to 'see different teaching styles and learn new ideas for their own teaching' (Zhang *et al.*, 2015: 158) or to 'learn new pedagogical strategies (...) and realize that they all struggle with similar issues' (Borko *et al.*, 2008: 434). Another advantage of 'peer' videos lies in the fact that, in contrast to 'other' videos, the teachers who perform in the video are usually present during the process of analysis and can therefore comment on their teaching, and have it evaluated by the observers (cf. Zhang *et al.*, 2015). In spite of these merits, the implementation of 'peer' videos can also be demanding in terms of cooperative video analyses and discussions. As Zhang *et al.* (2015: 159) conclude, 'for some teachers it was unclear whether the point was to support one another, (...), to encourage and improve good teaching, to be nice, or to be critical in a constructive way'. Teachers' behaviour in group discussions is a sensitive matter not to be underestimated, which is why it is addressed further in the fourth section.

'Other'/'published video'

Biaggi *et al.* (2013: 26, trans.) showed that the implementation of 'other' videos serves well to provide novice teachers with illustrative examples of how to apply 'teaching features relevant to learning'. What is more, 'published videos' can also trigger teachers' 'comparative reflection' (Zhang *et al.*, 2011: 461), i.e. they lend themselves well to teachers' comparison of their own performances with that of others. Put differently, this kind of video offers teachers the opportunity to study aspects associated with their own teaching (cf. Seago, 2004). This kind of 'social comparison' is often seen as a 'motivator for performance' (e.g. Baecher *et al.*, 2013: 191).

A downfall of this video type, namely the frequent lack of contextual information such as background knowledge about the class, the lesson plan or learning materials, has been acknowledged by a number of researchers (e.g. Seidel *et al.*, 2011; Zhang *et al.*, 2011). Needless to say, a shortcoming like this may seriously hamper in-depth video analyses. Approaches to overcome this difficulty are outlined in the section titled 'Digital Features'.

'Own', 'peer' and 'other' videos: Emotions involved

No matter whether teachers observe their own teaching videos, their peers'/colleagues' performances or that of complete strangers, they do so individually or in cooperative settings. For the latter, researchers have continuously highlighted the importance of creating a respectful and appreciative discourse atmosphere that allows for 'critical colleagueship' (Lord, 1994, as cited in Sherin & Han, 2004: 164). Borko *et al.* (2008) clearly state that for video-based discussions among colleagues to become fearless, open and productive, a strong professional community of mutual trust needs to be created. This demand is primarily based on their finding that teachers tended to be 'cautious and hesitant to explore pedagogical issues in great depth' (Borko *et al.*, 2008: 432), especially at the beginning of their video-based PD programme. Moreover, feelings of embarrassment occurred among teachers who would rather criticise their own than their colleagues' teaching until a professional and safe discourse atmosphere emerged. Lefstein and Snell (2011) noticed qualitative differences between preceding individual written analyses by in-service literacy primary school teachers and the comments teachers made during collaborative video analyses. Teachers hesitated to share their insights in a collaborative discourse setting as they were engaged in face-saving acts and frequently defended their own or their peers' performance against 'perceived attacks' (Lefstein & Snell, 2011: 510). This finding is somewhat contradictory to the one made by Krammer and Hugener (2014: 29, translation H.N.), who state that pre-service teachers 'experienced the work with their own videos as motivating (...), resulting in curious, open, honest and respectful analytical discourse'. Quite interestingly, however, students tended to become less interested in 'other' videos towards the end of the semester. In an attempt to explain this, the authors assume that the decline in interest might be due to students being less personally affected by 'other' than their own videos (Krammer & Hugener, 2014: 30). In fact, this view is shared by Seago (2004: 263) who defines 'other' videos as 'teaching that is emotionally distant'. Although this argument seems reasonable in a specific context, it loses some of its explanatory power when confronted with findings made by Kleinknecht and Schneider (2013: 19) who reveal that teachers who watched 'other videos' experienced more negative (disappointment or anger) and positive feelings (enjoyment or well-being) than teachers who observed their own videos.

Digital features

A number of suggestions of how to add value to video-supported PD via digital features have been made. Goeze (2010) argues that computer-assisted learning environments help to enrich teaching videos as learning sources, a position shared by Digel (2013: 3) who further emphasises that 'Online Case Laboratories' enable viewers to interactively work on video cases in 'formal, nonformal and self-directed learning processes'. The inclusion of hyperlinks not only offers the viewer insights into the performing actors' perceptions derived from interviews conducted prior to teaching, but it also provides theoretical knowledge, thereby offering the analyst a more profound understanding of the teacher's behaviour and creating a 'multiple-perspective' video perception (Goeze, 2010: 140, trans.). Hyperlink information may be used to increase or decrease video analyses tasks in terms of difficulty. An increase in demand follows from the complexity that hyperlink information adds to a 'case', whereas their guiding function might simplify video analysis (Goeze, 2010: 140). Overall, findings indicate that digital video enrichment through hyperlinks positively influences pre-service teachers' 'diagnosis of teaching and learning situations' (Goeze, 2010: 140, trans).

The employment of digital features to enhance teachers' PD via video has been taken one step further by Zhang *et al.* (2015) who assign teachers an active role in creating their own videos for analysis. Drawing on Yerrick *et al.* (2005: 359) and their concept of 'digital video editing' with a program called iMovie, Zhang *et al.* (2015: 156) emphasise the importance of having teachers autonomously select and upload their own videos, as this approach offers them 'active control (...) by selecting and editing clips for others to view'. They further argue that this kind of control leads teachers to engage in 'deeper reflection on their practice' (Zhang *et al.*, 2015: 161).

Teacher agency is also stressed by Hannafin *et al.* (2015: 164) who introduce the 'Video Analysis Tool' as a digital means for 'teachers and supervisors to assess as well as to compare and contrast identical video excerpts from different, unique perspectives'. The strength of the 'Video Analysis Tool' is that it puts analysts in the position to synchronise and compare their observations by coding relevant teaching situations, for instance those in which desired teaching practices occur. Coding also plays a significant role in a 'digital video analysis tool called Studiocode' (Prusak, 2015: 193). Here, teachers code teaching videos according to predefined categories (e.g. specific teacher behaviour). These categories are then marked on a timeline. A coded video may then be further analysed using Studiocode (Prusak, 2015: 194). Similarly, the tool 'Edthena' puts analysts in the position to 'code segments of uploaded video to highlight areas of pedagogical strengths or points of growth' (Parsons *et al.*, 2015: 272).

Summary

It has been shown in the previous sections that various challenges and opportunities are put forward by different kinds of videos, the former of which may be compensated for by digital features. In a negative sense, this complexity is further aggravated by the fact that research findings are far from consistent (cf. Sherin *et al.*, 2011). In a positive sense, videos pave the way towards multiple learning opportunities, provided they are embedded within a carefully designed learning environment with clear goals and adjusted to learners' needs. The ways the theoretical insights just outlined have informed the design of the aforementioned MsTa seminars (introduction) are illuminated in the next two sections.

Using Videos in Multilingual-Sensitive Professional Development Classes

Outline and objectives of the courses

During the winter term of 2015/2016, two seminars aiming at the development of EFL pre-service teachers' PV were offered at Goethe University Frankfurt/Main. The seminars were located in the second module of the EFL teaching curriculum and ran for 13 weeks (weekly 90-minute sessions).

They were based on an understanding of PV as outlined in the introduction of this chapter, albeit with a specific focus on heterogeneous EFL classrooms. Students were supposed to identify and describe heterogeneity-relevant teaching situations, i.e. instances that uncover pupils' diversity. Further, students were to evaluate teachers' performances in terms of whether they qualify as heterogeneous-sensitive. For example, students' ability to spot situations where the teacher offers pictures for visual learners, or creates spaces for multilingual language work for pupils with various native tongues serves as an indicator of their developing PV.

In both classes, special emphasis was put on EFL learners' linguistic backgrounds as a pivotal dimension of heterogeneity in EFL classrooms. More precisely, EFL learners' language (learning) biographies were treated as both a prerequisite for and goal of EFL teaching. Owing to the inconsistency of findings in terms of the effects different kinds of videos may have on PD, the analyses of 'own' and 'peer' videos were preceded by the provision and discussion of theoretical texts on heterogeneous-multilingual foreign language teaching and learning. This theoretical foundation helped to pave the way for students to apply their theoretical knowledge to the videos implemented, a deductive approach termed 'recognition of the paradigmatic' (Goeze, 2010). The theoretical input primarily served to direct students' attention during video analyses and to maximise the potential benefits videos can have on PD. During later sessions, students learned about EFL learners' different cognitive styles, learning styles and learning strategies (cf. e.g. Dörnyei, 2005; Lightbown & Spada, 2013) and about differing levels of motivation, anxiety or willingness to communicate (cf. e.g. Pawlak, 2012) as further aspects of heterogeneity.

After this theoretical introduction, students were introduced to the notion of PV and the attempt to propel it with different kinds of videos in the fifth session. After this session, videos of different types were used. Details will be discussed in the next section.

Video types implemented

At the onset of both MsTa seminars, the author of this text taught two microteaching lessons herself, which were both videotaped and used for critical analysis in class. Both microteachings were conducted in simulated, highly heterogeneous EFL learning groups. While the teacher performed a structured lesson, she by no means considered her 'pupils'' (enacted by seminar participants) heterogeneity, i.e. she neither included heterogeneous-sensitive materials nor did she make any attempt to make use of her pupils' linguistic backgrounds as resources for EFL learning. The decision to offer students a rather unfavourable example of teaching taught by the author of this chapter was based on the rather negative emotions often associated with the analysis of 'own' videos. The attempt here was to create a learning environment within which students could contribute their thoughts openly, and to show students how to criticise lessons in a respectful and constructive manner.

In the subsequent sessions of the classes, 'own' and 'peer' videos were used. As for the former, students were asked to prepare mini lessons of 20 minutes in groups of four to five students. The task was to design lessons in such a way as to take into consideration the heterogeneity of an imaginary learning group the composition of which was concretised with the help of 'role cards'. Role cards included information about each 'pupil', his or her learning profile and language background to help students elaborate heterogeneous-multilingual-sensitive lessons. The role cards remained the same throughout the entire seminar to offer students the possibility to adjust their lesson plans and accompanying materials such as worksheets to a learning group characterised by stable, theory-informed heterogeneity features. The lessons were then performed in the course of sessions 6–13 by one or two group members who acted as 'teachers', while 10 of their peers acted as EFL learners, i.e. pupils. Note here that the role cards helped 'pupils' play their roles. Whereas all students had access to the role cards prior to teaching, this was not true for the lesson plans designed by the students (for organisational reasons). The remaining students were observers of the lessons. All mini lessons were video-recorded and put on the seminars' digital learning platform for analysis. To guide and facilitate video analyses, observation sheets to be filled out in the course of teaching by the observers and reflection tasks to be worked on after teaching were provided, both of which included items that addressed the question as to what extent the teacher's behaviour is to be considered heterogeneous-sensitive. After recording, students first analysed the video individually at home as a preparatory task for the upcoming session, at which the same video was analysed collaboratively. Hence, the overall design of the seminars was influenced both by instructional and problem-based concepts (Kleinknecht & Schneider, 2013: 212).

Participants

A total of 54 students (11 male, 43 female) participated in the two seminars. Their EFL teaching experiences ranged from none to several lessons a month as substitute teachers in local schools. Participants were preparing to become teachers in diverse school types and by the time they participated in the courses, they had either recently begun their studies (second to third semester) or were more advanced students (fourth to tenth semester).

Course evaluation

The two seminars were evaluated in order to better understand the strengths and weaknesses of 'own' and 'peer' videos specifically for the development of PV in the context of EFL MsTas. In this contribution, I will focus on three aspects that can inform future teaching practice:

(1) How do pre-service EFL teachers evaluate their own and their peers' teaching videos, especially regarding developing their multilingual-sensitive PV?
(2) What emotions are evoked by 'own' and 'peer' videos in MsTa seminars?
(3) Which digital features further strengthen the merits and compensate for the weaknesses of video-based PV, according to pre-service EFL teachers?

To answer these questions, a post-seminar questionnaire with five open-ended questions was distributed. Items elicited students' free text responses as to whether and to what extent 'own' and 'peer' videos lend themselves to support their PD and what kind of digital features they considered helpful for this purpose. Students' comments were collected and identified as 'positive', 'mixed' or 'negative', and then structured based on their content. The exact wording of each questionnaire item is included at the beginning of the following sections.

Evaluation of 'own' videos in the MsTa seminars

The questionnaire item that addresses students' learning experiences with 'own' videos reads as follows: 'Please describe as precisely as possible what you learn when you analyze your own video'. Out of 42 respondents, 30 (71.4%) reported positive learning effects followed by 9 students (21.4%) who explained that they had experienced mixed effects and 3 students (7.1%) who reported negative effects.

The opportunity to compare their self-designed lesson plans with the actual teaching performance turned out to be the most prominent merit of 'own' videos in the MsTa seminars, as the following comments show:

(1) 'Since I knew how the lesson was planned, I could analyse whether my performance actually corresponded to our plan'
(2) 'I was surprised that our plan was not as good as we thought. It is the teaching which tells you how complicated the entire matter is'
(3) 'I was deeply involved in preparing the lesson plan, so while teaching I knew immediately that I should have acted differently in specific situations. When I watched the video again later, I clearly saw the reasons behind my mistakes, so I can avoid them in the future'

While in the first statement the lesson plan qualifies as a basis for comparison with actual teaching, the second one indicates that teaching also functioned as a touchstone for the quality of the lesson plans. The last comment reveals that through the implementation of 'own' videos, slippery thoughts that occurred in the process of teaching could be pinned-down and became subject to post-teaching analysis. This finding is supported by students who became more 'self-confident' as they noticed a discrepancy between the way they felt while teaching and their appearance on video:

(4) 'It was very interesting to see that the way you feel when teaching appears very differently from the outer perspective'
(5) 'I saw that I looked much more confident on the video than I actually was. This is a very positive learning effect'

Many students agreed that 'own' videos enabled them to get a fuller picture of classroom situations:

(6) 'It was new and eye-opening to see how much was going on in the classroom, things I didn't notice when I was performing'

Further, they stated that they learned a lot about themselves as future teachers when observing their own videos:

(7) 'I learned a lot about my habits and the way I appear. The video helps me to preserve the good things and avoid the bad ones later'

The vast majority of students stressed that they were much more critical with their own teaching (no matter whether they performed as teachers or not) than with their peers', especially since they were well aware of their 'strengths and weaknesses'. Interestingly, their critical perspective almost exclusively focused on their physical appearance and related issues, and not on didactic decisions associated with heterogeneous-sensitive teaching:

(8) 'I evaluate myself much more critical than my peers do, I know about my weaknesses (posture, intonation, pronunciation)'
(9) 'My speaking pace was too fast, some words were too complicated for the pupils and my eyes were half-closed. It might have looked as if I was tired or arrogant'

While Comment 9 shows that students were highly concentrating on their appearance as teachers at the expense of didactic considerations, Statement 10 indicates that this student related her observations to pupils' perspectives as well. Similar comments support the assumption that, though firmly rooted in a focus on the teacher, some students evaluated teacher behaviour from pupils' perspectives:

(10) 'I learned a lot about the effects my appearance had on the pupils'
(11) 'It was interesting to examine teacher–pupil interactions'

Somewhat paradoxically, some of the features that made 'own' videos valuable tools for learning also turned out to account for their challenges. More precisely, students highlighted that it was difficult for them to analyse 'own' videos objectively, especially since they were absorbed by their own (physical) appearance:

(12) 'I was always looking at my moves, not on my teaching skills'
(13) 'I cannot separate self-reflection from reflection on teaching'
(14) 'I tried to analyse the teaching, but I was distracted by my outer appearance' (fT)

Despite these limitations, it is argued here that students' awareness of the fact that 'subjective' self-reflections cannot replace in-depth analyses of didactic issues, is in itself a PV learning success. In this regard, work with 'own' videos was successful. Importantly, though, the students' responses did not provide evidence that specific skills related to multilingual-sensitive teaching were developed while working with 'own' videos.

Evaluation of 'peer' videos in the MsTa seminars

As for students' analyses of their peers' videos, the following item was included in the questionnaire: 'Please describe as precisely as possible what you learn when you analyse your peers' videos'.

Forty-one students answered the question, 28 of whom (68.3%) revealed positive and 3 (7.3%) mixed learning effects. Ten students (24.4%) ascribed rather negative effects to their peers' videos.

Students generally agreed that working with 'peer' videos was much more 'distanced' and 'objective' than working with their 'own' videos. They emphasised that with 'peer' videos, they could 'really concentrate on the lesson content' and that they 'felt free to look out for the main structure of the lesson, as well as the comprehensibility of instructions'. Further, students' remarks strongly suggest that their focus shifted from being highly teacher-centred to a more pupil-oriented one:

(1) 'My focus shifted towards pupils. I tried to find situations in which pupils created a heterogeneous classroom. But there was no focus on teacher appearance'
(2) 'I really looked at how pupils reacted to the teaching method. The teacher's physical appearance was not important any more, I concentrated on teacher–pupil interaction (which is far more important)'

Not only did pupils become the main target of observation, the same is true for didactic issues. Students frequently mentioned that seeing 'peer' videos offered them opportunities to 'see different styles of teaching and problem solutions' and 'learn about new methods'. 'Peer' videos were even described as a 'treasure trove for teaching approaches which lend themselves to multilingual-sensitive teaching' that 'serve as a valuable orientation for future teaching'.

Beyond providing a pool of didactic and methodological approaches, 'peer' videos triggered in-depth didactic reasoning. Students were eager to stress that this kind of video made them ponder questions such as 'why did the teacher act the way he did' or 'are there better ways to deal with this problem?'. It is important to note here that the implementation of 'peer' videos seemed to bridge the gap between merely self-related and didactic-oriented reflections, which was often perceived when students analysed their 'own' videos:

(3) 'When I watched the video I asked myself questions like "Would I have acted differently in this situation? Does the way the teacher behaved correspond to my criteria of appropriateness?"'
(4) 'I can adapt the teacher's positive sides. I would have been overstrained with some situations, so it is helpful to see how my peers dealt with it'

As with 'own' videos, one of the aspects associated with 'peer' videos qualified as an advantage and a disadvantage simultaneously, namely the fact that students did not have access to lesson plans before analyses. One student stated that this assisted him in 'concentrating on the actual lesson progress'. However, he was clearly outnumbered by those students who criticised the absence of contextual information. Students' comments show that this limitation to an 'outer perspective' impeded their analyses in various ways: first, they stressed that while observing, they were forced to solely rely on 'visible teacher performance' which, in turn, prevented them from putting what the teachers did in relation to his or her initial intentions. Many students pointed out that this led them to 'evaluate teachers' mistakes equally strict'. Put differently, a more fine-grained evaluation would have been possible if 'the genesis of mistakes had been traceable'.

Based on the findings presented in this and the preceding section, it can be stated that, according to the students involved, 'peer' videos, especially if complemented by rich contextual data (information about 'pupils'', lesson plans), might be better suited for the purpose outlined above than 'own' videos.

'Own' videos in the MsTa seminars: Emotions involved

To gain insights into students' emotions when watching their own videos, the following item was included in the questionnaire: 'Please describe as precisely as possible how you feel when you analyse your own video'.

Out of 29 respondents, 19 (65.5%) clearly stated that this experience was accompanied by highly negative feelings such as fear, nervousness, shame, anger and embarrassment:

Students primarily ascribed their negative emotions to the fact that they were afraid of not appearing self-confident while teaching. Many were concerned about 'what my peers might think' of them, especially since they found that 'the others seemed to be much more self-confident'. One student even explained that he could not prevent himself from feeling 'awkward' and 'inhibited' although he was aware that the reasons behind these feelings were unfounded.

Another emotion frequently mentioned was 'disappointment', particularly when students were unsatisfied with their teaching. As strong as the emotions described are, students indicated that they disappeared when their video was watched repeatedly.

The remaining students stated that they had mixed or positive feelings when their own videos were analysed (4 and 6 respondents, i.e. 13.8% and 20.7%, respectively). Positive feelings included 'excitement', 'interest' and 'fun' but were not explicated further.

'Peer' videos in the MsTa seminars: Emotions involved

A total of 25 students responded to the item: 'Please describe as precisely as possible how you feel when you analyse your peers' videos'.

Contrary to the feelings associated with the analysis of 'own' videos, a majority of 12 students (48%) mentioned positive emotions when observing 'peer' videos, followed by those who had mixed, negative or no feelings at all (6, 4 and 3, i.e. 24%, 16% and 12%, in order).

Positive emotions mainly resulted from not having to 'overcome a personal barrier' and included being 'relaxed', 'motivated' and 'excited'. Others pointed out that their positive feelings stemmed from the 'absence of mental pressure' and 'timidity'. It is also worth mentioning that many students expressed their 'utmost respect' for their peers and they were 'pleased' when their peers performed well. However, their peers' performances caused negative feelings as well. Some felt 'embarrassed' or 'angry' on account of 'bad' teacher behaviour, others felt like 'judges' and 'very uncomfortable' during discussions because they did not want to 'expose' or 'discredit' their peers' efforts.

Interestingly, a number of students indicated that they felt 'neutral' when observing 'peer' videos, or that they did not have 'any specific emotions'. Note that this case is absent in the context of 'own' video analyses.

Negative emotions as observed with 'own' videos are not necessarily a hindrance to developing PV, but these emotions potentially constitute a challenge absent in the case of 'peer' videos. This should be reflected by any didactic design using 'own' videos to develop PV as it relates to multilingual-sensitive teaching.

MsTa and digital features

To gain insights into what kinds of digital features students find useful for further PD seminars, they were offered the subsequent questionnaire item: 'Imagine you had the opportunity to embed teaching videos in a web-based learning module without any technical limitations to foster students' PV. What kind of digital features would you implement and how could they be used?'.

To begin with, students opted for a preservation of the general seminar structure, i.e. the provision of theoretical input by the instructor, followed by an alternation of lesson development and guided video analyses. Students' additional proposals can be grouped into three main categories, namely the attempt to integrate commentaries, to provide differing analysis options and, finally, to segment videos.

As for the integration of commentaries, students recommended comment links that offer teachers' thoughts about their lesson plans and a justification of the way they acted while teaching. Similarly, it was suggested to include a time line or subtitle bar to provide space for the analysts' comments. It was argued that it is important to be able to turn the commentaries off or on as required, to allow for both a 'first and unbiased observation' as well as 'fine-tuned analyses'. It was also suggested to include bookmarks and to create an account for each user so the bookmarks can be commented on any time.

The request to provide commentaries was closely interwoven with the attempt to offer different analysis options. First, students highlighted the importance of selecting and uploading a selection of 'own' videos they consider worth discussing. Second, these videos should be analysed from multiple perspectives, i.e. by themselves, their peers and 'expert analysts' to trigger self- and peer reflection and to permit analyses comparison. To ensure in-depth analyses, they further suggested adding a feature that captures classrooms from various camera perspectives. Lessons should then be watched from distinct perspectives either simultaneously or separately. By far the most progressive proposition was made by a student who stated that

(1) 'it would be interesting to display the teacher's and pupils' attention. If we had a digital feature for this, very much like an infrared camera, we could capture eye-tracking movements and analyse what captured pupils' attention when and why. So we could find ways of how to direct their attention better'

Most students were well aware of the cognitive load involved in a task such as observing various classroom perspectives at the same time. Students' general desire to divide videos into parts supports this assumption. In this context, students' recommendations ranged from straightforward ideas as in Comment 2 to sophisticated proposals as in Comment 3.

(2) 'Videos should be divided into sequences to be analysed in chronological order. Each sequence should lend itself to the analysis of different aspects such as classroom management or heterogeneous-sensitive teaching approaches'
(3) 'It would be useful to insert a section which provides the lesson plan as a kind of "table of contents". Users could then jump from "chapter" to "chapter", so they are not forced to analyse the entire video chronologically'

Overall, students seem to be well aware of the opportunities digital features can add to work with videos, expecting similar functionalities as offered by commercial video platforms.

Summary and Discussion of Findings

Students' questionnaire-based responses allow for tentative answers to the questions posed in the section titled 'Course Evaluation', thereby illuminating the usefulness of 'own' and 'peer' videos in terms of the influence they might have on pre-service teachers' ability to reflect on the multilingual-sensitivity of teaching as a constitutive part of the general heterogeneity these future teachers will more than likely meet in their future teaching careers.

As for Question 1, it is safe to say that the majority of students found both 'own' and 'peer' videos to be valuable learning resources. 'Own' videos not only offered opportunities to compare lesson plans and teaching, they also enabled students to get a fuller picture of classroom events, a finding in line with Zhang *et al.* (2011). Students frequently stated that they were absorbed by their appearance as teachers, which indicates a high level of 'immersion' (Seidel *et al.*, 2011: 262). Whereas being deeply involved helped students to spot their strengths and weaknesses, or 'areas of improvement' (Borko *et al.*, 2008: 434), it also led them to underrate their performance, an indicator of 'leniency bias' (Baecher *et al.*, 2013: 191) and to sharply criticise themselves. This clearly runs counter to Kleinknecht and Schneider's (2013) findings and rather supports Borko *et al.* (2008: 428) who found that while teachers 'criticised their own lessons (...) they were rarely critical of their colleagues'. As for 'peer' videos, findings are largely consistent with existing studies: students not only pointed out that 'peer' video analyses were much more distanced and objective (cf. Zhang *et al.*, 2015), they also stressed the fact that 'peer' videos provided numerous didactic and methodological approaches (Baecher *et al.*, 2013; Biaggi *et al.*, 2013). Another phenomenon that fits well into earlier insights is the fact that students' foci of analyses shifted gradually from being teacher-centred (as with 'own' videos) to being more pupil-related, although this shift is rather associated with discourse development than with video type in the research literature (cf. e.g. Sherin & Han, 2004). In sum, 'own' videos seem to have outperformed 'peer' videos in terms of their perceived positive influence on PV development (71.4% and 68.3%, respectively). However, this finding has to be interpreted cautiously: A number of students not to be underestimated (24.4%) deny 'peer' videos positive influences due to the absence of contextual information only, whereas more negative and mixed 'own' video influences may be traced back to an array of reasons. This encourages the interpretation that if students had had access to lesson plans prior to teaching, they would have evaluated 'peer' videos even more positively than they actually did. What is more, 'peer' videos triggered many more positive emotions among viewers than did 'own' videos. Hence, it is assumed here that 'peer' videos may serve slightly better than 'own' videos to foster PV through in-depth didactic analyses, at least as long as necessary conditions such as the provision of contextual information are met.

Regarding Question 2, it has become obvious that both types of video evoked differing emotions among students. Since more negative emotions were associated with 'own' than with 'peer' videos, researchers' call for discourse criteria such as openness and trust (cf. e.g. Sherin & Han, 2004) is underlined. Students were much more emotionally involved with their own teaching than with their peers', which runs counter to Borko *et al.* (2008), although single emotions such as 'anger' also occurred when observing their peers' teaching. Further, some students reported 'neutral' or 'no specific feelings' when viewing their peers' video, a circumstance that might explain the perceived increase in distance when analysing these videos (cf. e.g. Krammer & Hugener, 2014).

Concerning Question 3, students' answers to the relevant questionnaire item largely mirror digital tools used in current research projects (cf. e.g. Digel, 2013; Goeze, 2010). Students' desire to analyse videos from various perspectives and to receive a 'correct' solution to analysis tasks has been frequently mentioned. The question arises here whether digital features might also help fight the major disadvantage of 'own' videos, i.e. students' focus on their outer appearance while teaching and the negative emotions associated with 'own' video analysis. For example, it might be thinkable to transform the student teacher into a kind of avatar – the underlying assumption here is that an avatar prevents students from being entrenched in self-critical subjectivity at the expense of didactic analyses. Owing to the fact that the MsTa seminar participants were all rather inexperienced teachers and video observers, a circumstance that clearly accounts for some of the negative emotions associated with 'own' video analyses since they were perceived as 'very unfamiliar', a second questionnaire was distributed, the analysis of which is beyond the scope of this chapter. Suffice it to say that students indicated that, being novices, they would prefer to analyse 'peer' before their own videos as this approach offers them 'more safety' and 'orientation'.

The seminar reflection at hand allows for a tentative answer to the overall question raised in the title. Both 'own' and 'peer' videos seem to lend themselves to the development of multilingual-sensitive PV in pre-service teacher training classes. Needless to say, the preliminary findings made on the basis of the MsTa seminars are highly context specific and, therefore, lack external validity. Further, the questionnaire employed asked for students' self-evaluation and estimations, i.e. it did not 'measure' video-triggered PV growth in an empirical sense. To obtain more reliable insights into the impact 'own' and 'peer' videos can have on PV development, students' estimations need to be categorised in an empirical manner, and complementary tools such as vignettes and PV analysis tasks that are then accompanied by post-seminar questionnaires need to be implemented. The insights provided in this chapter might trigger such future research.

References

Baecher, L., Kung, S.-C., Jewkes, A.M. and Rosalia, C. (2013) The role of video for self-evaluation in early field experiences. *Teaching and Teacher Education* 36, 189–197.

Biaggi, S., Krammer, K. and Hugener, I. (2013) Vorgehen zur Förderung der Analysekompetenz in der Lehrerbildung mit Hilfe von Unterrichtsvideos: Erfahrungen aus dem ersten Studienjahr. *Seminar* 19 (2), 26–34.

Borko, H., Jacobs, J., Eiteljorg, E. and Pittman, M.E. (2008) Video as a tool for fostering productive discussions in mathematics professional development. *Teaching and Teacher Education* 24, 417–436.

Brophy, J.E. (ed.) (2003) *Using Video in Teacher Education*. Amsterdam: JAI.

Calandra, B. and Rich, P. (eds) (2015) *Digital Video for Teacher Education*. New York: Routledge.

Digel, S. (2013) Netzwerkgestützte Videofallarbeit: Ein didaktisches Konzept zur Kompetenzentwicklung von Lehrenden. *Magazin Erwachsenenbildung.at* 20, 2–9.

Dörnyei, Z. (2005) *The Psychology of the Language Learner: Individual Differences in Second Language Acquisition*. London: Lawrence Erlbaum.

Goeze, A. (2010) Was ist ein guter Fall? Kriterien zur Entwicklung und Auswahl von Fällen für den Einsatz in der Aus- und Weiterbildung. In J. Schrader, R. Hohmann and S. Hartz (eds) *Mediengestützte Fallarbeit: Konzepte, Erfahrungen und Befunde zur Kompetenzentwicklung von Erwachsenenbildnern* (pp. 125–145). Bielefeld: Bertelsmann.

Goodwin, C. (1994) Professional vision. *American Anthropologist* 96 (3), 606–655.

Hannafin, M., Recesso, A., Polly, D. and Jung, J.W. (2015) Video analysis and teacher assessment: Research, practice, and implications. In B. Calandra and P. Rich (eds) *Digital Video for Teacher Education: Research and Practice* (pp. 164–180). New York: Routledge.

Hellermann, C., Gold, B. and Holodynski, M. (2015) Förderung von Klassenführungsfähigkeiten im Lehramtsstudium. *Zeitschrift für Entwicklungspsychologie und Pädagogische Psychologie* 47 (2), 97–109.

Kleinknecht, M. and Schneider, J. (2013) What do teachers think and feel when analysing videos of themselves and other teachers teaching? *Teaching and Teacher Education* 33, 13–23.

Krammer, K. and Hugener, I. (2014) Förderung der Analysekompetenz angehender Lehrpersonen anhand von eigenen und fremden Unterrichtsvideos. *Journal für Lehrerinnenbildung* 1, 25–32.

Lefstein, A. and Snell, J. (2011) Professional vision and the politics of teacher learning. *Teaching and Teacher Education* 27, 505–514.

Lightbown, P.M. and Spada, N. (2013) *How Languages are Learned*. Oxford: Oxford University Press.

Lord, B. (1994) Teachers' professional development: Critical colleagueship and the role of professional communities. In N. Cobb (ed.) *The Future of Education: Perspectives on National Standards in America* (pp. 175–203). New York: College Board.

Maclean, R. and White, S. (2007) Video reflection and the formation of teacher identity. *Reflective Practice* 8 (1), 47–60.

Orlova, N. (2009) Video recording as a stimulus for reflection in pre-service EFL teacher training. *English Teaching Forum* 2, 30–35.

Parsons, S.A., Parker, A.K., Zenkov, K., DeGregory, C., Taylor, L., Kye, D. and Haury, S. (2015) Exploring the use of video coding in literacy and English teacher preparation. In E. Ortlieb, L.E. Shanahan and M.B. McVee (eds) *Video Research in Disciplinary Literacies* (Vol. 6; pp. 269–285). Bingley: Emerald Group Publishing.

Pawlak, M. (ed.) (2012) *New Perspectives on Individual Differences in Language Learning and Teaching*. Berlin: Springer.

Prusak, K. (2015) Generating expertise through the use of digital video. In B. Calandra and P. Rich (eds) *Digital Video for Teacher Education: Research and Practice* (pp. 181–199). New York: Routledge.

Rosaen, C.L., Lundeberg, M., Cooper, M., Fritzen, A. and Terpstra, M. (2008) Noticing noticing. How does investigation of video records change how teachers reflect on their experience? *Journal of Teacher Education* 59 (4), 347–360.

Rossi, P.G. and Fedeli, L. (eds) (2016) *Integrating Video into Pre-Service and In-Service Teacher Training*. Hershey, PA: Information Science Reference.

Seago, N. (2004) Using video as an object of inquiry for mathematics teaching and learning. In J. Brophy (ed.) *Using Video in Teacher Education* (Vol. 10; pp. 259–286). Oxford: Elsevier.

Seidel, T., Stürmer, K., Blomberg, G., Kobarg, M. and Schwindt, K. (2011) Teacher learning from analysis of videotaped classroom situations: Does it make a difference whether teachers observe their own teaching or that of others? *Teaching and Teacher Education* 27, 259–267.

Sherin, M.G. (2007) The development of teachers' professional vision in video clubs. In R. Goldman, R. Pea, B. Barron and S. Derry (eds) *Video Research in the Learning Sciences* (pp. 383–395). Mahwah, NJ: Erlbaum.

Sherin, M.G. and Han, S.Y. (2004) Teacher learning in the context of a video club. *Teaching and Teacher Education* 20, 163–183.

Sherin, M.G. and van Es, E.A. (2009) Effects of video club participation on teachers' professional vision. *Journal of Teacher Education* 60 (1), 20–37.

Trautmann, M. (2010) Heterogenität: (k)ein Thema der Fremdsprachendidaktik? In A. Köker, S. Romahn and A. Textor (eds) *Herausforderung Heterogenität: Ansätze und Weichenstellungen* (pp. 52–64). Bad Heilbrunn: Klinkhardt.

Trautmann, M. and Wischer, B. (2011) *Heterogenität in der Schule: Eine kritische Einführung*. Wiesbaden: VS Verlag.

Van Es, E.A. and Sherin, M.G. (2008) Mathematics teachers' 'learning to notice' in the context of a video club. *Teaching and Teacher Education* 24 (2), 244–276.

Wallace, M.J. (1979) *Microteaching and the Teaching of English as a Second or Foreign Language in Teacher Training Institutions*. Edinburgh: Scottish Centre of Education Overseas.

Wallace, M.J. (1981) The use of video in EFL teacher training. In *ELT Documents110 – Focus on the Teacher: Communicative Approaches to Teacher Training* (pp. 7–21). London: British Council.

Yerrick, R., Ross, D. and Molesbash, P. (2005) Too close for comfort: Real-time science teaching reflections via digital video editing. *Journal of Science Teacher Education* 16 (4), 351–375.

Zafer, S. (2015) Watch your teaching: A reflection strategy for EFL pre-service teachers through video recordings. *Procedia: Social and Behavioural Sciences* 199, 163–171.

Zhang, M., Lundeberg, M., Koehler, M.J. and Eberhardt, J. (2011) Understanding affordances and challenges of three types of video for teacher professional development. *Teaching and Teacher Education* 27, 454–462.

Zhang, M., Koehler, M. and Lundeberg, M. (2015) Affordances and challenges of different types of video for teachers' professional development. In B. Calandra and P. Rich (eds) *Digital Video for Teacher Education: Research and Practice* (pp. 147–163). New York: Routledge.

Ziegler, G. (2013) Multilingualism and the language education landscape: Challenges for teacher training in Europe. *Multilingual Education* 3 (1), 1–23.

Concluding Remarks

Learning in Multilingually and Digitally Mediated Spaces: The MCALL Approach

Gabriela Meier

This volume is a response to two recent developments in education that are both related to globalisation: on the one hand, the increasing *linguistic diversity* in school populations and, on the other hand, the *digital revolution* that led to new ways of being, learning and socialising. The contributions to this book, exemplifying the multilingual computer assisted language learning (MCALL) approach, show that these developments bring with them opportunities and challenges related to our understanding of how people learn and what roles different stakeholders can play in this. An important recognition in this book is that the MCALL approach to learning can be fun (Buendgens-Kosten & Elsner) and motivating (Pohl, Cutrim Schmid), yet also effective in terms of linguistic achievements (Alvarez) and deep learning processes (Meyer *et al.*). What becomes clear in this book is that MCALL opens up new and experimental ways of learning and teaching.The multilingual turn has so far been more of a theoretical movement rather than a game-change in mainstream practice. In turn, digital technologies have changed the way young people communicate and socialise (Meyer *et al.*). In some countries, digital resources have increasingly become a part of education and entered classrooms in the form of smart boards, computer suites, tablets, educational apps and games, etc. From this, it follows that combining the multilingual and digital dimension to support teaching and learning in classrooms harbours new opportunities and challenges compared to traditional classrooms. In this concluding section, I will discuss these and offer a summary of what I deem are the main topics emerging from this book (in bold), which together point to the need for a radical change in the way we understand school education. A discussion of the implications for theory, practice and research, as well as some important limitations, will round off this conclusion.

Opportunities and Challenges

Learner autonomy is an important strand that leads through the book, as both the multilingual approach and the digital approach require or enable learners to work more independently. Using MCALL means that students can direct their learning in more autonomous ways (Alm), using their multiliteracy and digital literacy for their own purposes. This, however, conceptualises learners and teachers in new roles and constitutes important shifts in understanding: (1) towards understanding *language learners* as language researchers, explorers, detectives, analysts, collaborators, guides and local experts (Pohl), as well as minority language experts (Si'ilata) or as experts (Meyer *et al.*) who gain 'symbolic power' through their digital competence (Hallet); and (2) towards understanding *teachers*, as coaches offering a structure for learning, and as a resource to support learning, but not as the sole authority of learning. Furthermore, it is important to note that the digital dimension means that teachers can facilitate MCALL approaches to learning without sharing their learners' languages (Elsner/ Buendgens-Kosten), and teachers can learn from the learners as developing experts (Si'ilata), thus developing a more **collaborative understanding of learning.** Furthermore, the MCALL approach, as shown in this volume, can empower learners to make their own choices and communicate knowledge across disciplinary, cultural and linguistic boundaries in a variety of modes (Hallet) as creative and responsible citizens (Meyer *et al.*). Furthermore, depending on the lesson design, learners can choose the materials and languages they want to engage in (Brunsmeier/Kolb). This means that learning is individualised, enables learning at different speeds, in different ways and based on different languages (Meyer *et al.*). Learners choose languages that they deem best for the job at hand, and teachers have to understand that engagement with a language other than the 'target' language may not indicate disinterest or reluctance to learning (Brunsmeier/Kolb), but may well mean that learners use real-life MCALL skills to get the job done. In this way, the MCALL approach resembles what young people do outside the classroom when they use digital devices in autonomous ways for everyday purposes.

Another important point is that the MCALL approach is a **multimodal approach** (Elsner & Buendgens-Kosten; Buendgens-Kosten & Elsner), including sound, music, maps, diagrams, photographs, emoticons, etc., that support and scaffold comprehension of content for different learner types. Clearly, conventional classrooms are also multimodal insofar as input is supported by body language, pictures, drama, etc., but an important difference between the conventional and the MCALL approach is that learners in the digital sphere are more in control as they can often repeat, look up words or content in different languages, to understand. Indeed Meyer *et al.* argue in their chapter that engaging with content through different languages is 'the key to deep learning'. Thus, the digital dimension potentially facilitates opportunities for self-regulated and autonomous learning, while the multilingual dimension offers opportunities for deep learning.

Digital multilingual materials are available through educational digital media, especially designed for use in classrooms or through materials that are publically available through the internet. Materials designed for educational purposes can have game character (see Buendgens-Kosten & Elsner) or facilitate communication through telecollaboration (see Cutrim Schmid). These have the advantage of offering *safe, tailored, age-relevant resources* and spaces for learning, but they have the limitations that they only offer certain planned language options (e.g. Mali story in Buendgens-Kosten & Elsner). In addition, the choices and functions are normally predetermined by material designers. Furthermore, such software applications may be outdated quickly and schools would need repeated funding to purchase updates if they are indeed available. Based on the chapters presented in this book, educational digital media, therefore, offer safe, age-appropriate resources, but we must not forget that there are linguistic and technological limitations. The open internet, in contrast offers a wide language choice compared to educational digital media. Using the internet, learners can read content in several languages or switch the language of the user surface and navigation tools. The choice depends on – and is limited by – the envisaged target audiences. Publically available online content is available in majority languages, but also in minority and obscure languages beyond those the teacher can speak or the materials designers can anticipate. The greater choice offered by the publically available internet facilitates greater freedom and learner agency that is limited only by infrastructure and any access configurations.

Having said this, I would like to make an important point, namely that content on the open internet is potentially inappropriate (e.g. porn, violence), dangerous (e.g. grooming, hackers), misleading (e.g. fake news), addictive (e.g. gaming, gambling) and illegal (e.g. the dark net). Another risk of greater autonomy and choice is that learners may get easily distracted and may check their Facebook updates instead of subject-specific content. This book does not specifically discuss *potential risks associated with internet use* for educational (or any) purposes. Therefore, this book should be read in conjunction with relevant guidance for classrooms (e.g. Rooney, 2014), for administrators (e.g. Greene, 2014) and with literature on relevant policies (e.g. European Commission, 2017) or critical media literacy (Buckingham, 2016; Redmond, 2015). Clearly, it is not just learners who need to be tech-savvy, as Buckingham (2016: 180) argues, also educators need to 'adopt a more critical stance toward the celebration of technology in education and the kind of techno fetishism that is mistakenly seen by some as the cutting edge of educational change'. This leads us to an important point made by Dausend, namely that *technology alone does not make a good lesson*, and that, as with all teaching materials, lessons need to be planned carefully, with clear objectives. Thus, publically available digital materials offer linguistic choice but are associated with important risks that need to be carefully managed through a risk assessment and appropriate filter software.

The MCALL approach, as it is presented in this volume, shows that *different languages serve different functions.* These functions are similar to those found in conventional contexts (see Cook, 2001; Moore, 2013). Particularly that in minority or migrant contexts, the use of languages that children grow up with can be comforting (Pohl) and facilitate expression of identity and belonging (Si'ilata, Melo-Pfeiffer). Additionally, first languages are a preferred medium to resolve conflicts (Dausend), help thinking and aid comprehension (Alvarez). All languages, however, can be used for socialising. This is, in my opinion, the most important point, and a golden thread that runs through all chapters. When given the chance, learners use various languages above all as a means of communication, for collaboration and to make friends with peers locally and elsewhere. This is socially significant, as this, on the one hand, enables openness towards others (Cutrim Schmid) and, on the other hand, makes education directly relevant and applicable to the learners' social lives (Pohl, Si'ilata, Cutrim Schmid, Dausend).

Linking to the above, the MCALL approach can support *communication locally, regionally, nationally and internationally*, namely between peers inside a single classroom (Brunsmeier & Kolb), between classrooms in different locations or countries (Cutrim Schmid), to maintain relationships between people in different countries (Alm) and to involve families in school life (Si'ilata). This authentic and potentially multilingual communication between real people harbours potential for learners to develop empathy with children elsewhere (Cutrim Schmid) and teachers can develop empathy with their learners' positions and thus better support their learning (Si'ilata). This is a clear departure from how, particularly foreign languages, used to be taught when I went to school, admittedly that was a long time ago. In the 1980s, we studied and practiced French in the classroom with the idea that we will use it at some stage in the future for work and/or travel, and some of us did find opportunities to use the language and others did not. The main change illustrated here is that there is a shift from *language learning* as a goal to *communication* as a goal (Alm).

In these new roles, *learners need a series of skills and competencies* to navigate and communicate across languages in digital and analogue environments. These are *linguistic and crosslinguistic* skills and awareness (Cutrim Schmid, Si'ilata, Brunsmeier/Kolb), *meta-cognitive* skills (Cutrim Schmid, Pohl), such as transferable skills from previous language learning experiences. Specifically, reflective skills can be developed to enable awareness of 'what it means to "know" a language, how foreign languages are learned, and the role of English as lingua franca', as well as social and collaborative skills (Cutrim Schmid), digital skills (Hallet) and critical media literacy (Pohl). Challenges mentioned in this book are that positive transfer from one language to another is not automatic and switching between languages can also be a source of confusion, especially between languages from different language families (Alvarez). Furthermore, Alm shows that multilingual learners are aware that multilingual communication can alienate certain groups, and learners may thus opt for a lingua franca that can be understood by all (Alm).

The MCALL approach, the way it is presented in this book, seems to offer much in terms of *affective dimensions*. This way of learning and teaching is shown to have an effect on motivation (Si'ilata, Cutrim Schmid), identity (Melo-Pfeiffer) and self-esteem (Pohl, Cutrim Schmid). From this point of view, the MCALL approach can give learners greater autonomy, recognise their plurilingual and social expertise, as well as their real-world knowledge, while facilitating the development of new social contacts to solve tasks that are relevant to the learners' lives in the here and now, rather than studying a language that could be potentially used at some stage in the future. Thus, I see great potential in this new conceptualisation of learners as contributors to group learning, as it potentially validates all learners' biographies and expertise.

An important observation made in this book is that the *monolingual habitus*, as described by Gogolin (1994) still *exists at personal and institutional level* (Alvarez, Buendgens-Kosten & Elsner). In 2017, more than 20 years later, the assumption that learning, and especially language learning, works best in one language based on the communicative approach, is still widespread (May, 2014; Meier, 2017; Weber, 2017). While some institutions insist on the use of one language, some learners feel that adhering to the monolingual approach gets them better grades (Alvarez). It seems that multilingualism is more instinctively acceptable at lower grades, or for private communication, but less so at higher grades and when it counts. The monolingual habitus is in line with the monolingual myths identified through the multilingual turn (Meier, 2017), which include the native speaker myth (native language competence as a suitable goal for learning), the sequential acquisition myth (that languages need to be learnt one after the other) and the language separation myth (that languages need to be kept separate to avoid confusion). However, Buendgens-Kosten and Elsner argue that the monolingual habitus is on shaky ground (Buendgens-Kosten & Elsner), and perhaps the MCALL approach could be instrumental in bringing about a paradigm shift, making the 21st century not only that of the digital revolution but also that of that of multilingual education.

Implications and Outlook

Practically, the MCALL approach could be seen as a response to recent calls for greater pedagogic guidance of how teachers can draw on different languages for learning (May, 2014; Meier, 2017; Weber, 2017). It is a critical approach since it is very much about autonomy and empowerment of learners; it offers cross-curricular opportunities as different language subjects (L1, L2 and L3) as well as content and language subjects can be bridged through this approach. Thus, it provides some ideas of how the MCALL approach can be used in a context-sensitive, flexible and multilingual way (cf. Meier, 2017).

In order to implement the MCALL approach, teacher education is important (Si'ilata): It is important to enable pre- or in-service teachers to reflect on assumptions of which they may not be aware (Meier, 2017; Meier, 2018). Si'ilata shows how a project using multilingual resources challenged deficit views teachers held about minority language speakers, and enabled teachers to empathise with the position of their learners, which had not been the case previously (Si'ilata). As is argued by Si'ilata, any teacher can enact plurilingual approaches, but they need support – above all to gain awareness of any unreflected acceptance of the monolingual habitus and potential deficit views they may have.

Theoretically, I argue that sociocultural theory as understood by neo-Vygotskian theorists (e.g. Lantolf, 2011), or as underpinning the multilingual turn (May, 2014), is a useful lens to understand the MCALL approach. Sociocultural theory emphasises that learners first make sense of new material in social interaction with others (primary plane), before they are able to cognitively internalise what they have learnt (secondary plane). Given that communication and collaboration play an important role in the MCALL approach, it can be argued that linguistic, content and social learning happen through using different languages to engage with real-life tasks. Sociocultural theory suggests that in order to achieve their full potential, and to develop from less autonomous to more autonomous language users, learners need support in their zone of proximal development. This is the metaphorical space where learners, with the help of others, can achieve more than they could have achieved or understood on their own. In sociocultural theory, this process is referred to as mediation. Mediation, from this perspective, is based on tools, which can be symbolic, concrete or social. The MCALL approach makes use of the social tools of teachers, peers, groups, real or imaginary, enabling social interaction. It makes use of symbolic tools by using various languages to make sense of the task in hand, and it makes use of concrete tools in the form of digital devices, software, dictionaries, and local or distant, again real or imaginary, materials and environments. The tools are therefore multimodal and may meet different learner needs. The MCALL approach, as presented here, emphasises the development of competencies, skills and awareness of a linguistic, social and digital nature, and how these can be developed in collaboration and through communication with others. Another important aspect of sociocultural theory of learning is the development from other-regulation, dependency on more capable others, to self-regulation, or a state of autonomous engagement with social, symbolic and concrete tools to develop understanding and further their own learning. This also means that the learners will choose those languages they deem most suitable to get the job done, rather than those prescribed by a teacher (Melo-Pfeiffer, Si‘ilata).

As mentioned above, the chapters in this volume point to a departure from conventional understandings of schooling. The latter is largely confined to the classroom, it is usually conceived as monolingual, predictable to a certain degree, related to everyday life in limited ways and largely reliant on the teacher. The MCALL approach, as presented here, takes learning beyond the classroom, uses different languages and accepts unpredictability of learning, as learners jointly negotiate tasks that are relevant to their local everyday life (Pohl). However, the book also points out that learner autonomy is not something learners automatically have, but it needs to be developed with the help of teachers and others (Dausend) in their zone of proximal development, I would argue especially in contexts where learners may be used to greater reliance on the teacher. Further guidance or scaffolding is required to learn to switch languages (Elsner/Buendgens-Kosten), and how to develop cross-linguistic transfer skills (Si‘ilata). Guidance in this is particularly needed in contexts where learning is traditionally monolingual.

In addition, the MCALL approach departs from the convention of expecting and evaluating monolingual texts as the norm: A refreshing multilingual reward system validating linguistic, communicative, pragmatic and action achievements is described by Brunsmeier and Kolb, and Alvarez describes recognition of using the first language for thinking and to scaffold comprehension. This way of recognising achievements is formative and does not affect formal grades. Clearly, there is great value in formative assessment, especially from a sociocultural perspective. However, in my view, such competencies are increasingly important life skills and more formal recognition of these should also be considered in curricula of the 21st century.

Combining multilingualism and CALL is an emerging but still new field of research, and more research is required to further theorise and validate any preliminary assumptions and conclusions that are offered in this volume. Such research could include questions in relation to how the potential of plurilingualism can be recognised and exploited more systematically, and how this could be integrated into classrooms to scaffold learning (Cutrim Schmid). Research could address the increasingly blurred boundaries between learning inside and outside of classrooms, including the virtual dimension. Particular attention should be paid to research regarding any risks and potential harm associated with the autonomous use of online materials.

Returning to the introduction, in which Buendgens-Kosten and Elsner asked the question as to whether there is a special relationship between CALL and multilingualism, and whether any such connection justifies a whole book, I would wholeheartedly say yes it does, as the MCALL approach to teaching and learning recognises new ways of communication and learning in a multilingual world and offers a pedagogic response to recent linguistic and technological developments. In addition, it has potential to offer greater social justice in education as it recognises languages not only of elites but of all learners and teachers as valuable resources for learning.

Acknowledgements

I would like to thank the editors for giving me the opportunity to contribute the concluding chapter to this book and for their valuable feedback on a previous version of this.

References

Buckingham, D. (2016) Do we really need media education 2.0?: Teaching media in the age of participatory culture. In C. Greenhow, J. Sonnevend and C. Agur (eds) *Education and Social Media: Toward a Digital Future* (pp. 171–186). Cambridge: MIT Press. http://www.jstor.org/stable/j.cttlc2cqn5.17.

Cook, V. (2001) Using the first language in the classroom. *Canadian Modern Language Review/La Revue canadienne des langues vivantes* 57 (2), 402–423.

European Commission (2017) Alliance to better protect minors online. See https://ec.europa.eu/digital-single-market/en/alliance-better-protect-minors-online (accessed 5 September 2017).

Gogolin, I. (1994) *Der monolinguale Habitus der multilingualen Schule.* Münster/New York: Waxman.

Greene, B. (2014) *The School Administrator's Responsibility for Implementing the Safe and Appropriate Use of Technology in Our Schools.* Amazon Digital Services.

Lantolf, J.P. (2011) The sociocultural approach to second language acquisition: Sociocultural theory, second language acquisition, and artificial L2 development. In D. Atkinson (ed.) *Alternative Approaches to Second Language Acquisition* (pp. 24–47). Abingdon: Routledge.

May, S. (2014) *The Multilingual Turn: Implications for SLA, TESOL and Bilingual Education.* New York: Routledge.

Meier, G. (2017) The multilingual turn as a critical movement in education: Assumptions, challenges and a need for reflection. *Applied Linguistics Review* 8 (1), 131–161.Moore, P.J. (2013) An emergent perspective on the use of the first language in the English-as-a-foreign-language classroom. *The Modern Language Journal* 97 (1), 239–253.

Meier, G. (2018) Multilingual socialisation in education: Introducing the M-SOC approach. In *Language Education and Multilingualism: The Langscape Journal* (Vol. 1, pp. 103–125). Berlin: Humboldt-Universität zu Berlin. https://edoc.hu-berlin.de/handle/18452/19672

Redmond, T. (2015) Media literacy is common sense: Bridging common core standards with the media experiences of digital learners. *Middle School Journal* 46 (3), 10–17. http://www.jstor.org/stable/24342146

Rooney, A. (2014) *Internet Safety (Let's Read and Talk About).* London: Franklin Watts.

Weber, J.-J. (2014) *Flexible Multilingual Education: Putting Children's Needs First.* Bristol: Multilingual Matters.

Index

For Product Safety Concerns and Information please contact our EU Authorised Representative:

Easy Access System Europe

Mustamäe tee 50

10621 Tallinn

Estonia

gpsr.requests@easproject.com

www.ingramcontent.com/pod-product-compliance
Ingram Content Group UK Ltd.
Pitfield, Milton Keynes, MK11 3LW, UK
UKHW021842150926
8657IPUK00004B/92

9781788921473